# 9/11

## AND ITS REMEDIATIONS IN POPULAR CULTURE AND ARTS IN AFRICA

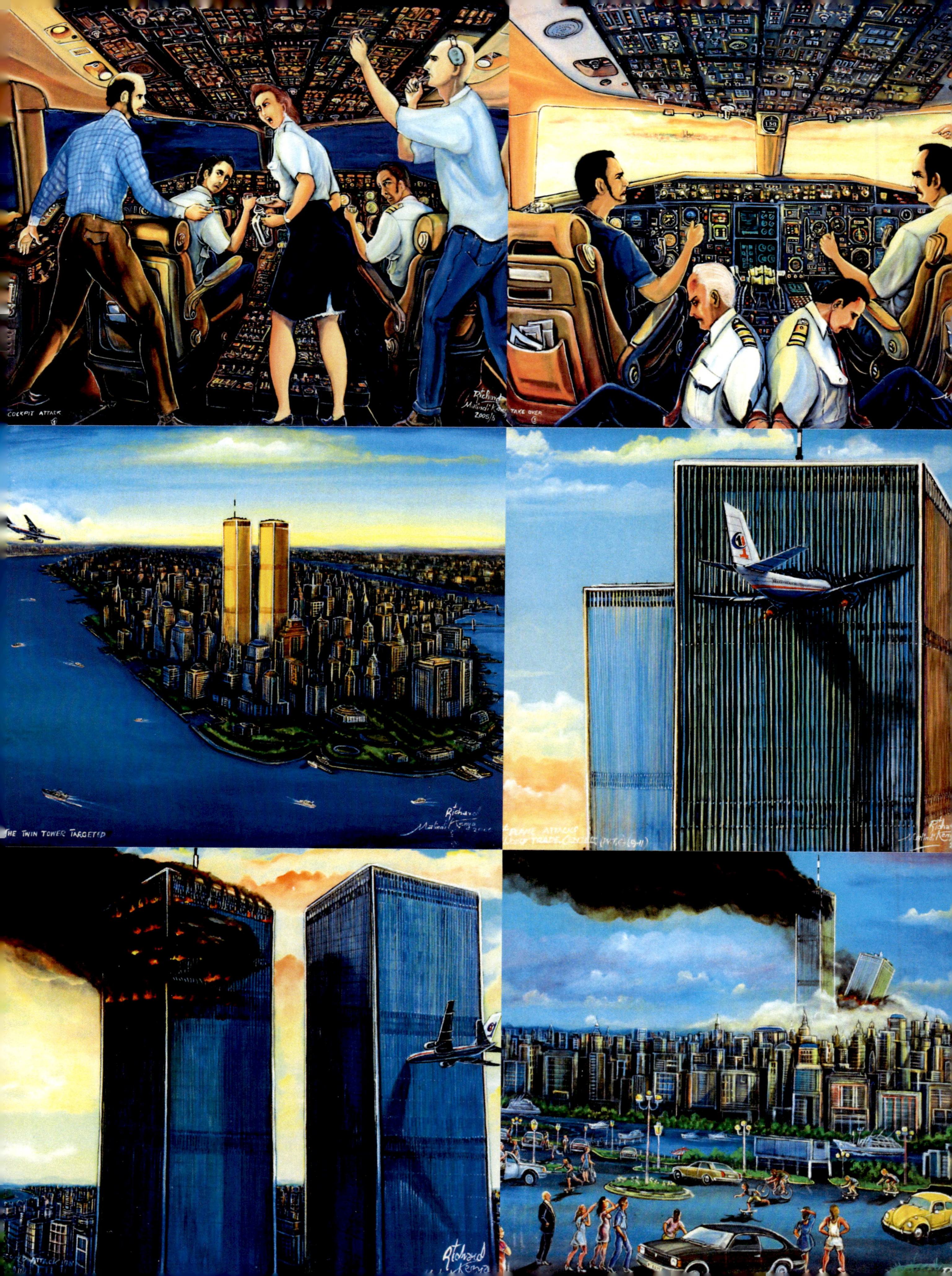
COCKPIT ATTACK
Richard
Malindi Kenya
2005/5
TAKE OVER
HE TWIN TOWER TARGETED

# 9/11
## AND ITS REMEDIATIONS IN POPULAR CULTURE AND ARTS IN AFRICA

**EDITED BY**

Heike Behrend
Tobias Wendl

**CONTRIBUTERS**

Heike Behrend
Abdalla Uba Adamu
Nura Ibrahim
Duncan Omanga
Tobias Wendl

**Richard Onyango, Six paintings from the series September 11,** acryl on canvas each 80 x 99,5 cm, 2006. Courtesy CAAC Collection Jean Pigozzi Geneva.

**IMPRESSUM**

Published in 2015 by LIT Verlag Berlin.

Series title:
Kunst und Visuelle Kulturen Afrikas / African Art and Visual Cultures – Vol. 3.
Freie Universität Berlin

Series editors: Kerstin Pinther and Tobias Wendl

Volume edited by Heike Behrend and Tobias Wendl with contributions by Abdalla Uba Adamu, Heike Behrend, Nura Ibrahim, Duncan Omanga and Tobias Wendl

Layout and typography: Sabine Rostock
Copy editing: Mitch Cohen
Editors' assistance: Hanna Prenzel

Cover: „Day of Agony". Poster Nigeria 2001 Collection Heike Behrend.
Backcover: Mounir Fatmi Save Manhattan 3, Installation VG Bildkunst, Bonn 2007

Bibliographic information published by the Deutsche Nationalbibliothek.

The Deutsche Nationalbibliothek lists this publication in the Deutsche Nationalbibliografie; detailed bibliographic data are available in the Internet at http://dnb.d-nb.de.

ISBN 978-3-643-90627-4

A catalogue record for this book is available from the British Library.


Contact: Fresnostr. 2 D-48159 Münster
Tel. +49 (0) 2 51-62 03 20, Fax +49 (0) 2 51-23 19 72, E-Mail: lit@lit-verlag.de
http://www.lit-verlag.de

Distribution: In the UK: Global Book Marketing, e-mail: mo@centralbooks.com
In North America: International Specialized Book Services, e-mail: orders@isbs.com
In Germany: LIT Verlag Fresnostr. 2, D-48159 Münster, Tel. +49 (0) 2 51-620 32 22,
Fax +49 (0) 2 51-922 60 99, E-mail: vertrieb@lit-verlag.de
In Austria: Medienlogistik Pichler-ÖBZ, e-mail: mlo@medien-logistik.at
e-books are available at www.litwebshop.de

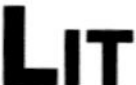

## CONTENT

Heike Behrend

**INTRODUCTION:
9/11 AND ITS REMEDIATIONS IN POPULAR
CULTURE AND ARTS IN AFRICA** 8

Abdalla Uba Adamu

**THE REMEDIATION OF EVENTS:
9/11 IN NIGERIAN VIDEOS** 38

Nura Ibrahim

**9/11, ISLAM AND THE VISUAL MEDIA
IN NORTHERN NIGERIA:
A SEMIOTIC ANALYSIS OF TWO SELECTED
PRE AND POST 9/11 POSTERS** 58

Duncan Omanga

**(RE) MAKING ENEMIES:
REPRESENTATIONS OF THE TERRORISTS IN
PRE- AND POST-9/11 EDITORIAL CARTOONS IN KENYA** 84

Heike Behrend

**9/11 IN A PHOTO STUDIO:
THE LIKONI PHOTOGRAPHERS AT THE
"STEIRISCHER HERBST" IN GRAZ, AUSTRIA** 98

Tobias Wendl

**9/11 IN THE VISUAL ARTS OF AFRICA AND BEYOND** 112

Heike Behrend

# INTRODUCTION: 9/11 AND ITS REMEDIATIONS IN POPULAR CULTURE AND ARTS IN AFRICA

This collection of articles and images on 9/11 in popular culture and visual arts in Africa is the outcome of two conferences.[1] Most of the authors are from Africa, from specifically Kenya and northern Nigeria, and it is their voices, their perspectives, and the images they collected that form the core of this publication. Numerous studies have explored the relationship between 9/11, terrorism, media, and popular culture in the USA (for example, Hoffmann 2011; Werckmeister 2005; Hentschel 2008; Schopp and Hill 2009; Heller 2005). But up to now, African and Western scholars have not made the responses and remediations from people in Africa, far away from Manhattan's Ground Zero, the subject of research.[2] In addition, the critical questioning of the attacks in post-September-11 American culture seems to have been difficult, avoided, and largely silenced under the Bush regime (Zizek 2002; Butler 2004), since to do so would have been easily interpreted as siding with the enemy.

The images of 9/11 presented and commented on here give evidence of manifold local reworkings of 9/11 that reflect on and explore the fundamental ambivalence toward the event and its mass mediation. Far from homogenizing feelings of sorrow and despair all over the world, the images of 9/11 and the ensuing War on Terror created very different responses and interactions in Africa that reflect and explore the effects of marginalization in a globalized world. They bring in what otherwise has been excluded and delegitimized in the West. They show how technical images of 9/11 were redirected and forced to admit perspectives their authors and readers might not have expected them to contain. They reflect on the moral implication of distance and give insights into the various ways distant conflicts are translated into intense proximities. And they allow us to approach the distant views of others who – for many reasons – are hostile to what they call the "West".

We have turned, above all, to popular culture and contemporary art in Africa (and the Diaspora) as the main site for understanding the different and often contradictory responses, negotiations, and prefigurations of 9/11. In fact, this volume is also an attempt to transcend the divide between popular culture and contemporary arts and to shift the assumed site of popular culture away from its identification with the lower strata of society. Instead of clear-cut oppositions between the arts and popular culture, we opt for a much more fluid set of possibilities and interactions between the two. We are interested, in particular, in the interfaces between popular culture and contemporary arts, their mutual engagement with each other (see the contribution by Tobias Wendl in this volume), and in the various strategies of popularization as part of globalization and

[1] The first preparatory meeting of all participants was held in 2007 in Mombasa, Kenya, generously funded by the Volkswagen Foundation; the second, in November 2009, saw all the contributors gathered again, this time at the Institute of African Studies in Cologne, Germany, financed by the Fritz Thyssen Foundation to discuss the book's general theoretical approach and the specific individual contributions. I would like to thank not only VW and the Thyssen Foundation but also friends and colleagues such as Jigaal Beez, Johannes Harnischfeger, Karl-Heinz Kohl, Elfi Mikesch, Eran Schaerf, Rüdiger Seesemann, and Bruno Sotto Mayor for their kind assistance and generous contributions. In addition, I am grateful to Ingeborg Eggink and Mirjam Shatanawi from the National Museum of World Cultures (Tropenmuseum) in the Netherlands for providing this publication with posters from their collections. Birgit Meyer also kindly contributed representations of Osama bin Laden to this volume. Many thanks also to Mitch Cohen for correcting the texts' English.

[2] The exception is Krings (2009); see also Behrend (2013:138ff).

localization processes. As we will show, popular practice rather often seems to be "in advance" of art practice in its vision of the world. The artist and composer Karlheinz Stockhausen, for example, expressed his admiration for the perfect calculation of the Al Qaida attack as a piece of art by Lucifer, thereby connecting to Baudelaire's aesthetic Satanism (Werckmeister 2005:58). Anselm Kiefer, who received the Peace Prize of the German Book Trade in 2008, declared Osama bin Laden to be the creator of the "most perfect" image. Boris Groys and Jeff Koons, too, articulated their envy of bin Laden, the indisputable "Master of Iconoplitics". In fact, not only on the level of violence and death, but also on the level of aesthetics, 9/11 created images so powerful, sublime, and monstrous that it changed the very texture of "reality", "reality" surpassing fiction (Kahana 2014:77).

Though strongly shaped by the logics of the market, the popular remediations of 9/11 presented in this volume provide sharp, bitter, ironic, and satirical insights into a particular cultural moment and its diverse reworkings in local contexts in Africa. While the War on Terror continues with increasing force and brutality in various parts of Africa and the Middle East, this volume deals only with the time span from 2001 to 2011, ending with Osama bin Laden's killing.

## REMEDIATION

The notions of mediation and remediation offer suitable entry points into the interface of a global event such as 9/11 and technical media. "Remediation" highlights the mobility and instability of images as they circulate across different media, creating new framings, meanings and audiences. Remediated images are not essentially repetitions of the same thing as they pass from medium to medium. Instead, they are "repetitions with a difference" that force us to consider the eventness of reappearance rather than assume their technological inevitability (Deleuze 2004 cit. Larkin 2013:251).

According to Bolter and Grusin (1999), remediation follows a double logic: that of "transparent immediacy" and of "hypermediacy". The logic of transparent immediacy implies that media technologies are erased from the representations they produce, making it seem as if these representations offer immediate access to reality. The technical apparatus is rendered invisible and creates the illusion that the representation is an authentic presence.

In contrast, "hypermediacy" asserts multiple acts of representation and acknowledges that technology itself is real, that it is gradually becoming our second nature. In this logic, reality is not supposed to lie beyond representation, but

Fig. 1
**WTC on slippe**
Senegal ca 20(
photographec
Karl-Heinz Ko

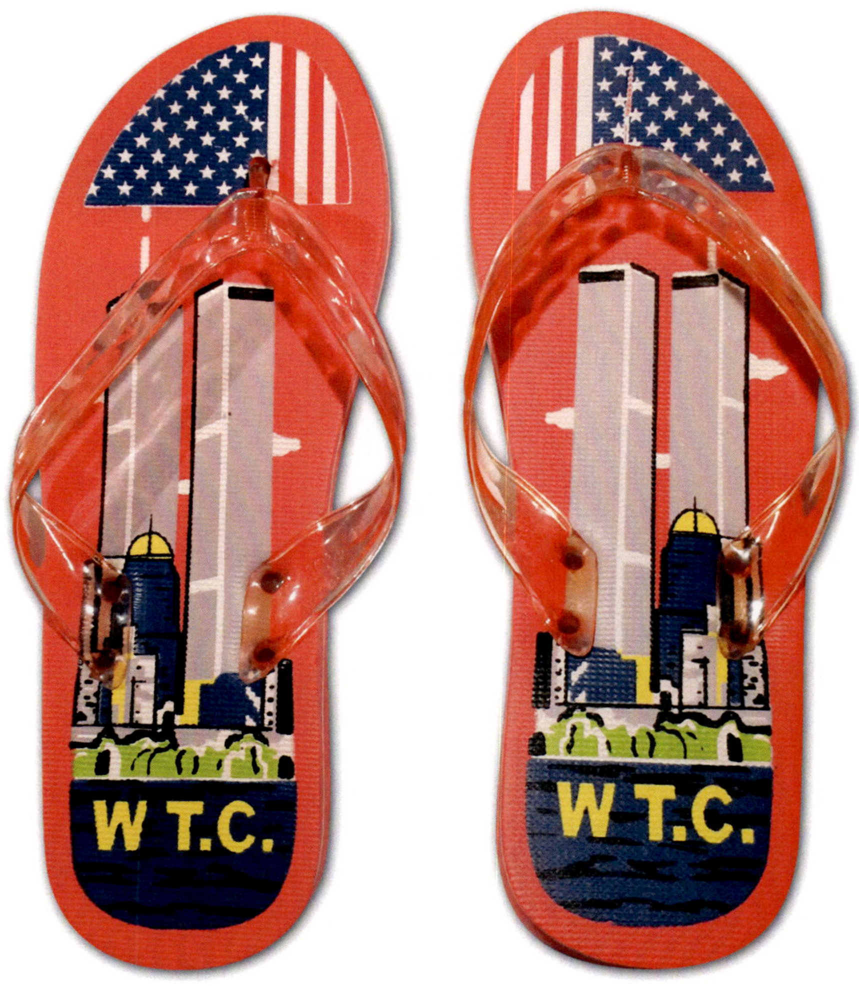


to be constituted by it. Hypermediacy claims immediacy and authenticity not beyond media, but instead through media.

This perspective on remediation is intriguing because it highlights the paradox that immediacy and authenticity – although by definition opposed to media and allegedly unmediated – are produced by media. Yet, the circulation of images and texts is not just an effect of technology but also a consequence of cultural debates. Images may be contested to the point of rejection, counter-violence, and destruction (see Behrend 2013). Images, particularly when circulating across different cultural contexts, may provoke an incessant process of valuation, devaluation and revaluation (Larkin 2013:242). Contradicting the (technical) logic of mass media, images of 9/11 generated not only a flow of new visibilities, immediacies and proximities but also distances, ruptures and withdrawal.

In fact, as a highly contested event, remediations of 9/11 have also prompted attempts to de-authenticate it, not to locate it in the present but to relegate it to a more secure past, to censor or debase it by putting the icon of the Twin Towers, for example, on the sole of a pair of slippers (that were sold in Senegal; personal communication from Karl-Heinz Kohl – figure 1) or to elevate and venerate it as some sort of relict. Thus, we have to take into account that processes of remediation are not only determined by technologies, but are also strongly shaped by historically and culturally situated media practices and hence subject to power relations.

### 9/11 AS ABSOLUTE EVENT

9/11, the attack on and the destruction of the World Trade Center in 2001, has been described as an "absolute event" that radically changed the course of history, the relations of power, and the conditions of its analysis (Baudrillard 2003). 9/11 reinforced not only a rather old opposition between the Christian West and Islam, but also deeply remodeled and modified the very foundations of Western political communities by changing state legislation and suspending civil rights and liberties as security measures and counter-terrorism policies. 9/11 also led to the declaration of a unilateral War on Terror, a war against a global network of terrorists that questioned the conventional definition of war as being waged between nation states. In fact, a new order of (counter-) terrorism, war and mass murder, policing, surveillance and espionage began, culminating in 2013 in the disclosure of classified National Security Agency files, revealing the extent to which a massively secret state apparatus had monitored the everyday life of people all over the world (Kahana 2014:81).

Yet, in the very year 2001, the U.S. celebrated the commemoration of the 60th anniversary of Pearl Harbor. As Clement Chéroux has shown, the American media inundated audiences with books, television, radio shows, and a gigantic Hollywood production titled "Pearl Harbor", all dedicated to the "day of infamy". In the months leading up to 9/11, the destruction and billowing clouds at Pearl Harbor had pervaded American visual culture and, so Chéroux, led to a specific intericonicity in the ways the images of the events of 9/11 were constructed: 9/11 as a second Pearl Harbor (Chéroux 2011:275ff).

Besides "Pearl Harbor", long before 9/11, American writers and filmmakers had already pictured New York's annihilation in a stunning range of ways by earthquake, fire, flood, atom bomb, ghosts, glaciers, giant ape King Kong, and meteors in popular media. The visions of New York's destruction formed a common narrative, inscribed in various popular forms of communication. As Max Page (2008) suggested, two contradictory messages were spoken over and over again directly after 9/11: "It was unimaginable" and "it was just like a movie". Despite repeated observations that 9/11 was "unimaginable" and an "absolute event", the destruction of New York had been imagined in popular media for decades and the language of disaster movies shaped the initial response to 9/11. Following Hollywood's spectacular visual codes, news coverage of 9/11, too, became "infotainment" (Chéroux 2011:279).

Interestingly, the Bush administration, too, called on Hollywood to help facilitate its response to the attacks. In November 2001, the White House met with Hollywood executives to find out how Hollywood films could assist in framing the "right ideological message" and how to communicate it to the American people (Zizek 2002 cit. Schopp and Hill 2009:14).

The World Trade Center with its Twin Towers, in particular, had served since the early 1970s as a familiar landmark and symbol of Manhattan, New York, and Western capitalism. In advertisements by Becks brewery, the cigarette brand Philipp Morris, and British Airlines, the WTC was consistently used in a stylized form. Especially in a mid-1980s advertisement for British Airways, not only were the Twin Towers shown in the background, but their reflecting surface was also broken by the shadow of a passing airplane, thereby strongly anticipating the images of the terror attack that occurred sixteen years later (Hoffmann 2011:15). This raises important questions about the status of popular culture and its relation to prophecy, the mediation of politics, disasters, advertisement, and entertainment.

From this perspective, 9/11 can be seen as a "repetition with a difference" (Deleuze 2004) and the fulfillment of popular prophecies. Yet, following Baudrillard, the event's absoluteness can be described also in terms of an impossibility to provide an exchange of deaths. According to him, 9/11 is a unique, singular, and absolute event because the members of Al Qaida who created it turned their deaths (as suicide) into an absolute weapon, into an offensive and efficient sacrifice. While the U.S. government attempts to exclude death, to lead a "clean" war in which drones and other digital technologies do the killings at a distance, with an ideal of "zero dead" (at least for its own soldiers), the suicide killers of Al Qaida have challenged their adversaries on a level where they cannot respond, with a violence that includes their own deaths (Baudrillard 2011:21ff).

## IMAGE ACTS

The images created of 9/11 have been considered image acts, images that are not only representations of an event, but also turn into actors themselves (Bredekamp 2010; Paul 2011:135). Comparable to the photographs taken of the atomic bombs on Hiroshima and Nagasaki, 9/11 too seems to have been planned to create above all striking images of destruction for global consumption through the mass media (Paul 2011:135). It is not by chance that Al Qaida chose the city with the largest media density and the fastest transmission structure worldwide. When planning their strategy, Al Qaida successfully relied on the logic of modern mass media: while the first attack on the North Tower of the WTC, the symbol of U.S. economic dominance, drew the attention of the media, the second attack became itself the object of real-time reporting. Never before 9/11 has an event been mediated so often in pictures (and sounds) and for the first time in "real time" (Paul 2011:137).

Terrorist strategies and the logic of the (re)mediation and commercialization of mass media entered into an almost symbiotic relationship, the media turning into collaborators and mediators between the terrorists, the state, and the public (compare Paul 2011:143ff). Though images have long been part of war and war propaganda, with 9/11, so it seems, they have gained a new quality in the new asymmetrical wars. The 9/11 attack wounded the U.S. state on the level of the spectacle and inflicted an "image defeat" (Retort 2005). The images of 9/11 give evidence of the increasing power of images at this specific moment in history when, with 9/11, a "war of images" or "iconoclash" was unleashed (see Mitchell 2005:11ff; Latour 2002; Bredekamp 2003). The images of 9/11 most conspicuously embodied the anxiety over image-making and image-smashing, idolatry and iconoclasm, through the spectacle that ushered in a New World Order defined by terrorism. Paradoxically, the iconoclastic act of destroying the Twin Towers was turned into a "creative destruction" in which secondary images of defacement or annihilation were created at the same moment that the target image was attacked (Mitchell 2005:18).

Some pictures of 9/11 were so powerful that they stepped out of their frames, broke through the TV screens, and created shock waves (Paul 2011:137). Even for people living far away from New York, the remediated images of the threat turned into a threat themselves (Becker 2013:10). Event and image enhanced each other, turning the consumption of the pictures of the event into the event. In fact, images have created a new level of conflict and reality in the contemporary asymmetrical wars. Consequently, history has to be envisaged as in part determined by struggles occurring on the level of the visual, struggles that may evolve around visual media (Pinney 2004:8), and the question of what should be given to see and what should be withdrawn from visibility.

Although images have become combatants also in earlier wars, as well, since

[3] For operational images translated into the domain of arts, see, for example, Harun Farocki's installation "Serious Games"(2010) or his "Eye/Machine" trilogy of (2000-03).

1991 and the Kuwait War and especially since 2001, warfare has tightened the complicity of war and image, as well as the relationship between violence and technology. New image technologies provided, for example, "operational" images, images produced by machines and for machines that point to another transformation, use, and understanding of images.[3] Operational images were "seen", above all, by ballistic missiles that used them to adjust their trajectory in flight; they were also "seen" by other automated systems to navigate, select, and connect to specific parts of their surrounding environment (Canales 2014:5). These operational images have radically changed the relation between everyday surveillance and weaponized vision. They are no longer envisioned to represent something, but instead are employed as recognition and tracking tools for military use (van Tomme 2014:26ff), and they question anew concepts of authorship, authority, responsibility, and control. In fact, the proliferation of digital image technologies has led to a polarization between an operational and a more informative sphere of images, creating a divide between images that are not made to be seen and those that are allowed to circulate in public and private domains (Werckmeister 2005:7).

At the same time, as Ariella Azoulay (2008) has suggested, the global dissemination of (digital) photography has created a space of political relations that are not mediated exclusively by the state. While, on the one hand, the camera modified the way individuals are governed and the extent of their participation in the forms of governance, on the other hand, photography created a new sphere of relations between people, a new encounter between people. In situations of war or disaster, photography can provide a mobile and global recording kit for contesting violations of citizenship. Through the "civil contract of photography", photographs can establish a tribunal and allow readings of injuries inflicted on others as a civic skill.

As Baudrillard suggested, technical images absorbed 9/11 so that it could be consumed. In the process of absorbing the images of 9/11, reality and fiction became inseparable and the fascination of the event was, above all, fascination by technical images (Baudrillard 2003:30). It is not by chance that photographic images and video provided the bulk of images that became iconic. Photography and film/video are indexical and seem to stabilize the referent and give it recognizable meaning, and by repeating Hollywood's syntax and lexicon they allowed addressees to decode images and sequences rapidly, so that the effects of reality – or the phantasms of realism – were multiplied (Lyotard 1993 cit. Kahana 2011:79).

As the ongoing War on Terror shows, extreme violence became a constituent part of images. The intentional staging of images in social media – for example, of humiliated corpses of U.S. elite soldiers dragged through the streets of Mogadishu, the hanging of Saddam Hussein, the beheading of Western journalists made public in videos in the Internet, and the torture photographs from Abu Ghraib – and the images of victims on both sides have become effective weapons and a means of gaining power and trans-national support. In the Internet, where the circulation of images makes it easy to bypass national boundaries and censorship by the state, images of 9/11 and the War on Terror have generated the proliferation of counter-images in an uncontrolled way and provoked new visual practices. For example, the pictures of imprisoned U.S. soldiers and those killed in action in Bagdad were answered with the photographs of Saddam's sons who had been killed and whose corpses were exposed to the mass media. The mutual mirroring of brutal killings and the spiral of violence and counter-violence was paralleled by a visual struggle with no end in sight. Following the oppositional logic of war and caught in the relationship of mutual visual outbidding, increasingly cruel images were met by the opponent's images of violence. With the killing of bin Laden, the "Master of Iconopolitics", in 2011, however, this oppositional politics of images was suspended, at least, for a short time. I will come back to this subject at the end of this introduction.

Yet, in spite of the mutual logic of image and counter-image that largely determined the politics of images on both sides, we have to keep in mind that the War on Terror is an asymmetrical war in which the visibility of death and the dead is dealt with in an unequal way. While the U.S. military made few efforts to keep the body bags of killed soldiers out of the public's view, Allan Sekula has suggested that the shadow side of these glorious images of these "precisely enumerated first world bodies" are the other bodies, THOSE of the victims of the U.S. military, too many to show and too many to count.[4] The West's popular media discourse is all too often complicit in silencing THOSE bodies (van Gelder 2014:58ff). The Western audience is spared the image of THOSE deaths caused by drones or by other means of digital warfare, "as if the refusal to show and to count them was the crowning virtue of a higher morality, a humanist revulsion against the quantification of death" (ibid.). Though unmediated in Western media, the tragedies of the deaths of THOSE bodies are very real; they leave behind desperate relatives and are mourned, remembered, and sometimes invoked in demands for revenge.

[4] See the exhibition by Allan Sekula, "War without Bodies", in 1991 at Harvard University.

## THE ARCHIVE OF 9/11

9/11, the War on Terror, and the ensuing war of images created its own archive of pictures. It included not only photographs by professional photographers, but also photos and videos taken by amateurs who used their camera phones, for example, to capture events. The spectacular quality of the images of the destruction of the WTC as they were mediated around the globe, however, were countered locally in New York by a proliferation of originally private photographs displayed in small and spontaneous memorial sites or shrines that sprang up immediately around the city and, in particular, beside St. Paul's Chapel. Besides photographic portraits of missing and dead people and images of the (still standing) Twin Towers, candles and messages indicated painful loss and the attempt to create meaningful sites to counter the absences. In addition, in the rubble from 9/11, in the murky refuse of dust, debris, and human remains, 8,000 photographs were found; these were scanned and placed on a website where families and survivors could view them (Sturken 2007:208). Thus, the intense networks of media that defined the events of 9/11 give evidence of an increased fluidity between public and private media, between old and new media, and between amateurs and professionals (ibid.:168ff). The same holds for the display of private photographs of victims killed by U.S. Forces in Iraq, other parts of the Middle East, or northern Africa. Here, too, (small) shrines have been established in private and public spaces showing photographs of the dead as living. Thus, there is a mutual mirroring of practices in dealing with victims, marking their absence with private photographs in various public spaces. In a way, these more private images acted as counter-images to the iconic photographs that came to define 9/11.

While certain images became icons, others disappeared, were censored, or were made inaccessible or unshowable. When I visited Ground Zero in spring 2002, no photographs of the destruction of the Twin Towers were on display; only when requested were they taken out of cases and boxes where they were kept hidden. At the same time, Ground Zero, a space filled with photographs, was itself relentlessly photographed (Sturken 2007:168). Ground Zero evolved into a central touristic site offering souvenirs and all kinds of kitsch as a means to connect to 9/11. These souvenirs also participated in a kind of re-enactment of the catastrophic event itself and contributed to the commercialization and trivialization of the catastrophic events as part of an emerging disaster tourism.

Most of the photographs and videos taken by professionals and amateurs were digital and became part of the Internet. The Internet evolved like a kind of super medium, a global digital archive that allowed people from all parts of the world to publish and to download and rework the images of 9/11 and the War on Terror on a local level and then to re-globalize them.

Although a global archive of images has been produced that is shared by both sides in the war of images, this does not lead to a homogenization of meanings and affects but, as this volume attempts to show, to quite different, sometimes even opposed significations produced through the reworkings of images, montages, and captions. For example, the photographic portraits of the 19 Al Qaida members engaged in 9/11, which the FBI had published as "wanted" photos, were remediated by jihadists, inserted and reworked into posters that celebrated them as martyrs of 9/11. Such practices underscore the immense possibilities that accompany the remediation of digital images and the potentialities of the archive.

## REMEDIATIONS OF 9/11 IN KENYA AND NIGERIA

The proliferation of technical images allowed people all over the world to participate in 9/11, thereby expanding the battlefield far beyond the nation states that later declared the War on Terror. While 9/11 created a new wave of nationalism and patriotism and a new culture of grief, memoralization, and celebration in the USA, in other parts of the world – often not directly involved in the War on Terror – the event inscribed itself in many different ways into national, regional, and local conflicts. Although Africa is far away from New York, there 9/11 transformed local geographies into parts of a larger geography of national outrage and global rage against terror (Appadurai 2006:95) and anti-terror.

Kenya and Nigeria have become deeply involved in the War on Terror and the struggles against new terrorist groups such as Al Shabaab and Boko Haram (Harnischfeger 2014), which claim to have connections to Al Qaida (Krech 2011). In contrast, in other countries such as Benin and Angola, where Christians and Muslims have been living peacefully together, 9/11 did not emerge as an event that strongly captured the popular imaginary.

In Kenya, in popular cartoons, in posters and videos in northern Nigeria, and in theater in Benin and other parts of Africa, the producers of popular arts created their own perspectives and options on 9/11, sometimes reifying dominant narratives and sometimes subverting them while also exploring the limits of the critical potentials in cultural practice.

In Kenya, 9/11 was not seen as an "absolute event", but as the repetition of a

[5] Not only the American embassy in Nairobi, but also that in Dar-es-Salaam, Tanzania was bombed.

previous traumatic incident that struck the capital in 1998.[5] Here the „distant suffering of others" was connected with the national trauma of the „Terrorist Embassy Bombing" in which hundreds of people were killed and thousands injured.[6] While the 1998 bomb attack created strong patriotic and nationalist feelings among Kenyans and triggered popular discourses about the place of Kenya in a globalized world (Kasfir 2005), after 9/11, many Kenyans realized painfully that the victims of the terrorist attacks in Africa and in the USA were not given the same media attention and support and that there were „second-rate" and "first-rate" victims, the former in Africa. In spite of protests demanding compensation from the U.S. government as were given to families of those killed in the 9/11 attacks, families of Kenyan victims so far have not received any payment. In this volume, Dan Omanga's paper analyzing the editorial cartoons of two Kenyan newspapers from 1998 to 2011 gives insights into changing attitudes toward 9/11 and the different representations of its (anti-)hero Osama bin Laden.

Since the 8th century, the Kenyan coast has hosted an Islamic population that during colonial times was increasingly marginalized economically and politically. Because two of the terrorists who were accused of being responsible for the "Embassy Bombing" in 1998 were identified as Muslims originating from Mombasa, Muslim inhabitants of Mombasa's Old Town were kept under strict surveillance, experiencing what it means to become the target of the United States' War on Terror.[7] (Seesemann 2007:168ff). They were forcefully silenced and, besides a few graffiti, there has not been much of a popular response to 9/11 by Kenyan Muslims. In addition, national campaigns were launched to reduce Muslims to a humiliated minority. Indeed, after 9/11, when the enemy had been named as a global terrorist network, many African states were able to identify with such naming of their own dissidents, anti-state activists, and violent minorities, and most states recognized that this was a name with infinite possibilities for political manipulations. As Arjun Appadurai has shown, the new "geographies of anger" followed a double logic: globalizing internal moral opponents and localizing faraway moral enemies. The new geographies of anger were thus the spatial and political outcome of complex interactions between faraway events and proximate fears, old histories and new provocations (Appadurai 2006:20,118,100).

In fact, Christian photographers from western and central Kenya dared to make 9/11 a theme in their photo studio (see my contribution in this volume) but only outside of Kenya in the "protected space" of an international art show, when invited to participate in the "Steirischer Herbst" in Graz, Austria. In October

[6] Actually, in Kenya, 9/11 was connected to a whole series of local "terrorist bombings" that began with the "Embassy Bombing" on August 7, 1998. This catastrophic event was followed by the bombing of the Israeli Paradise Hotel near Mombasa in November 2002 and the attempted shooting down of an Israeli passenger plane at the same time, the August 3, 2003 Mombasa Town Bombings, and the 2007 Ambassador Hotel Bombings in Nairobi. The latest catastrophic event is the terrorist attack by members of Shabaab on the Westgate Mall of Nairobi on September 21 2013, when more than 60 people were killed and more than 200 wounded.

[7] In a public talk as part of the election campaign at the end of September 2007, the Kenyan Minister of Foreign Affairs apologized to the Muslims of Kenya for the intimidation and discrimination they had experienced in recent years.

2001, a few weeks after 9/11, they remediated global images of 9/11 as part of their photographic practices. In their studio in Graz, they participated in the "war of images" and transformed the burning Twin Towers into a highly ambiguous popular spectacle for local consumption within the art world.

In northern Nigeria, which – in contrast to Kenya – has a strong Muslim majority and where Sharia law was established in 2000, 9/11 led to outbreaks of violence between Christians and Muslims (Danfulani and Fwatshak 2002). Many Nigerian Muslims celebrated 9/11 as a "victory" in the larger political struggle against the United States. As in Kenya, also in northern Nigeria, 9/11 was not conceptualized as an absolute event, but instead as having begun with the Gulf Wars. The first Gulf War had already created another node of anti-Americanism in northern Nigeria, expressed not only in widespread demonstrations to support Iraq, but also in a spate of naming newborn male babies "Saddam" and after 9/11 also "Osama" (see Adamu in this volume). As the contribution of Abdalla Uba Adamu in this volume demonstrates, two locally produced videos personalize the opposition between Muslims and the West and rework it into the antagonism between Osama bin Laden, celebrated as a folk hero, and George W. Bush, represented as some sort of primitive "bush devil".

In addition, in northern Nigeria, young men in particular downloaded certain pictures of events and persons involved in the War on Terror from the Internet and redirected and reworked them to admit another perspective serving the political project of radical Islam (see the contribution of Nura Ibrahim in this volume). In posters, downloaded photographs of bin Laden and Saddam Hussein were remediated, displaying both as popular heroes defending the interests of marginalized Muslims not only in northern Nigeria, but all over the world. In fact, it may be asked whether this highly intense proliferation of popular images – serving the cause of Islam – contributed to the creation of a new visual public realm in which images had not formerly played such a dominant role.

The two posters Nura Ibrahim discusses in this volume give visibility to polarities and structural conflicts. The photographs, carefully chosen, organized, and montaged, aim to make a political argument and proceed by means of an exposition of important differences that strongly dramatize the content and counter the West's officially recognized narratives. The posters are politically anchored with captions and the specific organization of their montage of images. In the case of the Saddam poster, the captions express a violent anti-Semitism, creating a strange alliance between radical right-wing and Nazi groups in Europe and Islamist movements in northern Nigeria. Interestingly, it is in the text – the captions – that the enemy is imagined as American Jews who, in accordance with a theory of worldwide conspiracy, are seen behind American politics.

In the Saddam poster, photographs within a photograph are displayed that provide highly interesting insights into the local politics of images and the popular practices into which pictures have been inserted. Photographs thus appear as agents and "patients" of activity. One photograph, for example, depicts some high-ranking Iraqi military men marching on the portrait of President Bush. They are seen stepping with their feet on the face of Bush, an act of iconoclasm thereby humiliating, cursing, and "killing" him, as Nura Ibrahim suggests, based on the conversations he had with poster producers. In addition, two photographs show people demonstrating by holding the photograph of Saddam in their hands, expressing their affiliation with, loyalty to, and solidarity with him. In one photo, the corpse of Saddam Hussein is shown covered by a flag; a portrait depicting a living Saddam occupies a chair near the spot where Saddam's head is supposed to be. The presence of Saddam in the photograph is thus doubled in an ambiguous way. While the covered corpse signifies death, discontinuity, and loss, the photograph within the photograph visually counteracts his final disappearance by giving him "immortality". His corpse (under the flag) is shown not separated, but deeply connected to the nation, his living relatives, and his brothers-in-arms, thereby transforming his individual death into a collective and national event. Here, photographs within photographs turn into explicit political statements and are given to show acts of national glory, the humiliation of the enemy, and revenge.

It is not by chance that in northern Nigeria the local police confiscated and destroyed T-shirts with the portrait of bin Laden and political posters that celebrated Saddam Hussein, bin Laden, jihad, anti-Semitism, and anti-Americanism. They also arrested and punished the producers of such politically provocative media. In spite of protests by Muslims, the central government intensely fought radical producers of popular images and thereby contributed to the creation of an even stronger antagonism, especially among youth, as Nura Ibrahim suggests in his contribution. Thus, the negativity of the images that were not allowed in northern Nigeria but which we have decided to show in this volume provides insights into the official canon and its limits, the construction of the enemy, and the complex play of oppositions between the antagonists in the war of images. The images question censorship, the boundaries of mass media reproduction and the idea of an unstoppable circulation or flow of images.

**OSAMA BIN LADEN IN AFRICA**

Osama bin Laden became a less-than-global but more-than-local public "icon", providing a source of identification, political and religious affiliation, and embodied affective engagement, as well as of more commercially minded advertisement. In particular, the proliferation of decentralized consumer technologies of image making have made bin Laden's image increasingly available for personalized, popular appropriations of various kinds and have enabled his image to travel along more intimate and horizontal routes of circulation than those propelled by mass media circuits, facilitating its incorporation into diverse visual economies and communities of interpretation. In fact, his availability as image can be understood as a (counter-)effect of a national political order in which visibility and circulation via the image are a privileged means of recognition for all political and religious agencies and events (cf. Strassler 2014:100f).

Although forbidden by the central government of Nigeria, in various media his image was smuggled into public and private domains in northern Nigeria (and other parts of Africa). His photographic portrait was imprinted on T-shirts (figures 2) and sold to people who wanted to express their affiliation with or admiration for him. Posters and stickers of bin Laden (figures 3, 4, 5), too, were produced to demonstrate political protest against the policies of the U.S. government, its allies, and the central government of Nigeria, which many Muslim in northern Nigeria identify with the West. In the popular imaginary also outside of northern Nigeria, Osama bin Laden in particular emerged as a hero or at least a person of great power. In Angola, as Bruno Sotto Mayor, a Brazilian anthropologist has found out, a new type of sculpture emerged around 2004: the figure's head is covered by a turban and strongly resembles bin Laden's covered head. This sculpture belongs to the so-called Tchishi shi tradition among the Chokwe. The statuettes are "power objects" and are used today in the struggle against witches (personal communication from Bruno Sotto Mayor). In the iconography of these sculptures, the head is of special importance because it is filled with medicine. Thus, as an emblem of power, bin Laden's turban has been inserted also into the very modern "traditional culture" and "reworked" as part of a "fetish" or "power object" in the fight against witchcraft.

In 2002, in Ghana, the walls of a shop named Atomic in Odokor, a residential quarter of Accra, showed the painted portraits of Bush and bin Laden each holding a telephone receiver in his hands (figures 6,7). They depict Bush and bin Laden, two former allies and "best friends" who later turned into enemies, communicating with each other. In a conversation the owner explained that he had the two pictures painted to draw attention to his business (personal communication from Birgit Meyer). Without taking sides, the two images may be seen as a tacit commentary on the very incapacity of George Bush and bin Laden, two former allies and "friends", to communicate instead of fighting each other.

In 2009 in South Africa, party firecrackers labeled "Osama's Double Delight" were sold (figures 8, 9, 10); they bore the image of bin Laden. Jigal Beez, as he kindly informed me, found them in East London, where they were offered by an Indian shopkeeper. The firecrackers (whose producers remained anonymous) were said to be very noisy and to explode twice, thereby echoing the destruction of the two towers on the auditory level. They were said to fly completely uncontrollably through the air. Here, obviously in a rather ambivalent way, bin Laden's power is brought into play in a double (self-)destructive (suicidal) and iconoclastic way: on the one hand, he is celebrated as a strong power, causing loud noise and two explosions that, however, bring his self-destruction at the same time. Here we are confronted with a brilliant product of the popular imaginary that unites opposed characteristics in a highly ironic and performative way, celebrating and yet undermining the image of the folk hero on a visual and auditory level. Echoing the explosions of the Twin Towers, the firecracker also produces a peak and a paradox of visibility whose goal is its own destruction.

Unlike in northern Nigeria and Kenya, immediate reactions to 9/11 were absent in Benin and only after a few years did a few artists take up the subject. In contrast to Nigeria and Kenya, Benin is marked by a mostly peaceful co-existence among Christians, Muslims, and the followers of the rather inclusive local Vodun religion. Consequently, 9/11 stayed a distant event, an event of the suffering of others that was not translated into conflictual local political and religious relations. Yet, as Jacques Bossa, a young scholar from Benin, found out, the Beninese artist Master Cool made use of 9/11 in a popular musical comedy, connecting it to irony and humor as a critical potential. He inserted the vocabulary of the War on Terror into a popular song that explored the "battle of the sexes" between men and women. In a song called "wet bird" about an adulterous affair, at the height of sexual lust the woman ("wet bird") groans and shouts the name of Osama bin Laden. The song's text not only modulates 9/11 and the War on Terror into a sexual register, but also plays with the topic of betrayal: Osama bin Laden as the supposed former "friend", at first financially and militarily supported by President Bush, who later turned against his former ally and now is "fucked" by him, as Master Cool asserted in an interview with Jacques Bossa.

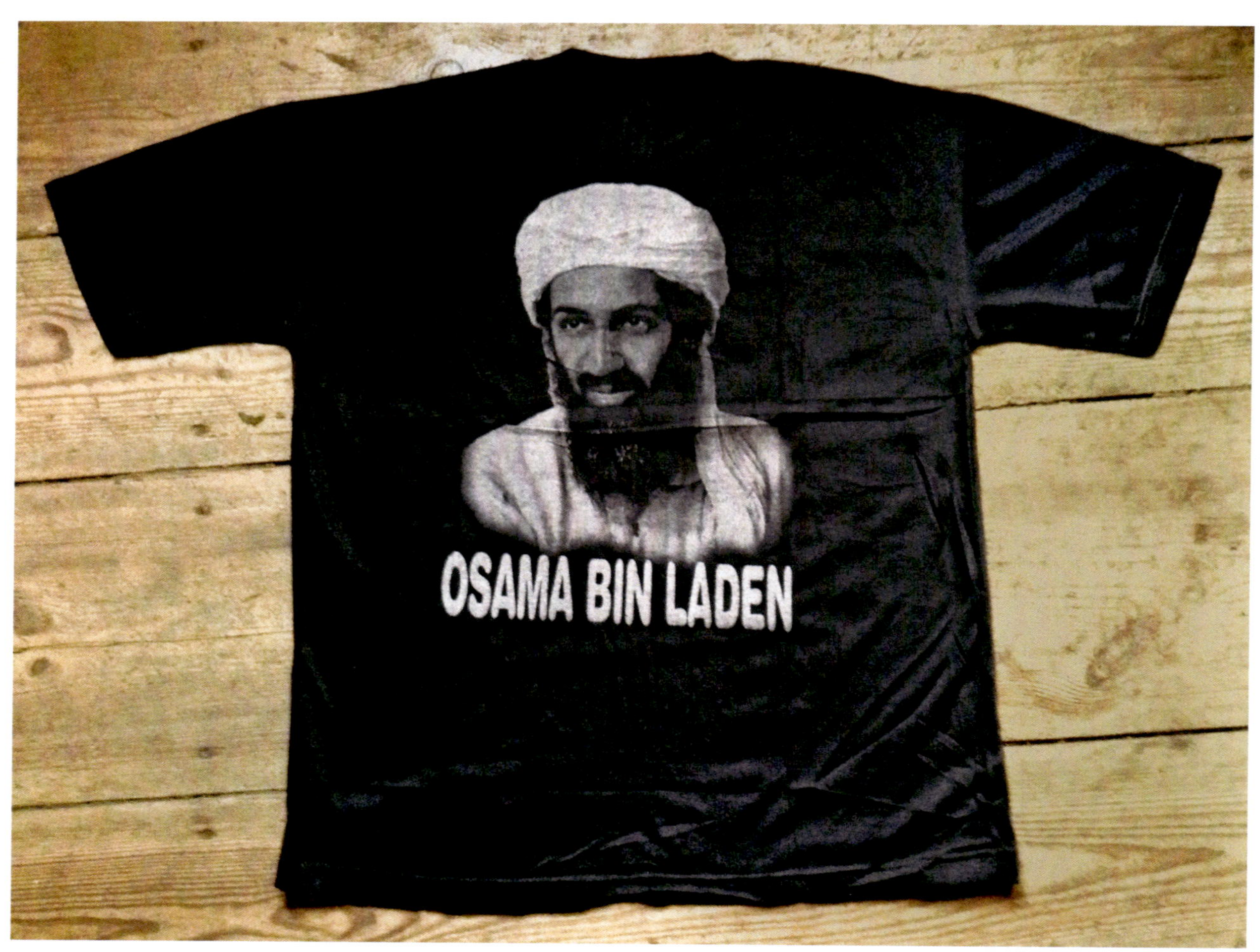


Fig. 2
**Bin Laden Tshirt**
bought in Nigeria
around 2002/3,
made in Indonesia

Fig. 3
**Osama bin Laden**
**Sticker,**
Nigeria ca 2002

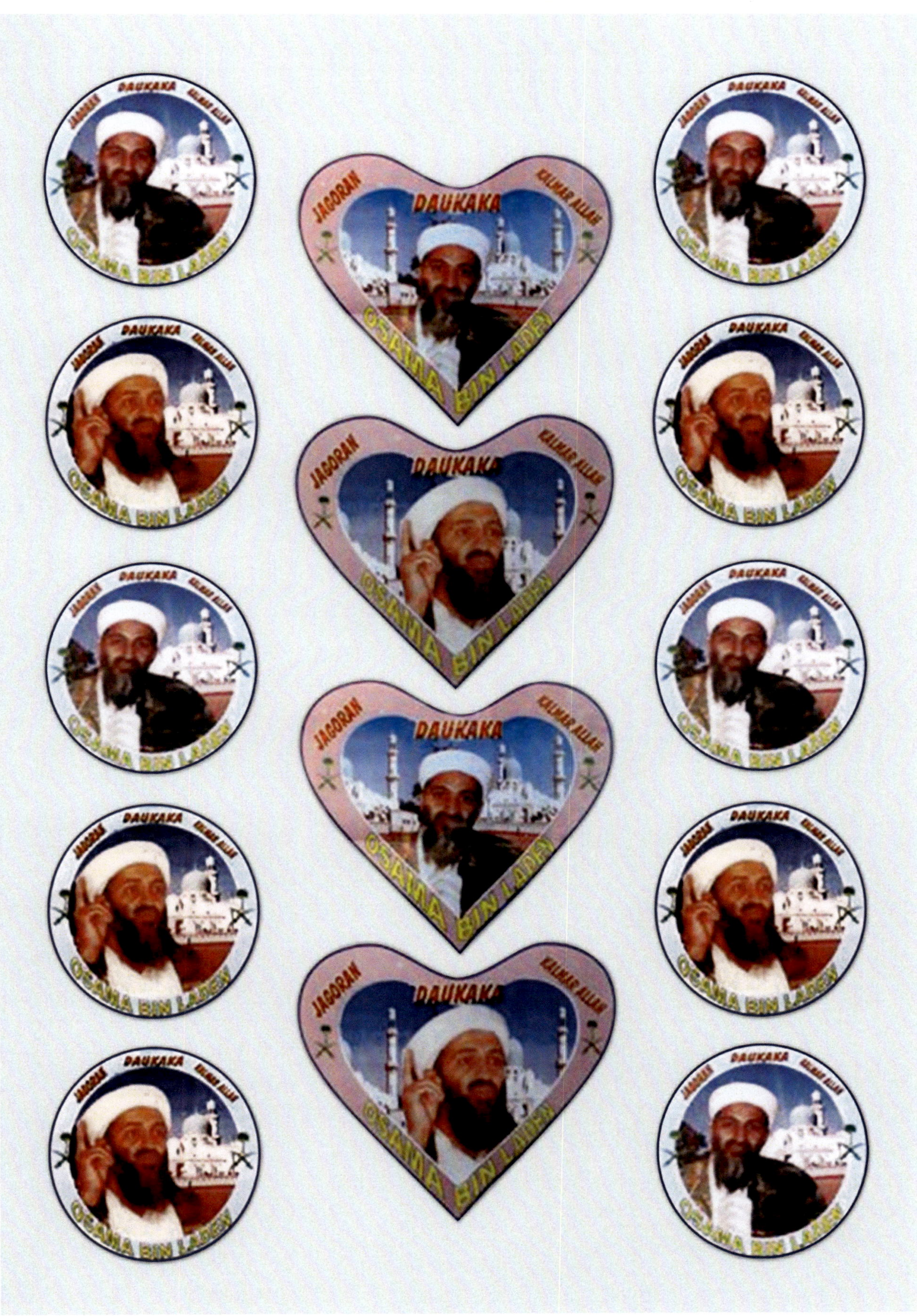
JAGORAN
DAUKAKA
KALMAR ALLAH
OSAMA BIN LADEN

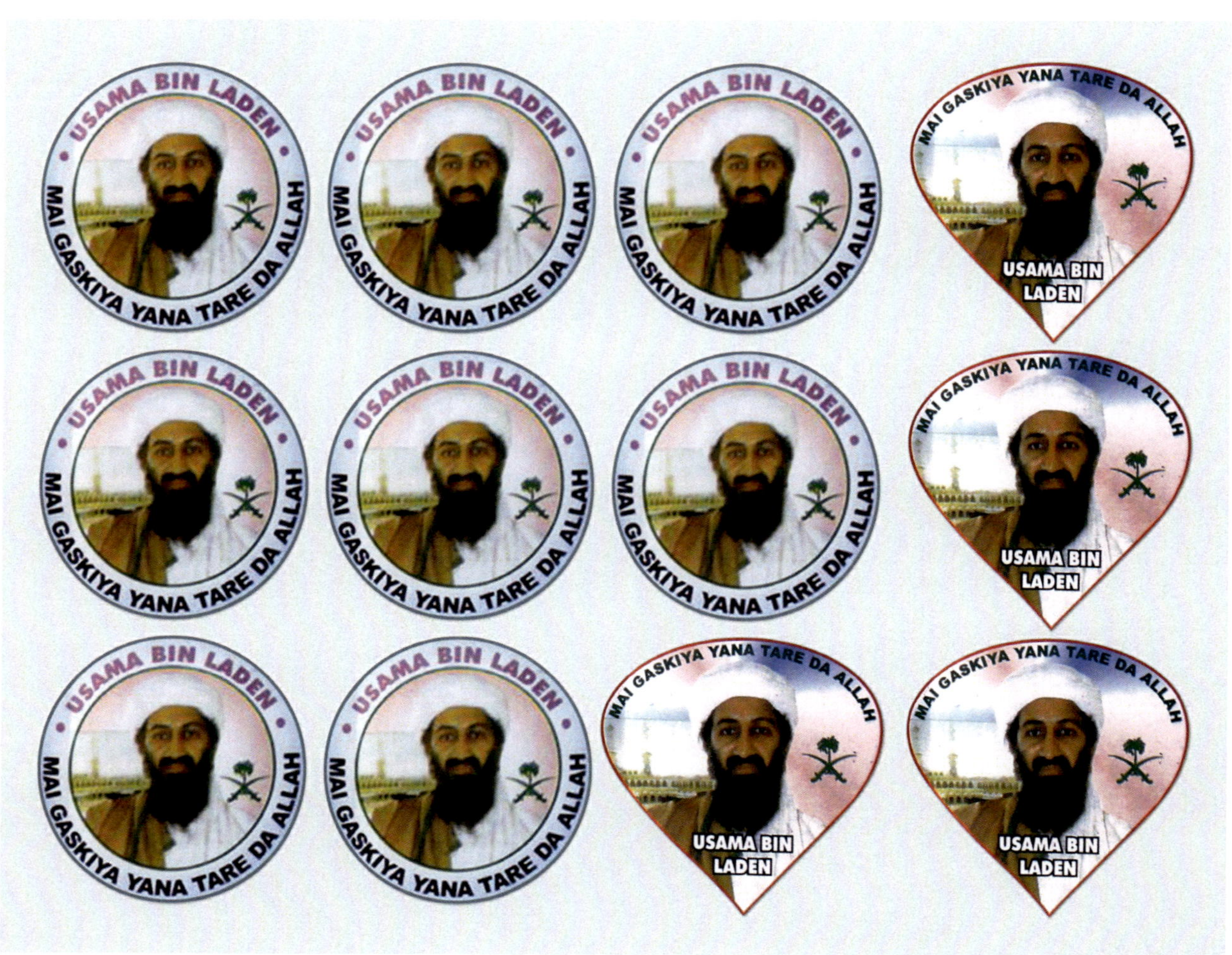


Fig. 4
**Osama bin Laden Sticker,**
Nigeria ca 2002

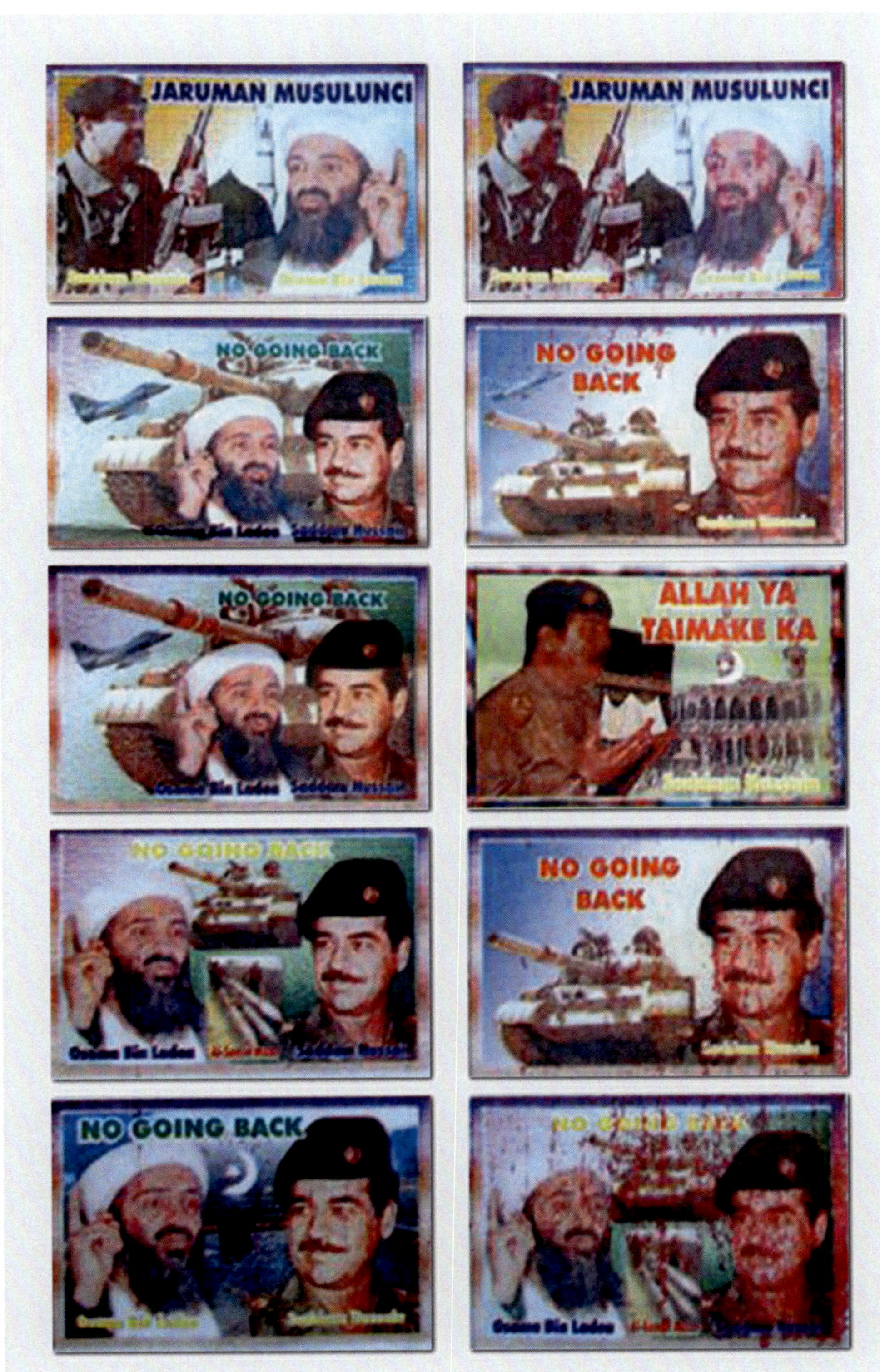


Fig. 5
**Osama bin Laden and Saddam Hussein Sticker,**
Nigeria ca 2002

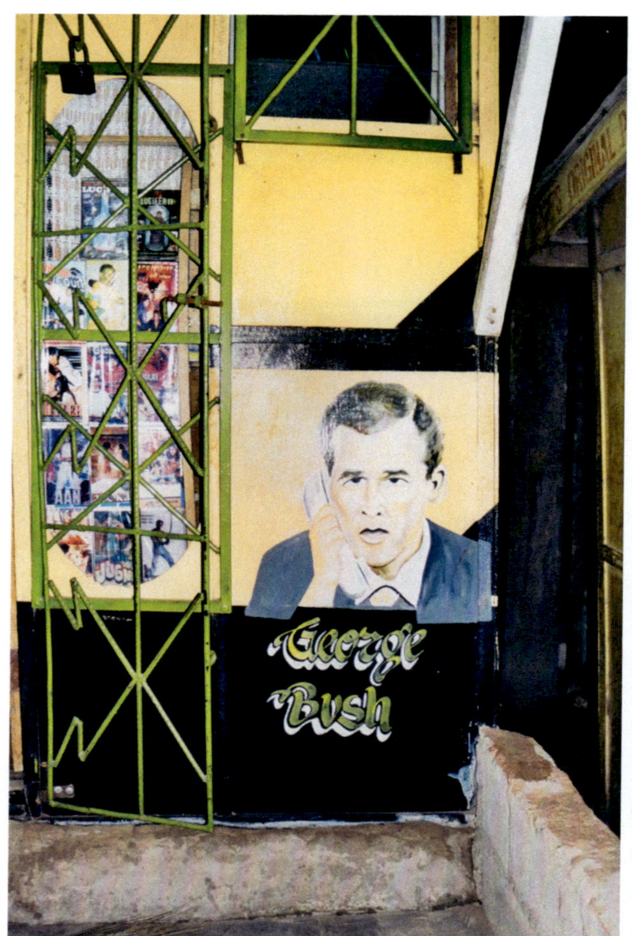


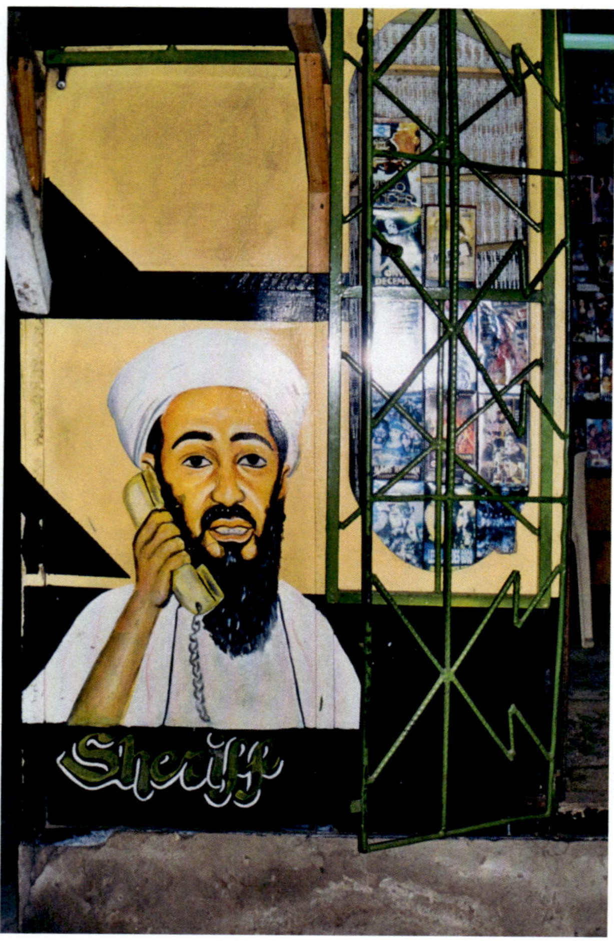


Fig. 6
**Painted portrait of George Bush,**
Atomic shop, Odokor, photographed by Birgit Meyer, Accra 2002

Fig. 8
**Painted portrait of Sheriff bin Laden,**
Atomic shop, Odokor, photographed by Birgit Meyer, Accra 2002

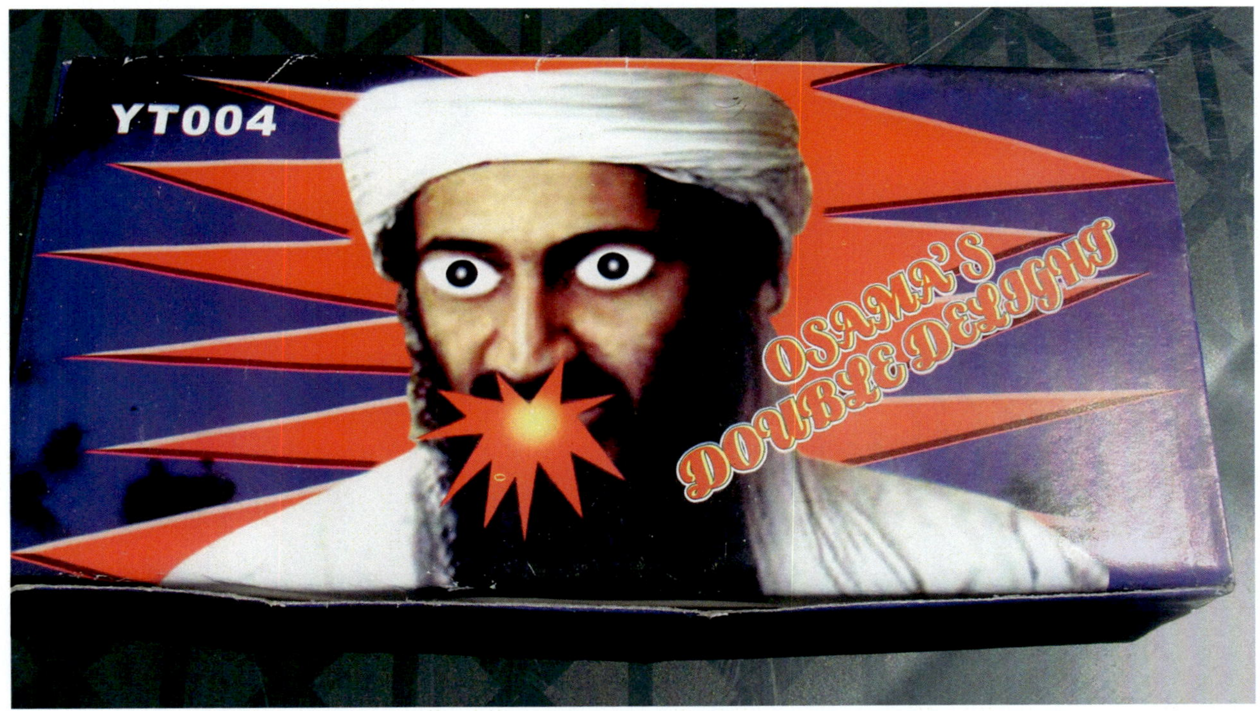


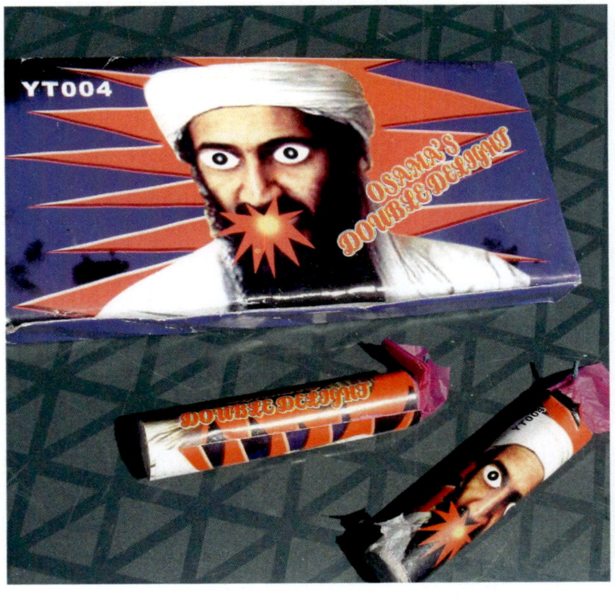


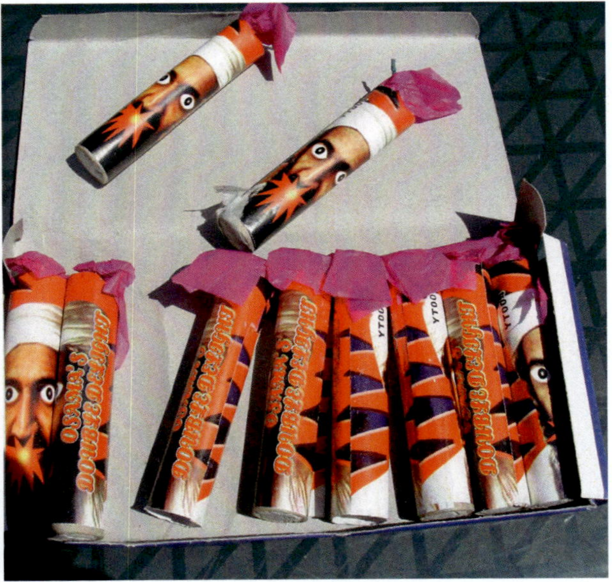

Fig. 8, 9, 10
**Fire Crackers**
**"Osama's Double Delight",**
South Africa ca 2009,
photographed by Jigal Beez

"Here is a married woman
My husband is out!
(phone rings)
Hi my chicken
Yes!
Take me, take me quickly
I am dying of desire
Ha (cries)
Oh my pilot!
Oh my plane!
Oh my bin Laden!
Oh my America!
Oh my bike!
Oh my boat!
Ho my sea! Oh my freight agent!
Oh my port!"

**THE DEATH OF OSAMA BIN LADEN**

Although Osama bin Laden never publicly admitted to have been the brain behind 9/11, the United States and its allies identified him as responsible for the attack and hunted him as Public Enemy Number One. In fact, the War on Terror was conceptualized (in a not very Christian way) as revenge, and when bin Laden was killed on May 2, 2011, ten years after 9/11, many Americans celebrated this event as a (final) victory that would ease their pain and shame while in other parts of the world people mourned bin Laden's murder and swore revenge.

For ten years, the U.S. government used every means to try to put a violent end to bin Laden. Finally, in the night of May 2, 2011, he was confronted in his bedroom and reportedly killed by two shots fired by one of the Navy Seals, Robert O'Neill, who recently broke his silence and gave interviews to the Washington Post, narrating in detail his story. The legitimacy of this act of killing, insofar as it was not self-defense, is highly questionable from an international law and human rights perspective (Diers 2011:309).

In contrast to the event of 9/11 that created a new flood and flow of images, the killing of bin Laden was characterized by a drastic scarcity, if not absence of images. A photograph of the "Situation Room", taken by Pete Souza, the chief photographer of the White House, was finally released on May 4, 2011.

This meanwhile famous photograph, which has inspired many artists, including Rimini Protocol, Franz Reimer, and Alfredo Jaar, does not show the victim of "Operation Geronimo", but instead President Obama, Hillary Clinton, Joe Biden, and other members of the national security team, who watch an event that is withdrawn from view. It shows the President and his staff following the operation and the killing in real time (though later it was said that when the actual killing took place a technical disturbance prevented viewing). The killing itself was not (re-)mediated. Photographs of the house, the bed, and the surroundings were released, but no images of bin Laden's corpse as a proof of his death. His funeral took place in the form of a secret interment in the sea to create no traces and no site of memory, thereby denying a pilgrimage site to any cult of martyrdom.

The absence of images of the killing of bin Laden marks a break in the U.S. government's politics of images. While, as mentioned before, images of the execution of Saddam Hussein and his killed sons were made public, images of bin Laden's killing and his corpse were withheld. They were neither displayed as evidence of his death nor as a trophy of victory. Instead, the US government dispensed with publishing the violated corpse of bin Laden, either out of respect for devout Muslims, the wish not to create a martyr icon, or the decision that gestures of triumph may be foregone. Yet, without a doubt, this restraint was due not only to moral or ethical reservations, but also to a media-political calculation (Diers 2011:311) to stop the mediation of ever more violent pictures as part of the war of images.

However, the iconic photograph of the Situation Room, too, has been reworked in various ways. An edition of an Orthodox Jewish New York weekly removed the two females; and Osama bin Laden was resurrected in the Situation Room by photo-shopping his head onto the body of the Vice President, thereby depicting him as a spectator of his own killing (ibid.:325). Interestingly, a former personal assistant to Obama maintained that the President refused to be in the Situation Room during the bin Laden raid and was photo-shopped into the famous photograph.

In spite of the attempts to avoid showing images of bin Laden's killing and his corpse, faked images of bin Laden's dead body appeared immediately in the Internet and were downloaded and montaged into posters and calendars, for example in Uganda and Nigeria (figures 11, 12). The attempts to efface the images of bin Laden's death were thus countered by the production of secondary images of effacement that entered the global flow and were reworked in various ways in local contexts. The decision to withhold images of the dead bin Laden did not lead to closure.

The death of bin Laden has not succeeded in ending the War on Terror. Instead, after bin Laden's death (and even before) new Islamist groups emerged, such as IS in Syria and Iraq, Boko Haram in Nigeria (see Harnischfeger 2014), and Al Shabaab in Kenya (Engelhardt 2014, Hansen 2013), the latter two claiming connections to Al Qaida. It is as if the terror network of Al Qaida has expanded, multiplied, and emerged with various new territorialized centers from which wars are fought against the enemies of (radical) Islam. And after bin Laden's killing, the war of images continues, too, with unprecedented force. In August 2014, the U.S. Department of State put an extremely violent propaganda film into YouTube that made use of some sequences of the videos of decapitation that IS had published. This film is part of the American anti-terror campaign "Think again, turn away" and provides an example of the aforementioned logic of visual outbidding that uses the most violent and dreadful images the enemy has produced as part of his terror campaign as a counter-measure. Following the logic of remediation, so it seems, no event is truly "over" if it can be referenced, reenacted, rehashed or recapitulated in the interest of thickening the media plot (Spyer and Steedly 2013:18).

Fig. 11
**"45 Minutes"**,
Killing bin Laden,
Poster, Nigeria, 2011
(collection Behrend)

# 45 MINUTES

Osama bin Laden

Barrack Obama

THESE ARE PEOPLE KILLED BY AMERICAN PRESIDENTS

Saddam Hussein

George Bush Jr.

PABLO ESCOBAR of Colombia

George Bush

GOING

Manuel Noriega of Panama

Ronald Reagan

Col. Muammar Abu Minyar al-Gaddafi

Omar Al Bashir

Robert Mugabe Zimbabwa

JANUARY JANVRIER 2011

| Lun | Mar | Mer | Jeu | Ven | Sam | Dim |
|---|---|---|---|---|---|---|
| Sun | Mon | Tue | Wed | Thur | Fri | Sat |
| 30 | 31 | | | | | 1 |
| 2 | 3 | 4 | 5 | 6 | 7 | 8 |
| 9 | 10 | 11 | 12 | 13 | 14 | 15 |
| 16 | 17 | 18 | 19 | 20 | 21 | 22 |
| 23 | 24 | 25 | 26 | 27 | 28 | 29 |

FEBRUARY FEVRIER 2011

| Lun | Mar | Mer | Jeu | Ven | Sam | Dim |
|---|---|---|---|---|---|---|
| Sun | Mon | Tue | Wed | Thur | Fri | Sat |
| | | 1 | 2 | 3 | 4 | 5 |
| 6 | 7 | 8 | 9 | 10 | 11 | 12 |
| 13 | 14 | 15 | 16 | 17 | 18 | 19 |
| 20 | 21 | 22 | 23 | 24 | 25 | 26 |
| 27 | 28 | | | | | |

MARCH MARS 2011

| Lun | Mar | Mer | Jeu | Ven | Sam | Dim |
|---|---|---|---|---|---|---|
| Sun | Mon | Tue | Wed | Thur | Fri | Sat |
| | | 1 | 2 | 3 | 4 | 5 |
| 6 | 7 | 8 | 9 | 10 | 11 | 12 |
| 13 | 14 | 15 | 16 | 17 | 18 | 19 |
| 20 | 21 | 22 | 23 | 24 | 25 | 26 |
| 27 | 28 | 29 | 30 | 31 | | |

APRIL AVRIL 2011

| Lun | Mar | Mer | Jeu | Ven | Sam | Dim |
|---|---|---|---|---|---|---|
| Sun | Mon | Tue | Wed | Thur | Fri | Sat |
| | | | | | 1 | 2 |
| 3 | 4 | 5 | 6 | 7 | 8 | 9 |
| 10 | 11 | 12 | 13 | 14 | 15 | 16 |
| 17 | 18 | 19 | 20 | 21 | 22 | 23 |
| 24 | 25 | 26 | 27 | 28 | 29 | 30 |

MAY MAI 2011

| Lun | Mar | Mer | Jeu | Ven | Sam | Dim |
|---|---|---|---|---|---|---|
| Sun | Mon | Tue | Wed | Thur | Fri | Sat |
| 1 | 2 | 3 | 4 | 5 | 6 | 7 |
| 8 | 9 | 10 | 11 | 12 | 13 | 14 |
| 15 | 16 | 17 | 18 | 19 | 20 | 21 |
| 22 | 23 | 24 | 25 | 26 | 27 | 28 |
| 29 | 30 | 31 | | | | |

JUNE JUIN

| Lun | Mar | Mer | Jeu | Ven |
|---|---|---|---|---|
| Sun | Mon | Tue | Wed | Thur |
| | | | 1 | 2 |
| 5 | 6 | 7 | 8 | 9 |
| 12 | 13 | 14 | 15 | 16 |
| 19 | 20 | 21 | 22 | 23 |
| 26 | 27 | 28 | 29 | 30 |

Fig. 12
**Killing of bin Laden**
Poster, Nigeria, 2011 (collection Behrend)

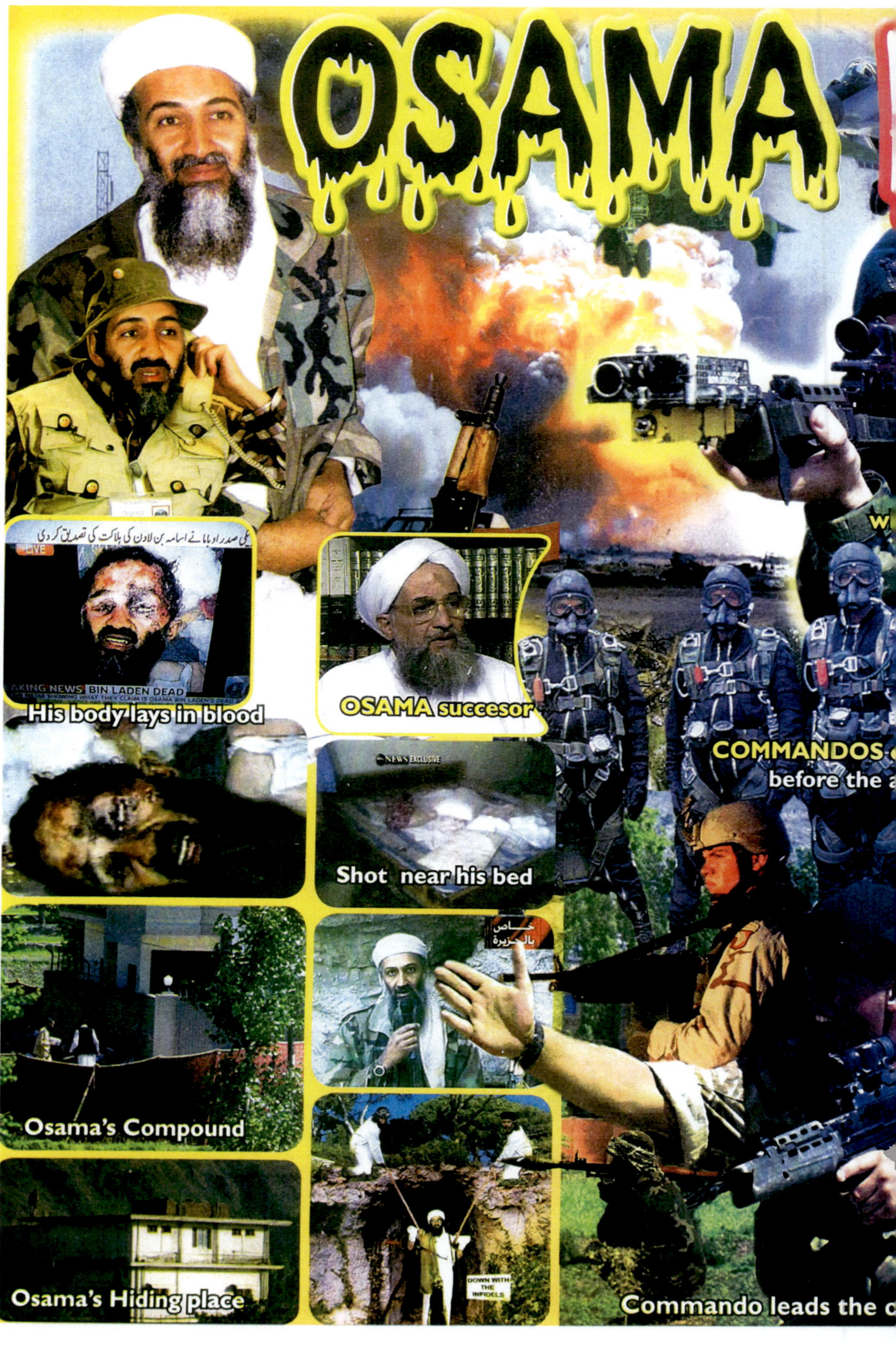

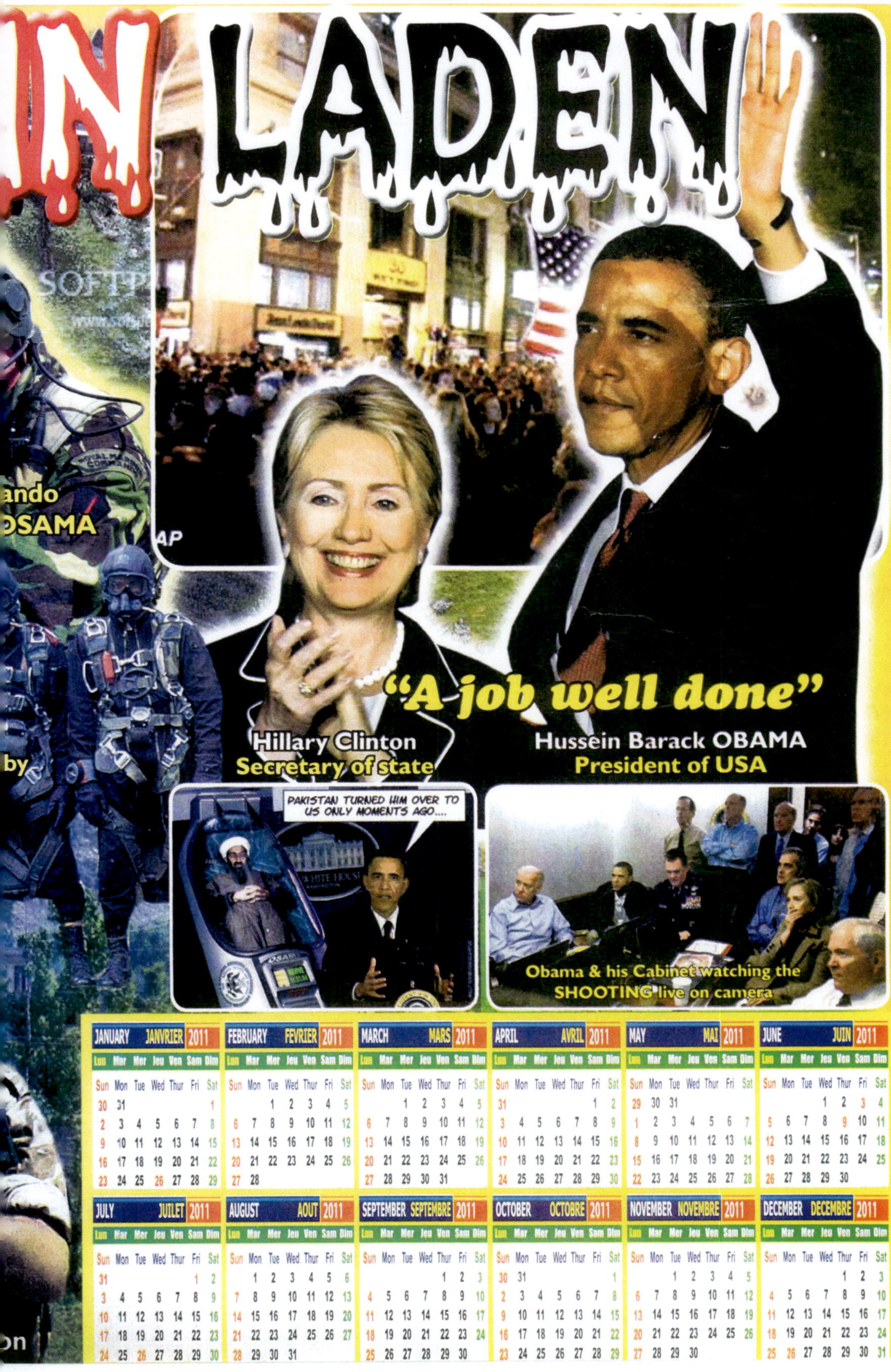

N
LADEN
ando
OSAMA
by
on
AP
"A job well done"
Hillary Clinton
Secretary of state
Hussein Barack OBAMA
President of USA
PAKISTAN TURNED HIM OVER TO US ONLY MOMENTS AGO....
Obama & his Cabinet watching the SHOOTING live on camera

## BIBLIOGRAPHY


Appadurai, Arjun, *Fear of Small Numbers. An Essay on the Geography of Anger*. Durham: Duke University Press 2006.

Azoulay, Ariella, *The Civil Contract of Photography*. New York: Zone Books 2008.

Baudrillard, Jean, *Der Geist des Terrorismus*. Vienna: Passagen Verlag 2002.

Behrend, Heike, *Contesting Visibility. Photographic Practices on the East African Coast*. Bielefeld: Transcript 2013.

Bolter, Jay, David and Grusin, Richard, *Remediation: Understanding New Media*. Cambridge, Mass.: MIT Press 1999.

Bredekamp, Horst, „Marks und Signs. Mutmaßungen zum jüngsten Bilderkrieg". In: Berz, Peter et al. (Eds.), *FAKtisch*. Munich: Fink 2003.

Bredekamp, Horst, *Theorie des Bildakts*. Berlin: Suhrkamp 2010.

Butler, Judith, *Precarious Life: The Powers of Mourning and Violence*. London: Verso 2004.

Chéroux, Clément, „The Déja-vu of September 11". In: Hoffmann, Felix (Ed.), *Unheimlich Vertraut. Bilder vom Terror*. Köln: König 2011.

Danfulani, Umar and Fwatshak, Sati, "Briefing: The September 2001 Events in Jos, Nigeria". In: *African Affairs* 101 (2002).

Deleuze, Gilles, *Difference and Repetition*. London: Continuum 2004.

Diers, Michael, „"Public Viewing" oder das elliptische Bild aus dem „Situation Room" in Washington". In: Hoffmann, Felix (Ed.), *Unheimlich Vertraut. Bilder vom Terror*. Köln: König 2011.

Engelhardt, Marc, *Heiliger Krieg. Heiliger Profit. Afrika als neues Schlachtfeld des internationalen Terrorismus*. Berlin: Links Verlag 2014.

Hansen, Stig Jarle, *Al-Shabaab in Somalia: the history and ideology of a militant Islamist group, 2005-2012*. New York: Columbia University Press 2013.

Harnischfeger, Johannes, "Boko Haram and its Muslim Critics. Observations from Yobe State". In: Pérouse de Montclos, Marc-Antoine (Ed.), *Boko Haram. Islamism, Politics, Security and the State in Nigeria*. Leiden: African Studies Centre 2014. pp. 33-62.

Heller, Dana, (Ed.), The Selling of 9/11. How a National Tragedy became a Commodity. New York: Palgrave Macmillan 2005.

Hentschel, Linda (Ed.), *Bilderpolitik in Zeiten von Krieg und Terror: Medien, Macht und Geschlechterverhältnisse*. Berlin: b_books 2008.

Hoffmann, Felix, „Visual Identities. An Introduction". In: Hoffmann, Felix (Ed.), *Unheimlich Vertraut. Bilder vom Terror*. Köln: König 2011.

Kahana, Jonathan, "Evidence of What? Harun Farocki and Trevor Paglen Picture Homeland Insecurity". In: Nils van Tomme (Ed.), *Visibility Machines: Harun Farocki and Trevor Paglen*. New York: Artbook D.A.P 2014.

Kasfir, Sidney L., "Narrating Trauma as Modernity. Kenyan Artists and the American Embassy Bombing". In: *African Arts* XXXVII/3 (2005), pp. 68-96.

Krings, Matthias, Marke "Osama": Über Kommunikation und Kommerz mit Bin-Laden-Bildern in Nigeria. In: *Peripherie*, 29 No. 113 (2009), pp. 31-55.

Larkin, Brian, "Making Equivalence Happen: Commensuration and the Architecture of Circulation". In: Spyer, Patricia and Steedly, Mary Margaret (Eds.), *Images That Move*. Santa Fe: SAR Press 2013.

Latour, Bruno, *Iconoclash oder Gibt es eine Welt jenseits des Bilderkriegs?* Berlin: Merve Verlag 2002.

Meyer, Birgit and Hughes, Stephen, "Editors Guest Preface". In: *Postscripts* 1/2, 1/3 (2005), pp. 149-153.

Mitchell, J. William T., *What Do Pictures Want? The Lives and Loves of Images.* Chicago 2005.

Page, Max. *The City's End. Two Centuries of Fantasies, Fears, and Premonitions of New York's Destruction*. New Haven: Yale University Press 2008.

Paul, Gerhard, "The Image as an Act and the New Wars of Images". In: Hoffmann, Felix (Ed.), *Unheimlich Vertraut. Bilder vom Terror*. Köln: König 2011. pp. 143-169.

Van Gelder, Hilde, "Reclaiming Information, Rebuilding Stories: Reinventing Fundamental Rights". In: Nils van Tomme (Ed.), *Visibility Machines: Harun Farocki and Trevor Paglen*. New York: Artbook D.A.P 2014.

Retort; Boal Iain et al., *Afflicted Powers: Capital and Spectacle in a New Age of War.* London: Verso 2005.

Schopp, Andrew and Hill, Matthew B. (Eds), *The War on Terror and American Popular Culture: September 11 and beyond.* Madison, NJ: Fairleigh Dickinson University Press 2009.

Seesemann, Rüdiger. Kenyan Muslims, the Aftermath of 9/11, and the War on Terror, in: Islam and Muslim Politics in Africa, (EDs) Soares, benjamin and Otoyek, René, New York (Palgrave) 2007, pp.157-176.

Spyer, Patricia and Steedly, Mary Margaret (Eds.), *Images That Move*. Santa Fe: SAR Press 2013.

Sturken, Marita, *Tourists of History. Memory, Kitsch and Consumerism from Oklahoma City to Ground Zero*. Durham: Duke University Press 2007.

Werckmeister, Otto Karl, *Der Medusa Effekt. Politische Bildstrategien seit dem 11. September 2001*. Berlin: Form+Zweck 2005.

Zizek, Slavoj, *Welcome to the Desert of the Real: five essays on 11 September and related dates*. London: Verso 2002.

Abdalla Uba Adamu

# THE REMEDIATION OF EVENTS:

# 9/11 IN NIGERIAN VIDEOS

## INTRODUCTION

The media coverage of the incidents of 9/11 and the subsequent Gulf War has reterritorialized and created a translocational connectivity of the event from a specific geographic location to an amorphous transnational arena where it is reworked and re-transcribed for domestic consumption on sites far away from its origin, but brought closer by the media. The central figures in the two incidents, former Iraqi President Saddam Hussein and Osama bin Laden of the Al Qaida network, were seen as heroes among the Muslims of northern Nigeria in particular. Posters, stickers, and, in the case of Bin Laden, T-shirts were produced to celebrate the two central figures. Many newborn male babies were named Saddam and Osama in the period following the escalation of the incidents. This created further visibilities and audibilities of the two figures and accentuates the role of media in mediating their acceptance and celebration as folk heroes in a political context different from their original environments.

However, the most textual interpretation of the events – sourced from CNN and Middle Eastern satellite TV broadcasts, especially Al Jazeera news channel – was the reenactment of the incident into two Hausa comedy video films. The first was *Ibro Usama* (2002), while the second was *Ibro Saddam* (2003). Both the films are parodies that, while giving a serious subject matter a light treatment, nevertheless communicate to the audience, principally the massive fan base of the actors Rabilu Musa Dan Ibro and Kulu, the actors' understanding of these global events.

This paper intertextually analyzes the intermedial shift of messaging from the satellite broadcasts of the event and its reworking into local African video dramas. In particular it looks at how the events leading to 9/11 – the Gulf War of 1991 – as well as the incident were reenacted based on the transnational satellite imagery and the re-interpretation of the textual messages of Osama bin Laden's broadcasts – which yields an insight into how a global event is reworked for a domestic audience.

## WARS IN THE PERSIAN GULF

Due to Iraqi support for various Arab and Palestinian militant groups such as Abu Nidal, the United States included Iraq in its list of state sponsors of international terrorism on 29 December 1979. The U.S. remained officially neutral after the invasion of Iran by Iraqi forces, which became the Iran–Iraq War. In March 1982, however, Iran began a successful counteroffensive – Operation Undeniable Victory – and the United States increased its support for Iraq to prevent Iran from forcing a surrender. After the Iran-Iraq War ended in August 1988, Iraq subsequently initiated a war with Kuwait on 2 August 1990.

Ignoring a United Nation's Security Council deadline to leave Kuwait in 1991, Saddam Hussein faced a U.S.-led coalition Gulf War that launched around-the-clock missile and aerial attacks on Iraq beginning in January 1991. The United States eventually drove the Iraqi Army out of Kuwait in February 1991, and occupied the southern portion of Iraq, as well as maintaining economic sanctions that were imposed on Iraq when Iraqi troops invaded Kuwait.

Subsequently, U.S. officials continued to accuse Iraq of violating the terms of the Gulf War's cease-fire by developing weapons of mass destruction that included anthrax, nerve gas, nuclear weapons, and other banned weaponry. The Iraqi government repeatedly denied possessing these weapons. Isolated military strikes by U.S. and British forces continued on Iraq sporadically, the largest being Operation Desert Fox in 1998. Western charges of Iraqi resistance to UN access to suspected weapons were the pretext for the crises between 1997 and 1998, culminating in intensive U.S. and British missile strikes on Iraq on 16-19 December 1998. The election of George W. Bush as U.S. President in 2000 saw a more aggressive policy toward Iraq, and after two years of intermittent activity, U.S. and British warplanes struck harder at sites near Baghdad in February 2001.

While the events of the Gulf War were still bubbling in the newsrooms, another incident loomed in the horizon. On the morning of 11 September 2001, 19 Al Qaida operatives hijacked four commercial passenger jet airliners. The hijackers deliberately crashed two of the airliners into the Twin Towers of the World Trade Center in New York City. Another team of hijackers crashed a third airliner into the Pentagon in Arlington, Virginia, just outside Washington, D.C. The fourth plane crashed into a field near Shanksville in rural Pennsylvania after some of its passengers and flight crew attempted to retake control of the plane, which the hijackers had redirected toward Washington, D.C. There were no survivors from any of the flights. Led by Osama bin Laden, a radical Islamist trained by the U.S. during the 1980s to conduct guerilla attacks against the Soviet Army in Afghanistan, Al Qaida formed a large base of operations in Afghanistan, which had been ruled by the Islamist extremist regime of the Taliban since 1996.

Osama bin Laden initially denied, but later admitted, involvement in the incidents through various podcasts. For instance, on 16 September 2001, bin Laden denied any involvement with the attacks by reading a statement that was broadcast by Qatar's Al Jazeera satellite channel: "I stress that I have not carried out this act, which appears to have been carried out by individuals with their own motivation." (Griffin 2009:28).

This denial was broadcast on U.S. news networks and worldwide. On 27 December 2001, in another podcast, Bin Laden states, "Terrorism against America deserves to be praised because it was a response to injustice, aimed at forcing America to stop its support for Israel, which kills our people" (Bergen 2006:370), but he stopped short of admitting responsibility for the attacks.

The United States responded to the attacks by launching a "War on Terror", invading Afghanistan to depose the Taliban, who had harbored the Al Qaida movement. The invasion began on 7 October 2001. The stated aim was to locate Osama bin Laden and other high-ranking Al Qaida members and put them on trial, to destroy the whole organizational structure of Al Qaida, and to remove the Taliban regime, which supported and gave safe haven to Al Qaida.

However, Iraq's subsequent refusal to disarm its alleged weapons of mass destruction as well as its support for terrorism as exemplified by the 9/11 incident served as triggers for another full-scale U.S.-led allied invasion of Iraq in March 2003.

### WAR NEWS AND MEDIAL REPRODUCTION

The Persian Gulf Wars were heavily televised wars. For the first time people all over the world were able to watch live pictures of missiles hitting their targets and fighters taking off from aircraft carriers. Allied forces were keen to demonstrate the accuracy of their weapons.

In the United States, the "big three" networks ABC, CBS, and NBC led the network news coverage of the wars. Still, it was CNN that gained the most popularity for its coverage, and indeed its wartime coverage can be seen as one of the landmark events in the development of the network. Newspapers all over the world also covered the war and Time magazine published a special issue dated 28 January 1991 with the headline "War in the Gulf" emblazoned on the cover over a picture of Baghdad taken as the war began. At the same time, the coverage of the war was new in its instantaneousness. About halfway through the war, Iraq's government decided to allow live satellite transmissions from the country by Western news organizations.

According to Jeanne Colleran (2003), re-echoing Paul Patton's "Introduction" to Jean Baudrillard's *The Gulf War Did Not Take Place*, the 1991 Gulf War was the first war in which images of the war were relayed live from the battlefront. The war became a "mediatized" (Colleran 2003:616) process in which the media transformed public events into commodities. Indeed, as Darren G. Lillker (2008) further argues, the theory of mediatization explains how the media shape and frame the processes and discourses of political communication, as well as the society in which that communication takes place. Thus, "from the moment the United States began military action against Iraq, television journalists and news anchors converted the war into a nightly (or in the case of CNN, constant) mini-series." (Colleran 2003:618).

As Colleran further argues, the spectacularity of the war coverage seems to provide such substantive and comprehensive insight that no further critical analysis is needed. The nature of the coverage therefore becomes an endorsement. Indeed, one could argue that the attackers used geopolitical strategies to further their cause in launching themselves from a low-density media coverage market to one in which their views and demands could be heard on a much larger scale. By providing massive coverage of the events, the U.S. media seem to have unwittingly given the perpetrators of the attacks a stage they needed. Further, one way the U.S. may have contributed to the support for terrorists' aim with media was by broadcasting and thus giving general publicity to the messages sent by bin Laden, obtained by whatever means necessary. By constantly reproducing what he said, the media increased the spectacularity of the theater of events. Consequently, by launching attacks against the U.S. at the heart of media focus, the attackers have found a weapon in one of the instruments of free society. Thus Jean Baudrillard argued, the attackers, "also appropriated for themselves the very weapons of the other dominant power – money, stock market speculation, computer and aeronautics technologies, the specular dimensions and media networks. They have assimilated all of these from modernity and globalization without deviating from their goal, which is to destroy them." (Baudrillard 2002:409).

The media coverage of these events, with images on magazine covers and satellite TV newsreels echoed around the world and giving Iraq the image of an underdog facing a massive onslaught from much more superior forces. In northern Nigeria, the established local and transnational Hausa radio stations of BBC World Service, Voice of America (VOA), Radio France International (rfi), and Radio Iran (Hausa Section) provided ample translation of the events from agency reports. In particular, Radio Iran provided a more slanted interpretation of the events in accordance with the ideological fault lines of the Sunni-Shiite divide in the Muslim world.

Thus, the media coverage of the incidents of the Gulf Wars and the War on Terror re-mediated and "co-territorialized" – through spontaneous messaging – the event from a specific geographic location to an amorphous transnational arena in which it was reworked and re-transcribed for domestic consumption on sites far away from its origin, but brought closer by the media; in essence, the events were remediated on the local level.

## TURNING AWAY FROM SUFFERING: FILM PRODUCTION AND 9/11

The reactions of the international film community, from both Hollywood and Bollywood, toward the reenactment of the incidents preceding and including 9/11 were more muted – perhaps out of respect for the sheer catastrophic nature of the events that they might be accused on cashing on. As Wheeler Winston Dixon noted:

"In the days and weeks after 9/11, Hollywood momentarily abandoned the hyper violent spectacles that dominated mainstream late 1990s cinema. Films were temporarily shelved, sequences featuring the World Trade Center were recut, and "family" films were rushed into release or production, to offer the public escape from the horrors of 9/11" (Dixon 2004:3).

Thus, as Quay and Damico further pointed out, Hollywood initially responded to the events of 9/11 by changing a number of its filmic productions out of concern that audiences would not be receptive to certain imagery soon after the attacks. At least 45 films were cancelled, altered, or delayed. Of particular concern were images of the Twin Towers, which were commonly included in films set in New York City; "after the attacks, the Twin Towers were quickly edited out of comedies." (Quay and Damico 2010:174).

Thus for many years there were no major Hollywood features reflecting on the 9/11 incident. Most of the early spate of Hollywood films dealing with the theme were either TV documentaries, for instance, *9/11: The Twin Towers* (2006) or acerbic docu-dramas such as *Fahrenheit 9/11* (2004). The only major feature films were *World Trade Center* (2006) and *United 93* (2006).

In India, the Indian film industry produced the first "conflict-commerce" (Krings

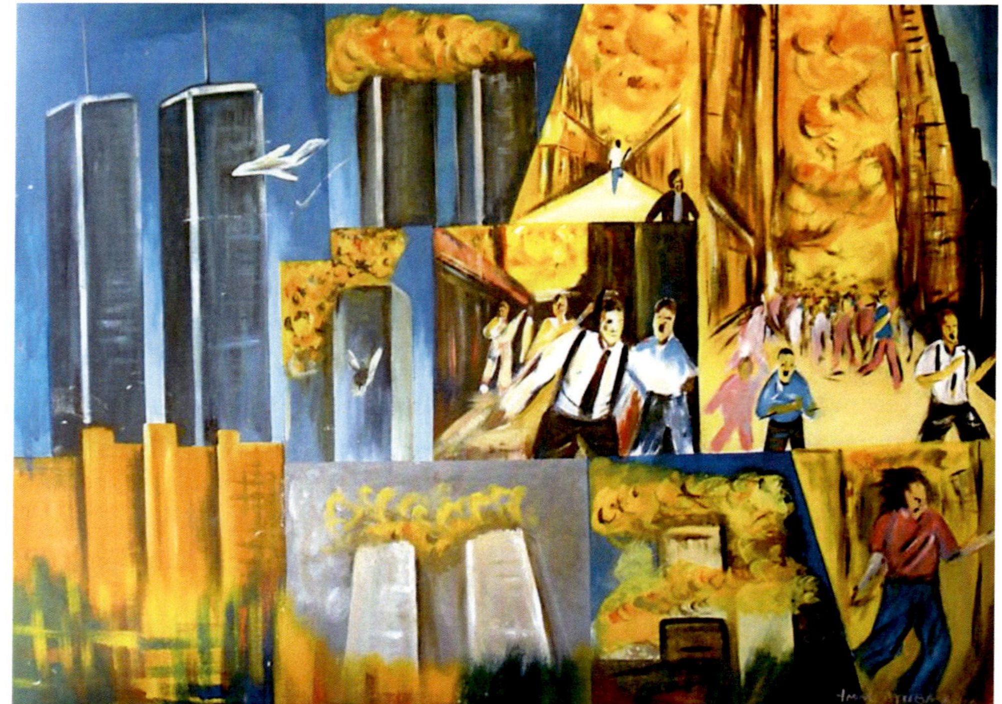

Fig. 1
**Wall painting of the 9/11 incident in a College in Kano**

2009:31) film in the form of *Yun Hota To Kya Hota* (2008). The story revolves around a group of people who were not connected to each other in anyway other than by ill fate. These were people from different parts of India who had travelled to the U.S. and were now boarding the ill-fated flights that crashed into the Twin Towers and Pentagon on 9/11.The story reenacts the horror of the hijacking and some of the incidents that occurred on board during those catastrophic minutes. Some of the characters in the film died in the accident while some survived – thus reworking the original live script of the incident in which there were no survivors in the aircraft.

Years later, in 2013, Kamal Hassan directed *Viswaroop* (Omnipresent), a Tamil spy thriller that shows a Muslim RAW agent plotting against a jihadi who wants to detonate a nuclear device in the heart of New York. Although others were produced in between, there was a studied effort on the part of the major film studios to respect the events of 9/11 and to avoid the theme altogether.

## NIGERIAN RESPONSES TO THE MEDIA SCREENPLAY

Whereas in the U.S. and other parts of the world there were commemorations of the 9/11 incident, in some parts of Nigeria there were *celebrations* of the event. In the process of the celebrations, almost all variety of media were used – presenting perhaps the most focused intermedial interpretation of the event – and became part of the cultural industries targeting youth in particular.

In Nigeria, the first local interpretation of the 9/11 event was in the form of protests against U.S. government led by the Kano State branch of the Nigerian

Council of Ulama [Council of Islamic Scholars] on 3rd October 2001. Muslim youth in both the northern and southern parts of the country also protested. For instance, on 11 October 2001 a group of Muslim women marched through the streets of Kano in northern Nigeria, protesting the U.S. attack on Afghanistan. The following day, 12 October 2001, Kano erupted into a violent protest against the war when thousands of youths led a protest march after Friday prayers. In southern Nigeria, the National Council of Muslim Youths (NACOMYO), which was based in Ibadan, mobilized its members to protest the U.S. action against Afghanistan on 6 November 2001.

By 19 October 2001, Osama bin Laden had become a folk hero in Kano, and his posters, downloaded from the Internet and culled from international news magazines, became hot commodities. A visual depiction of the event is painted on a large wall in the Art Class of the local Kano State School of Technology, seen in Figure 1.

The celebration of Bin Laden in Kano is reflected in the poster sales at a local market. According to a news report:

"One of the sellers of the portraits who simply called himself Abdulmumini told *Weekly Trust* that on a daily basis he sells between 150 and 200 copies of the portraits and that because of the excessive demand for the portraits, he had increased the price of the portraits from N50 to N100. He said in spite of the increase in price, there is still a mad rush for the portraits" (Kazaure 2001).

Further, in the same Kano, another dimension of the support for Osama bin Laden was reflected in the spate of naming babies after both Saddam and bin Laden. For instance, according to a BBC news report, in Kano, one hospital worker said there was currently "a season of Osama babies." "Osama bin Laden is my hero," said 36-year-old Sadiq Ahmed, father of a baby Osama. "My wife gave birth to our third child on 15 September and I named him Osama in honour of Osama bin Laden who has proved to the world that only Allah is invincible, by exposing America to shame despite its claim of being the strongest nation on earth." (BBC News 2002).

The posters and later T-shirts became the first transmedial ports of the domestication of the events, although more emphasis was placed by the cultural production industries on the Afghan War and its dramatis personae. Subsequently, T-shirts (apparently produced outside Nigeria, judging by their high

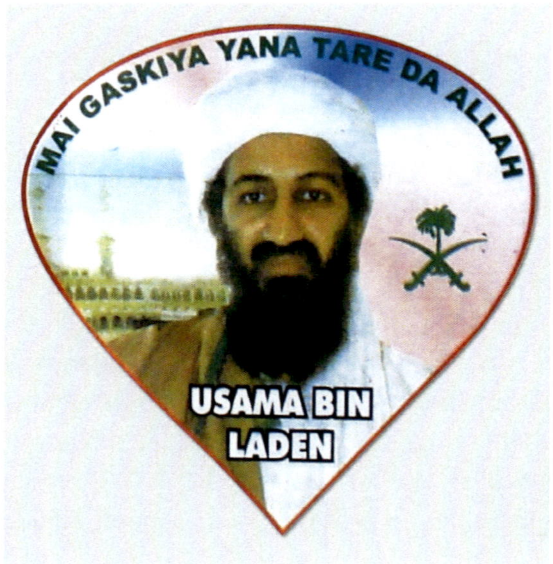

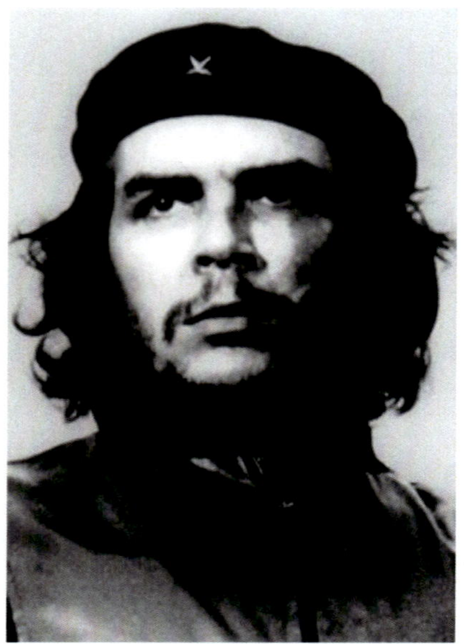

Fig. 2
**Cult Revolutionaries: "Osama bin Guevara"**

quality) with full-face pictures of Osama bin Laden appeared in the second-hand clothing markets ("gwanjo") in early 2002 and were in high demand particularly among migrant Islamic school pupils (almajirai) (see figure p. 24). The posters of Osama bin Laden were later made into stickers and these adorned commercial motorcycles as well as the backs of commercial buses throughout northern Nigeria. Significantly, these "war poster industries" were patronized predominantly by youth educated more Islamically than Westernly, who see Osama bin Laden as an Islamic hero.

Reynolds and Barnett argued in this sense that CNN's verbal and visual framing of 9/11 created higher visibility and subsequently made it possible for audiences away from the theater to adopt its iconography; for "to viewers the events of September 11 comprised an act of war so horrific that immediate military retaliation was not only justified but necessary." (Reynolds and Barnett 2003:86).

In all the posters, bin Laden was portrayed as romantic warrior, with his facial image having the same cult power as Ernesto "Che" Guevara's face that attained for millions of youth across the world in the 1960s when Alberto Korda's photograph of him received wide distribution and modification, appearing on T-shirts, protest banners, and in many other formats. The most romantic and photogenic of all Latin American revolutionaries, Ernesto "Che" Guevara has, "ever since his death, been associated primarily with this single image." (Shaw and Dennison 2005:193). As Karantonis noted, "in Latin America Che Guevara is a folk hero, symbolizing revolution against forms of oppression and the landed elite, as well as championing attitudes against U.S. intervention in Latin American affairs." (Ibid. 2005:29).

In a similar way, Osama bin Laden became an icon of Islamist revolution in northern Nigeria in a "War against America", giving him the same revolutio-

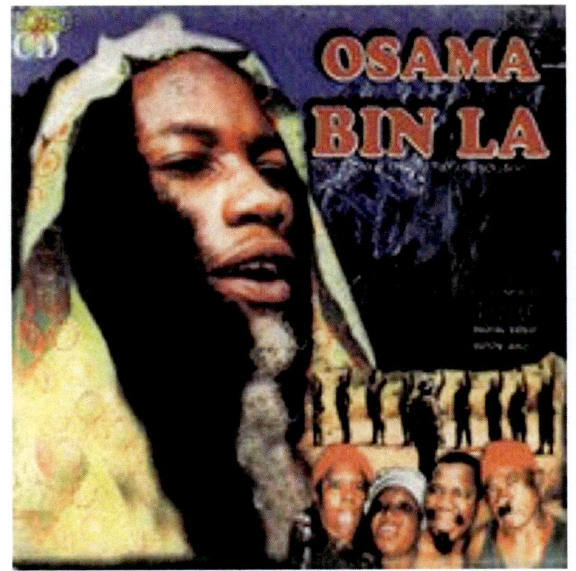


Fig. 3
**Osama Bin Igbo**
Nigerian Igbo version (2002)

nary cult status as Che Guevara. A comparison is shown in Figure 2.

The poster of Osama bin Laden, downloaded from the Internet, was overlaid on the background of the Grand Mosque in Mecca and the Saudi Arabian symbol of crossed swords next a palm date tree. The slogan in the Bin Laden picture, "Mai Gaskiya Yana Tare da Allah" (He who holds on to the truth is surely with Allah) is intended to portray bin Laden's almost prophetic qualities.

The imagery of Osama bin Laden and Che Guevara shared similar fates in the different communities. Bin Laden, like Che Guevara, was a political figure, but also the focus of a pop culture following among Muslim northern Nigerians, just like Che was an icon for 1960s youth in North America and Western Europe.

**NIGERIAN VIDEOS**

While posters, stickers and T-shirts of the 9/11 incident became the immediate first ports of call for intermedial shifts of the imageries of the incident – shifting locations from newsreels to physical cultural production media – visual reenactment of the incident was slower, as on the international level. The Nigerian film industry, Nollywood, vied with the Kano-based Hausa film industry, Kanywood, to produce the first film based on the event. The first film, however, was from Nollywood in 2002 and was titled *Osama bin La* (2002). It was in the Igbo language and created furor in Kano over its portrayal of Osama bin Laden as a crook and fraudster. Figure 3 shows the video's poster.

The Kano Government security agencies were concerned that the video found its way into Kano markets. The "Nigerian" film market Nollywood, controlled principally by Igbo merchants in Kano, exists virtually independently of the Hausa home videos in Kano and follows a different marketing and distributing network. The concern in Kano over *Osama bin La* was that it could generate riots – in a polity where Osama bin Laden was seen as an Islamic jihadist. The government quickly banned the video (even before the Censorship Board became aware of the film in the first place), and Hausa cassette dealers throughout northern Nigeria refused to stock it.[1] It has not been possible to obtain a copy of the video for deeper visual analysis.

[1] Based on fieldwork and interviews with Alhaji Abdulkadir A. Kurawa, then Executive Secretary of the Kano State Censorship Board, 23 April, 2002.

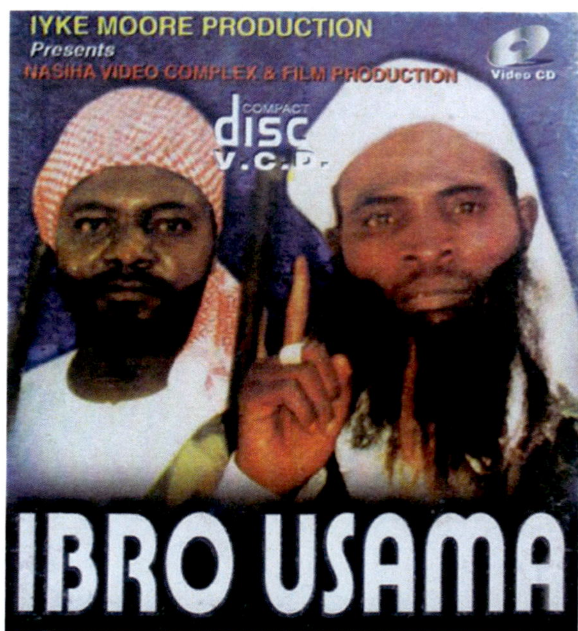


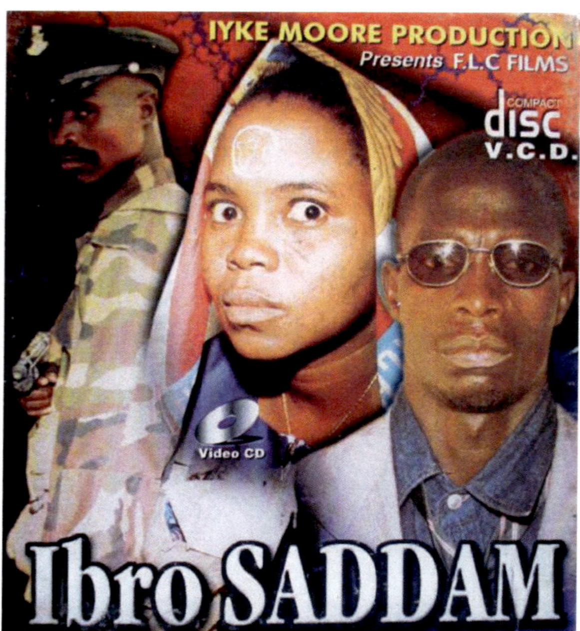


Fig. 4
**Prepping up for War on Insolence** – 9/11 in Hausa Video Films

This constant barrage of news items on 9/11 and "visual framing" provided the Kanywood Hausa film industry in northern Nigeria with opportunities of reworking the events in two films – *Ibro Usama* (2002) followed almost immediately by *Ibro Saddam* (2003). Both were comedies, as was Igbo *Osama bin La*. Hausa filmmakers therefore focused attention on the historical narrative of the events, tracing the roots of the incident. I will analyze the films, framing my analysis within the context of the intertextual felicity of the news coverage of the events and the plot of the films. The posters of the two films are shown in Figure 4.

The Ibro Usama poster in Figure 4 indeed reproduces the exact visual imagery of Osama bin Laden popularized in posters and car bumper stickers throughout northern Nigeria, with a single index finger raised to symbolize the oneness of Allah and total dependence on Him. The poster therefore carries its own spiritual conveyance in additional to the image of Osama bin Laden.

### *IBRO USAMA* AND THE "WAR ON INSOLENCE" ("YAKI DA FITSARA")

*Ibro Usama* and *Osama Bin La* were released within a few months of each other in 2002. And since the pattern of production of the Ibro series of films – called "chamama genre" – is based on cheap productions, I would suggest that *Ibro Usama* was a counterpoint to the Christian *Osama Bin La*. For while the latter ridicules Osama bin Laden, the first remained faithful to bin Laden's podcasts on the Internet – thus giving a more accurate script of bin Laden's motives and philosophies.

The two Hausa 9/11 films followed a reversed order in reenacting the Gulf Wars. For instance, *Ibro Usama* was supposed to cover the invasion of Afghanistan by U.S. troops in October 2001. The film was released in early 2002. *Ibro Saddam*, on the other hand, covered the incidents of the Kuwait War (1990) in 2003.

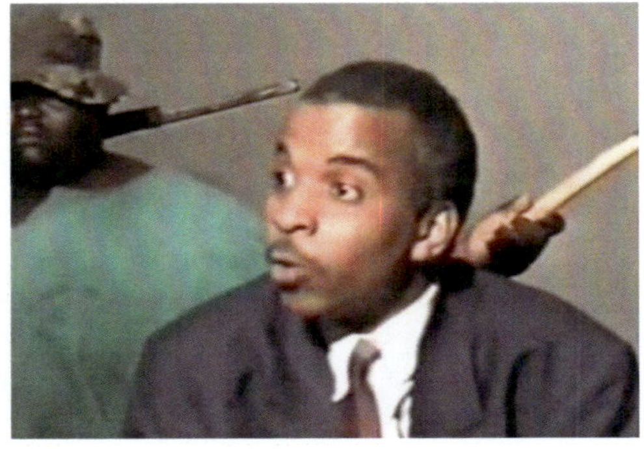

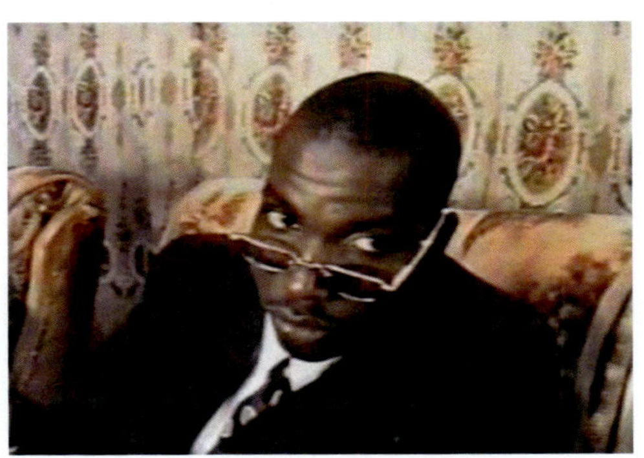

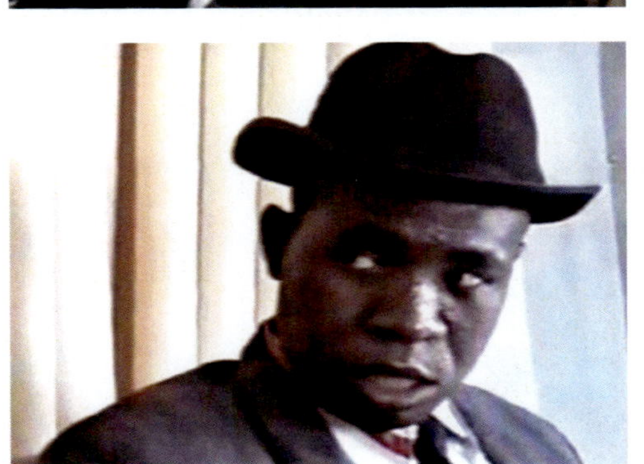

Fig. 5
**George "Bosho" Bush** Addressing his War Cabinet

Fig. 6
The Secretary of Defense, **"Donald Kwalle Henry Rumsfeld"**

Fig. 7
**"Tony Blair"** in his support for War on Insolence

While the two films were independently made, they do supplement each other in providing a historical reconstruction of the Gulf Wars and the War on Terror.

*Ibro Usama* (retaining the Hausanized version of Osama's name) details the American war against Afghanistan and the comic antics both sides went through to execute the war. The theme of the film was a declaration of "War on Insolence" (Yaki da Fitsara) declared by George "Bosho". The George Bush character is played by a light-skinned actor always in a suit, to portray as much "whiteness" as possible, as seen in Figure 5.

The War on Insolence was then declared on enemies the United States previously perceived as friends; the 9/11 attack on U.S. soil was seen as the attackers' insolence toward their former mentors. The U.S. Secretary of Defense, Donald Henry Rumsfeld, was played by an actor in a wooden manner to appear clueless about the war efforts. Figure 6 shows Alhassan Kwalle as Rumsfeld.

The script for the Hausa War on Insolence is heavily influenced by media images from newsreels, including buildings being blown up and helicopter gunship attacks (all culled from the Internet and pirated DVDs of conventional films), filtered through the lens of some northern Nigerians Muslims. Although the script for this comedic reference to the real War on Terror was poorly written, the Hausa *Ibro Usama* shows how the filmmakers perceive the war and convey it to their publics by scouring international news portals, creating a montage of remediations of the events in accordance with their own tastes.

In a shuttle diplomacy initiative, the Secretary of Defense, unusually accompanied by a bumbling British "prime minister" had the task of convincing allied nations to join the U.S. in the War on Insolence. The Blair character in *Ibro Usama* – shown in Figure 7 – is presented with a permanent bowler hat, providing an effective profiling of a typical British upper middle class power broker in the eyes of Nigerian filmmakers. Even the suit worn by the character is conservatively cut – at least in the fashion sense, if not the political.

From the start of the War on Terror in 2001, the British Prime Minister strongly supported much of the foreign policy of U.S. President George W. Bush and ensured that British armed forces participated in the 2001 invasion of Afghanistan and the 2003 invasion of Iraq.

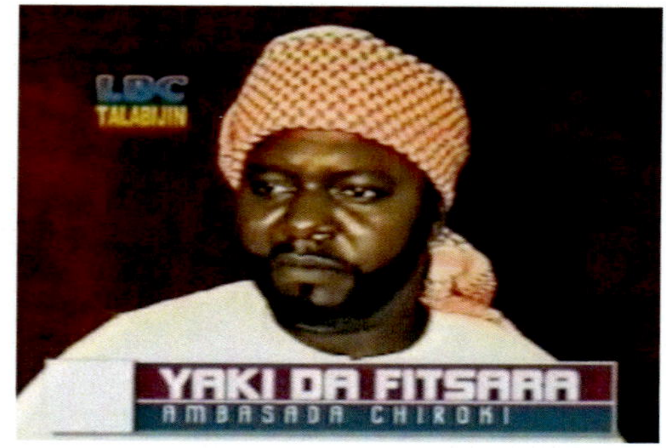


The War on Insolence cabinet eventually hatches a plan to obliterate Afghanistan, although the Secretary of Defense suggests asking Afghanistan authorities, the Taliban, to first hand over Ibro Usama to face justice for the atrocities committed against Americans, the refusal of which would lead to war between the United States and its allies against Afghanistan. In the real "Operation Enduring Freedom", as the Afghan war was codenamed, one of the five demands of the U.S. government to the Taliban was to deliver to the U.S. all of the leaders of Al Qaida. This was made on 20 September 2001.

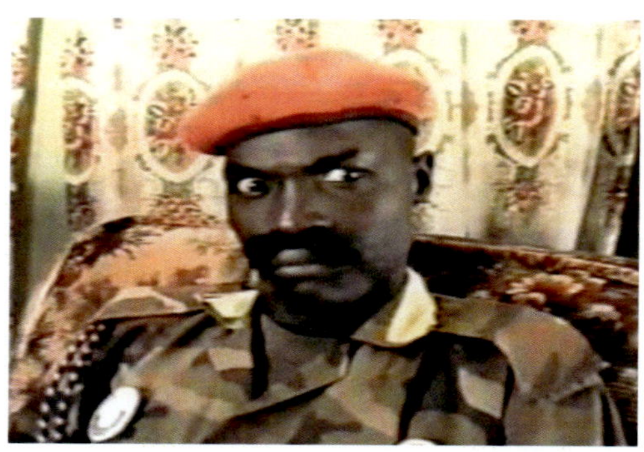

In *Ibro Usama*, the refusal of the Afghan Taliban leadership to "hand over" bin Laden to the Americans, exactly a day after it was made, was relayed to the world via satellite TV broadcast by the "Taliban Foreign Affairs Minister" as shown in Figure 8.

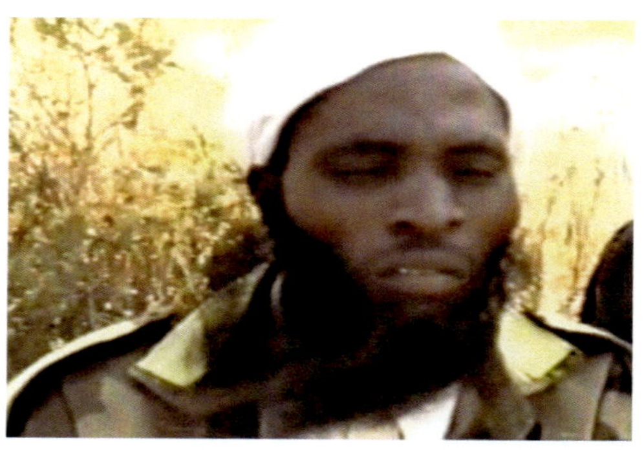

Fig. 8
**Not Handing Over Bin Laden**

Fig. 9
**Gen. Katakore Franks, U.S.** commander in Afghan war

Fig. 10
**Ibro as Bin Laden** training troops

The marquee across the screen, "Yaki Da Fitsara", meaning War on Insolence, turns the point of view of the war from that on terror to that on American insolence. The Ambassador warns of reprisals against any country providing logistic striking support to the NATO forces and their allies. The Ambassador then announces that they will not hand over bin Laden without sufficient evidence to link him explicitly to the Twin Towers' bombings; thus, the script remains faithful to the protestations of the offline bin Laden about his innocence of direct involvement in the Twin Towers attack.

Following the Taliban's repeated refusal to expel bin Laden and his group and end its support for international terrorism, the United States and its partners launched an invasion of Afghanistan on 7 October 2001 under the overall command of General Tommy Ray Franks. In Ibro Usama, Gen. Franks was played by a comedian, Katakore, as shown in Figure 9.

Bin Laden himself is depicted as a bumbling revolutionary with little game plan but constantly relying on prayers to Allah to help him fight his enemies. The screen shot in Figure 10 is taken from a "training session" in the bush of an African "Afghanistan" to prepare bin Laden's army for confrontation with the Americans.

Eventually a confrontation occurs between the Americans and bin Laden's spiritually motivated, if ill-equipped troops. The filmic narrative does not clearly indicate who won, simply fading out on Ibro Usama with captured American troops. The commanding officer then phones President Bosho and informs him that their segment of the war is over, as they have recorded a massive victory by capturing and securing the local market. This annoys Bosho and sends him into a screaming frenzy, followed by montages of slapstick comedy skits to the end of the film.

Fig. 11
**The demented Bush man** with wild staring eyes

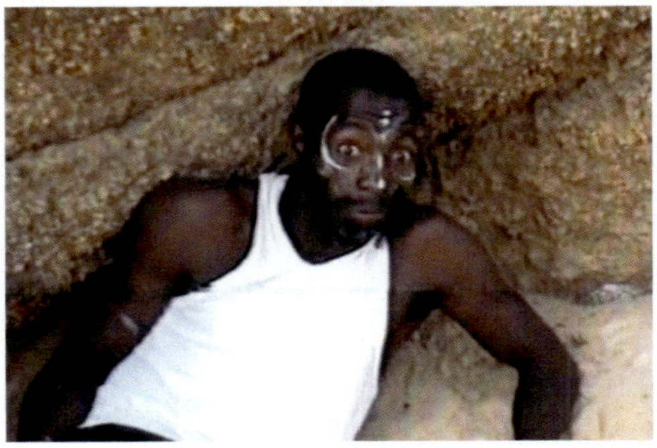

Fig. 12
**Ibro Saddam** rescuing a wild Bush

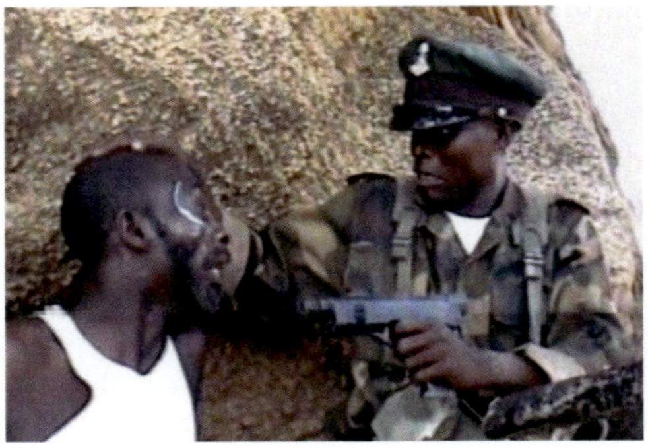

In the narrative of the Hausa video film *Ibro Usama*, almost every diplomatic initiative by the U.S. was depicted as resorting to either blackmail, arm-twisting, or outright corruption to convince the allies to join in the War on Terror. Although the allies are eventually persuaded to join the war efforts, they always insist on valid proof that indeed there is justification for the war. The film's central message is that the War on Terror was declared without sufficient proof and that it was initiated by the countries allegedly behind the initial terror attacks.

## *IBRO SADDAM* AND "NON-CLEAR" WEAPONS INSPECTION

The second Hausa video film that treats the tragedy of the 9/11 incidence was *Ibro Saddam*. It was released in early 2003, too early for the film to capture the invasion of Iraq in the same year. Instead, it provided a sort of prequel to *Ibro Usama* by going back to the Gulf War of 1991 and providing a historical tapestry on which to weave its plot, as well as to enable an understanding of the events in *Ibro Usama*, particularly the allusion to Iraq's possession of weapons of mass destruction.

The film starts with the Saddam character, Ibro Saddam, leading his troops in some military sortie. They encounter an incoherent wild "bush" man, with wide eyes and tribal marks painted all over his face, as seen in Figure 11.

Being a magnanimous leader, Ibro Saddam rescues the bush man, who happens to be a Christian, and rehabilitates him. When asked his name, the bush man simply said "Kulu Bush" (See figure 12, p. 51.)

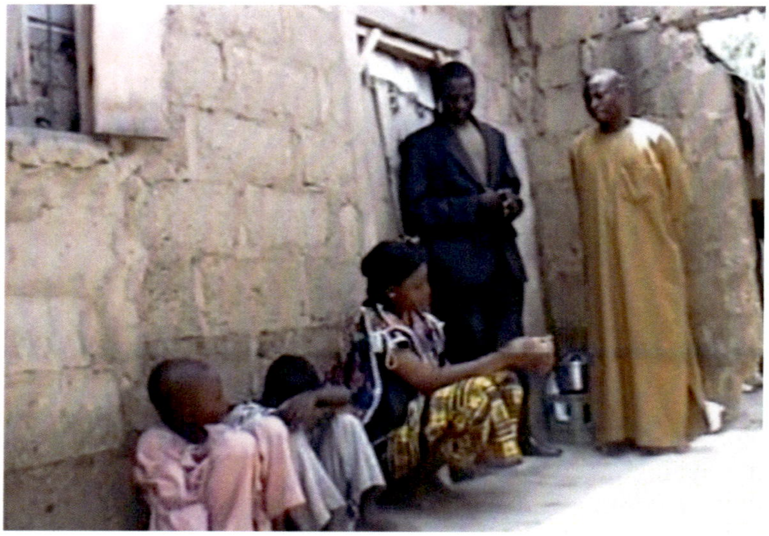

Fig. 13
**Magnanimous Saddam** – helping a widow and children

Thus, as in *Ibro Usama*, *Ibro Saddam* reverses the role of the antagonist, making him the protagonist and essentially shifting the point of view of the narrative to a more imaginative recollection that suits the audiences of the filmmakers. This is further confirmed by the series of scenes that show Ibro Saddam engaged in various humanitarian activities that establish his personality and acceptance among his people. In one scene, he enters a household where a widow is comforting her children who are crying because of hunger. The Saddam character chides her for not reporting her poor status to an agency created to assist women in her situation and proceeds to give her money to purchase food items, as in Figure 13.

Next he is shown severely punishing a villager for mistreating his goat, as another show of his compassion to all in his domain – both human and animal. In the end, the villager thanks Ibro Saddam for his compassion even to animals.

In another scene, Ibro Saddam's sheikhs counsel him against helping "Jews and Christians" as "masu hikima" (those who are crafty), saying Muslims should avoid association with Jews and Christians. The Saddam character insists on helping the downtrodden or less fortunate who happen to be within the purview of Islam. Thus, right away the Saddam character interprets one life mission of Islam as a more humane way of living.

All these montages serve the purpose of creating a sympathetic perspective of Ibro Saddam for the filmmaker's audiences – thus casting the real War on Terror as a post-imperialist device aimed at acquiring the mineral resources of a weaker country.

In the meantime, the homeless, uncivilized Christian rescued from the bush by Ibro Saddam emigrates to the United States and is renamed "George Kulu Bush". He adopts the surname of "Bush" because the bush in which he was found is his identity. He somehow enters politics and we see his posters ador-

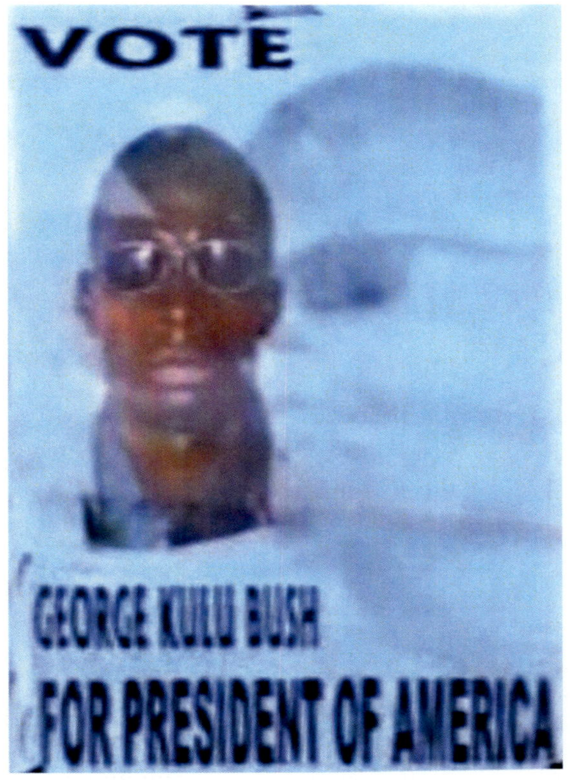


Fig. 14
**George Kulu Bush**
for American
President

ning walls where he is competing for the post of the President of the United States, as in Figure 14.

Yet despite being given a new lease on life by the magnanimous Ibro Saddam, Kulu Bush harbors a strong hatred for Ibro Saddam and plots to get rid of him and occupy his country (it is not clear if Kulu Bush himself is an Iraqi). There are scenes of how the people in the public sphere hate the new president for his threats of war and his aggression towards Ibro Saddam and how they fear that reprisals will have far-reaching consequences. Thus, the filmmakers see the conflict in Iraq as a personality clash between the leaders of the U.S. and Iraq, rather than as based on protecting world security or freedom and democracy.

After being elected as the President of the United States – and there is a scene in the film in which ordinary people debate the election results, claiming that Bush did not win – George Kulu Bush has two carefully chosen convicted criminals brought to him for briefing. The first is a rapist, while the second admits to violently killing a woman and her children. Their crimes impress Kulu Bush so much that he appoints the rapist director of intelligence services and authorizing him to go to Arab countries and spy on their mineral resources, particularly oil "wanda su ka fi mu" (which they have more of than we do). He appoints the convicted murderer head of his personal security, authorizing him to destroy anyone who even approaches him – thus creating the image of a paranoid president who appoints only criminals to positions of power and responsibility.

Seeking to settle old scores, George Kulu Bush decides to declare war on Ibro Saddam, his former savior. Thus, according to this montage, the subsequent war on Iraq is brought about by *Ibro Saddam's* befriending "Jews and Christians". This montage subsequently explores the political relationship between U.S. and Iraq, in which the U.S. considered Iraq an ally before things soured.

After two years during which the Americans had bombed Afghanistan, the director of intelligence reports that, after Afghanistan, the U.S. should look for a country that would be swatted like a fly so that the U.S. can take what it wants, particularly mineral resources like oil. President Kulu welcomes this idea and suggests swatting Ibro Saddam (although the actor flubs his lines in

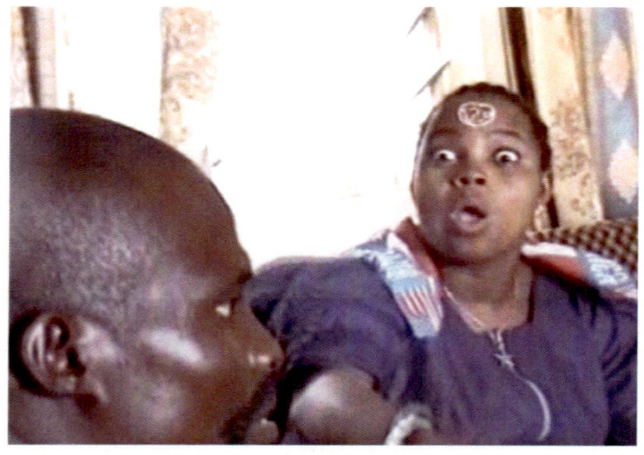

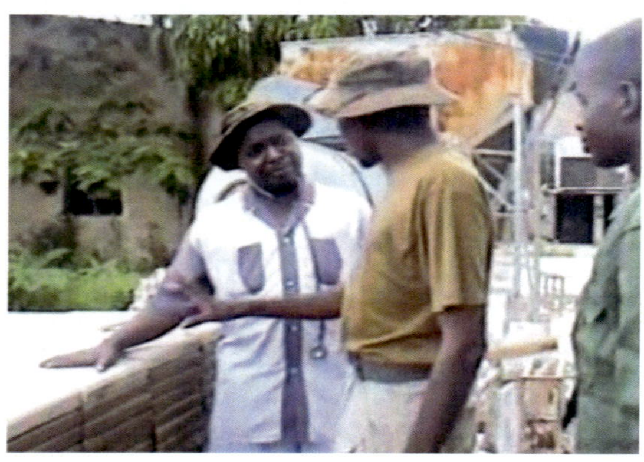

Fig. 15
**Unyielding Ibro Saddam** and the more aggressive United Nations representative

Fig. 16
Weapons inspector **Hans Chiroki Blix** looking for "Non-clear"/Nuclear weapons and "Ant-rest"/Anthrax

the dialogue and says "Saddam Hussain").

A two-pronged approach is adopted. The first is a media blitz to convince the world that Ibro Saddam is evil. The second is to send an inspection team to uncover any weapons, particularly those of mass destruction, that Ibro Saddam might have stockpiled, which will give the U.S. army enough justification to attack Iraq and arrest Ibro Saddam or preferably kill him by any means. As O'Shaughnessy pointed out, "The British and U.S. governments recognized that the propaganda war would be as critical as the physical war. International public opinion had to be at least neutralized if it could not be persuaded." (O'Shaughnessy 2004:211). The narrative of Ibro Saddam would seem to reinforce this fundamental fact.

The ultimate aim, though, is to weaken Iraq as a nation, get rid of Ibro Saddam, acquire the oil fields of Iraq for Americans, and appoint a stooge president who will kowtow to American will and wishes. This is revealed as part of a larger world domination strategy, for after obliterating Iraq, the next target is Syria. The task of this investigation is given to the United Nations because, as President Kulu Bush boasts, "It is ours, and when it investigates, it will only tell us the truth."

Subsequently, the United Nations is sent to Ibro Saddam. The UN, represented by a female actress, itself symbolic because the Hausa translation of United Nations, or "majalisar dinkin duniya" (the assembly of uniting the world) is feminine. This character accuses Ibro Saddam of forming "majalisar barke duniya" (the assembly of splitting the world), as seen in Figure 15.

In fact, this gender dimension is brought out in a heated argument between Ibro Saddam and the United Nations in which Ibro Saddam says he understands the UN insistence on inspections of his country for weapons of mass destruction but does not have to agree, whereupon the UN insists he has to accept the decisions of the body. Ibro Saddam then points out that he is only being merciful to the UN representative because she is a woman – otherwise he would have destroyed her. However, in the end, Ibro Saddam agrees to the inspection because he feels he has nothing to hide.

In this acquiescence, coupled with the earlier scenes of Kulu Bush ordering the UN to carry out weapons inspection because the United States "owns the United Nations", *Ibro Saddam* reflects a masculine understanding of the ineffectiveness of UN and further affirms that the UN is merely carrying out a U.S. agenda on Ibro Saddam's territory.

Then the United Nations Monitoring, Verification and Inspection Commission led by Hans Martin Blix, played by another comedian, Bashir Bala "Chiroki" as a bumbling, incoherent team leader, is sent to Ibro Saddam's territory. He goes about fumbling, stumbling, and generally mumbling on a search for weapons of mass destruction ("makaman kare dangi") and getting increasingly frustrated when he does not find any, despite the full co-operation of the locals, principally because the latter are not even sure what to look for or what it would look like when they actually see it. For instance, at one site, the chief inspector declares to the site's owners that the inspection team is there to search for "non-clear weapons" (uttered in English dialogue, rather than Hausa), as shown in Figure 16.

This word play between "nuclear" and "non-clear" reflects a subtle subtext in the film's narrative, as it acknowledges the UN Inspector's background in inspecting nuclear disasters, particularly Chernobyl in the Soviet Union in April 1986. Hans Blix was also the head of the Atomic Energy Commission.

The portrayal of the inspectors as fumbling further reflects an understanding of how ineffective the inspections were in finding the evidence Kulu Bush wanted in order to invade Iraq. They also declare they are looking for "ant-rest", another word play, this time on "anthrax"; and "uranium" becomes "reunion". At another inspection site, the team leader insists on "investigating" a woman (who is clothed in full hijab, the Muslim female dressing) in a private room – to the protestations of both the woman and his own troop commander. It would appear that this is introduced as a further reflection of the defilement of the sacred territory that is pure (even the hijab worn by the woman is pure white) – all in an attempt to sully Ibro Saddam's name. In the end, they find nothing worth reporting, and the film flounders to the end.

## CONCLUSION

In this essay I have explored the "remediation" of a series of political communication broadcasts in relation to the 9/11 incidents in the form of newsreels and looked at how these were reworked by the Muslim Hausa of northern Nigeria as local versions of the events. Although there are other forms of cultural production of the incidence, I have focused only on video films. It is significant that the Nigerian film industry seems to be the first to produce feature films about 9/11, releasing two films in 2002 (*Osama Bin La*, *Ibro Usama*) and one in 2003 (*Ibro Saddam*), although the latter is a prequel. Mainstream film industries, particularly Hollywood and Bollywood, seemed to have waited for what might be understood as a "decent waiting period" of at least five years before producing full feature films on the incident – and even then, they produced very few.

The narrative structure of the two Hausa 9/11 films was based on international reports of the events, particularly the Hausa translations of world news from Hausa services of BBC World Service, Voice of America, Radio France International (rfi), Deutsche Welle, and Radio Tehran. The events portrayed in the films reflect not only an understanding of the chronology of the Gulf Wars and their consequences, but also a jaundiced take on the wars themselves.

The two films clearly narrate the Gulf Wars from the point of view of America's antagonists (Bin Laden and Saddam Hussein), rather than the American protagonist views. The narrative structure therefore cast the Americans as aggressors – further reinforcing the oft-repeated anti-American mantra prevalent in many African countries. Thus, despite an attempt to present "facts" as they heard them through various media outlets, the filmmakers were able to inject perspectives that are sympathetic to bin Laden and Saddam Hussein, overturning the mainstream media's narrative structure of the stories to convert them into the actual protagonists. This reveals how texts and events are reworked in African societies that do not share the same political views as those of the majority of the Western nations.

## REFERENCES

Baudrillard, Jean, "L'esprit du terrorisme". *The South Atlantic Quarterly*. 101/2 (2002), pp. 403-415.

Bergen, Peter. L., *The Osama bin Laden I know: An Oral History of al-Qaeda's Leader*. New York: Free Press 2006.

Colleran, Jeanne M., "Disposable wars, disappearing acts: Theatrical responses to the 1991 Gulf War". *Theatre Journal* 55/4 (2003), pp. 613-632.

Dixon, Wheeler, "Something Lost – Film after 9/11". In: (ibid.) (Ed.), *Film and Television after 9/11*. Carbondale: Southern Illinois University Press 2004. pp. 1-24.

Griffin, David Ray, *Osama bin Laden: Dead or alive?* Northampton/Mass: Olive Branch Press 2009.

Karantonis, Antonio, *Perspectives of an Iconoclast: Writings in Latin American Studies and International Relations*. Victoria, B.C.: Trafford 2005.

Krings, Matthias, "Marke 'Osama'. Über Kommunikation und Kommerz mit Bin-Laden-Bildern in Nigeria". *Peripherie* 113/29 (2009), pp. 31-55.

Lilleker, Darren. G., *Key concepts in political communications*. London: Sage 2006.

O'Shaughnessy, Nicholas J., *Politics and propaganda: Weapons of mass seduction*. Ann Arbor: University of Michigan Press 2004.

Reynolds, Amy and Barnett, Brooke, "America under attack: CNN's verbal and visual framing of September 11". In: Chermak, Steven M. et al. (Eds.), *Media representations of September 11*. Westport, Conn: Paeger 2003. pp. 85-101.

Shaw, Lisa and Dennison, Stephanie, *Pop Culture Latin America!: Media, Arts, and Lifestyle*. Santa Barbara, Calif.: abc-clio 2005.

## ONLINE

BBC News, "Osama baby craze hits Nigeria". January 2002. http://news.bbc.co.uk/2/hi/africa/1741171.stm accessed January 14, 2015.

Kazaure, Musa Umar, "Kano Ulama declare support for Bin Laden". *Daily Trust* 2001, http://allafrica.com/stories/200110090433.html accessed January 14, 2015.

Kazaure, usa Umar, "Price of Bin Laden's portraits hikes". *Daily Trust* 2001, http://allafrica.com/stories/200110190407.html accessed January 14, 2015.

## FILMOGRAPHY

Dale, Richard, *9/11: The Twin Towers*. United States: Dangerous Films 2006.

Dare, Auwalu, *Ibro Usama*. Nigeria: Nasiha Video Complex Film Production 2002.

Greengrass, Paul, *United 93*. United States: Universal Pictures 2006.

Moore, Michael, *Fahrenheit 9/11*. United States: Fellowship Adventure Group 2004.

Munir, Kabeer.. *Ibro Saddam*. Nigeria: FLL Films 2003.

Chidebe, Mac-Collins, *Osama Bin La*. Nigeria: Jesus Team Productions 2002.

Shah, Naseeruddin, *Yun Hota To Kya Hota*. India: C.A.T. Productions 2006.

Stone, Oliver, *World Trade Center*. United States: Paramount Pictures 2006.

Nura Ibrahim

# 9/11, ISLAM AND THE VISUAL MEDIA IN NORTHERN NIGERIA:

## A SEMIOTIC ANALYSIS OF TWO SELECTED PRE AND POST 9/11 POSTERS

Since the incident of September 11, 2001, media channels have been swamped with images and stories about the fanatically held beliefs and hardhearted habits of Muslim communities around the world. The American War on Terror was the biggest media event in the history of media technologies, and its reverberations echo in many ways (Nisbet 2001). In northern Nigeria, where Muslims are the majority, the War on Terror was received pessimistically with demonstrations on the streets by youth. The War on Terror was seen as constituting a threat to the Muslim community all over the world and, as such, the event was interpreted as an unmistakable part of war against Islam. Occurring in the era of new media technologies, the conflicts received perhaps the widest media coverage in the history of publishing, spreading their impact far beyond immediately involved communities that have access to media technologies.

The focus of this paper is therefore on examining the relationships between local (alternative) media and global events. The paper analyzes commercially available street posters in northern Nigeria that capture and reinterpret the War on Terror. In these posters, images of the War on Terror from international magazines, newspapers, and most significantly from Internet websites have been remediated locally and transformed into new reconfigurations of these conflicts that have received little attention in media studies. They depict local perceptions of global conflict situations remediated as posters, a medium that constitutes the most vivid form of communication in alleyways in towns, cities, and villages, with vendors selling them.

Young people are the primary direct clients of American War on Terror posters. The majority of the poster producers in Kano are not formally trained; most are primary and secondary school dropouts. Only an insignificant number of them has attained higher education, and in entirely different areas. Their perspective on global events and their commercial interest shape the selection of images and the narratives of the popular posters.

Posters in northern Nigeria usually portray religious subjects: the shrines in Mecca and Medina, Quranic verses in calligraphic forms, but above all portraits of the Prophet's disciples, international scholars, and local sheikhs. With the War on Terror blaring away on multiple international media channels, pictures of people like Osama bin Laden, Saddam Hussein, Abu Musab Al-Zarqawi, Mohammad Ghaddafi, Sheikh Hassan Nasrullah, etc. are included favorably in the Muslim religious poster artwork, while at the same time George Bush, for example, is never depicted positively in the posters produced for sale.

## POSTERS AS COMMUNICATION CHANNELS

Bestley and Noble (2002) defined the poster as "a typically printed paper announcement that is displayed publicly and functions as a tool for the promotion of a product, an event, a sentiment or a cause through image and/ or text..." However, within the context of this study, the poster as a medium of communication refers to any large piece of printed paper designed to be attached to a wall or vertical surface.

Islamic poster art originated in Turkey and Cairo at the end of the 19th century, with calligraphies and images of Mecca and Medina. Believed to bestow "baraka" (blessings) and protection, these posters were framed and hung in shops and houses. When this art found its way to India around the turn of the 20th century, it evolved into a more vibrant and creative form, visibly influenced by the kind of Hindu calendar art produced by the printing press of Raja Ravi Varma founded in Bombay in 1892. The decline of classical calligraphic art contributed to (and was itself hastened by) the instant popularity of these Islamic posters.

## THE HISTORY OF POSTERS IN MUSLIM NORTHERN NIGERIA

In Nigeria, the detailed history of posters is yet to be written. But in an interview conducted by the author in 2007 in Kano Kurmi market, a poster producer revealed: "The history of posters in northern Nigeria began in the 1930s. Posters were imported by Hausa merchants from Egypt."[1] He further contended that the first set of posters to make an inroad into the Hausa land showed the Prophet and his disciples. Nowadays, posters from India and China, American film posters, Hausa film posters, and many political posters are prominent in Nigeria.

[1] Author's interview with Faila posters publisher Muhammad, A. at Kurmi Market/ Kano in 2007.

The main concern of this study is the political/religious posters that remediated the global event of 9/11. Generally, posters, like stickers, are another form of modern graffiti that provides individuals, denied other legitimate means of social communication, the opportunity to express their views on social, political, or religious matters or to voice their grievances and protest against injustice (Chiluwa 2008).

## STUDIES OF IMAGES

What we see, read, and hear in the visual media is the end product of a complex process. Posters, stickers, paintings, and billboards are made within a media organization in accordance with particular sets of activities and practices and by a number of different kinds of people. While the consumer is encouraged to see the output of the media as simple, straightforward, and natural, the makers of images are engaged in a highly organized and multi-layered system of production. Economic pressures are a key determinant in shaping this production process, but other factors such as culture, religion, politics, etc. are also important.

Assumptions about the autonomous efficacy of the images have surfaced frequently in public commentary, due to their transparency and their special ability to set the agenda for both news reporting and policy-making (Arrieta-Walden 2004; Back 2004; Folkenflik 2004). Prominent communications scholars such as Griffin and Zelizer vehemently contradict the popular assumptions about media images as "all-powerful forces", arguing instead that photographs in the press are typically constructed as generic symbols that serve to support dominant discourses. Griffin, for instance, maintains that pictures in the press predominantly function as "simple thematic cues" (2004:348). But Zelizer (2004:115) argues that aesthetic appeal and familiarity are privileged over photography's potential, thereby undermining the provision of newsworthy and critically important information. According to Yousuf (2004), the images carried by the religious posters in India also participate actively in what can be called the stereotyping of certain communities and of the genders. A young woman or a child, for example, if depicted anywhere, is always shown as an embodiment of perfect innocence and beauty.

The impact of posters as a tool of propaganda has also received much attention. In Belgium, for instance, election posters are an important means of political communication. Political broadcasts on public television are strictly limited (the principal parties are allotted airtime for five party political broadcasts, the smallest party only one) and commercial airtime cannot be bought (Van de Bulck 1993:471). Van de Bulck suggested "parties therefore see their poster campaigns as the backbone of their electioneering efforts".

In Nigeria, there is an apparent lack of research on posters generally and religious posters in particular. There is literature on a theme close to posters: that of religious stickers. Generally, as Chiluwa (2008:372) puts it, a sticker is "another form of modern graffiti which provides individuals, denied of other legitimate means of social communication, the opportunity to express their views on social and political matters or voice their grievances or protest against injustice".

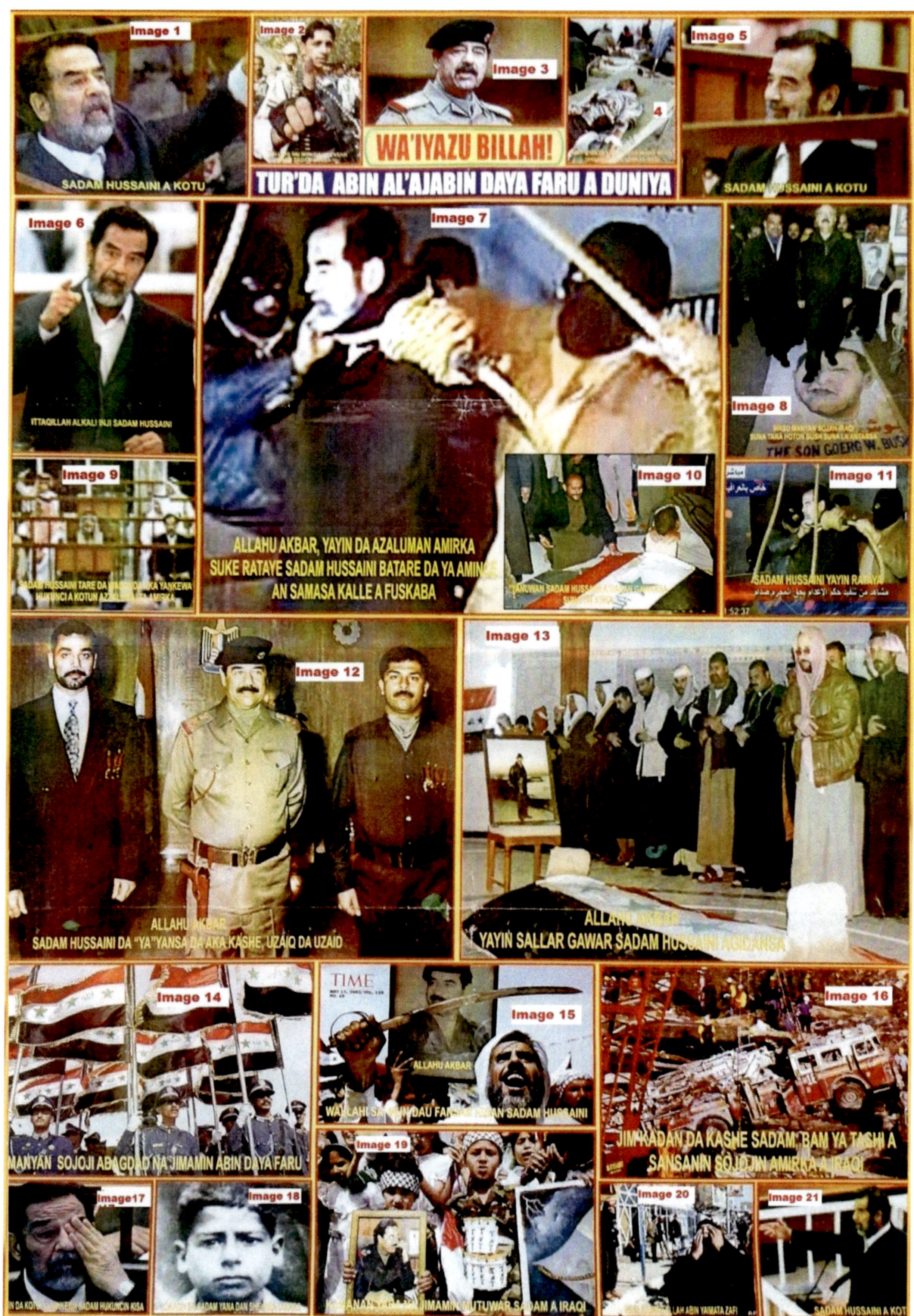
Image 1
SADAM HUSSAINI A KOTU
Image 2
Image 3
4
WA'IYAZU BILLAH!
TUR'DA ABIN AL'AJABIN DAYA FARU A DUNIYA
Image 5
Image 6
ITTAQILLAH ALKALI INJI SADAM HUSSAINI
Image 7
ALLAHU AKBAR, YAYIN DA AZALUMAN AMIRKA
AN SAMASA KALLE A FUSKABA
Image 8
Image 9
Image 10
Image 11
SADAM HUSSAINI YAYIN RATAYA
Image 12
SADAM HUSSAINI DA "YA"YANSA DA AKA KASHE, UZAIQ DA UZAID
Image 13
Image 14
MANYAN SOJOJI ABAGDAD NA JIMAMIN ABIN DAYA FARU
TIME
Image 15
ALLAHU AKBAR
Image 16
JIM KADAN DA KASHE SADAM, BAM YA TASHI A
SANSANIN SOJOJIN AMIRKA A IRAQI
Image17
Image 18
Image 19
Image 20
Image 21

## SEMIOTIC ANALYSIS OF SELECTED WAR ON TERROR POSTERS

This study is theoretically grounded within the perspectives of "framing theory" and "symbolic interaction theory". The two are complementary in the sense that framing looks intently at how the message is packaged, while symbolic interaction is concerned with how the symbolic meaning is extracted from the message. I believe that the aim of the study is best furthered by using the two theories.

Semiotic analysis, which refers to the "process of analyzing the effects of the production and reproduction, reception and circulation of meanings in all forms, used by all kinds of agents of communication" (Hodge and Kress 1988), can be applied to anything that can be seen as signifying something – in other words, to everything that has meaning within a culture. Even within the context of the mass media, semiotic analysis can be applied to any media texts (including television and radio programs, films, cartoons, newspaper and magazine articles, posters, and other ads) and to the practices involved in producing and interpreting such texts. Thus, this study employs this method to analyze the selected two posters.

## THE SADDAM HUSSEIN POSTER

Posters of Saddam Hussein, mainly collaged from images taken from Internet websites as well as international magazines (such as The Economist, Time, Newsweek), started appearing in the late 1990s, during the Gulf War, as massive montages on a single large sheet of drawing paper and pasted on street walls, in work environments (e.g. mechanic's and tailor's shops), in public transport, and even in some living rooms in northern Nigeria. The posters were designed as a propaganda medium to promote support for and affiliation with Saddam Hussein during the Golf Wars. Of the many posters available, I chose one, reproduced in Figure 1.

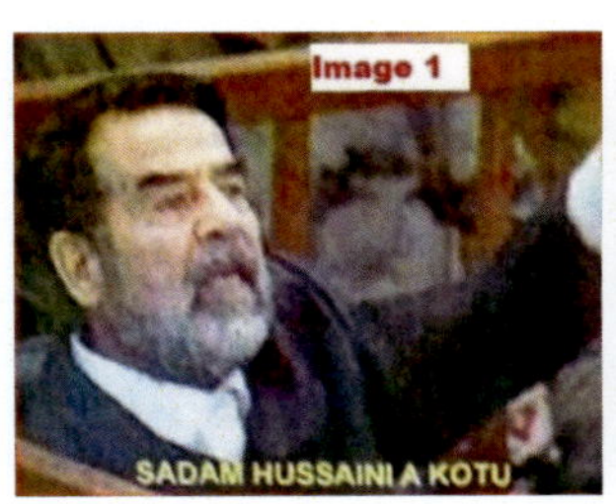


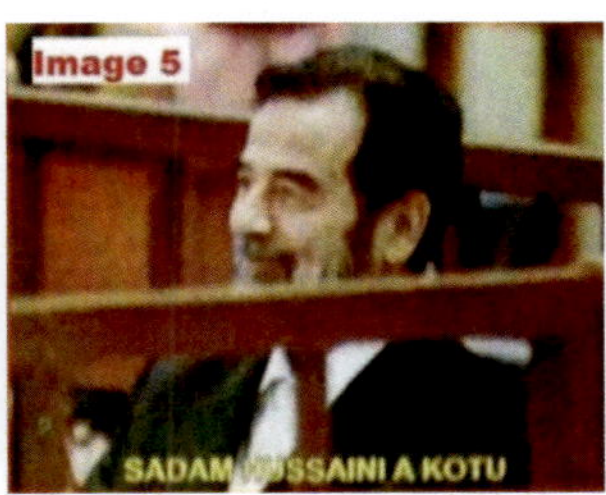


Fig. 1
**The Saddam Hussein poster**

Occupying the upper section of the poster are five photographs, four of Saddam Hussein depicted with different backgrounds and one of a young boy. All four photographs of Saddam Hussein are arranged to narrate the story of a military leader convicted by a court of law. In the first photograph, Saddam is seen raising his hand toward the judge in a challenging manner. This can be interpreted to mean that Saddam Hussein was fearless even in the Court.

Depicting him with a smile on his face in the courtroom is purposely done to tell the viewer that he is in a win-win situation. The Hausa written message accompanying the two photographs, "Saddam Hussein a Kotu" (Saddam Hussein in the Court) further communicates this sense of courage as well as stress in the courtroom.

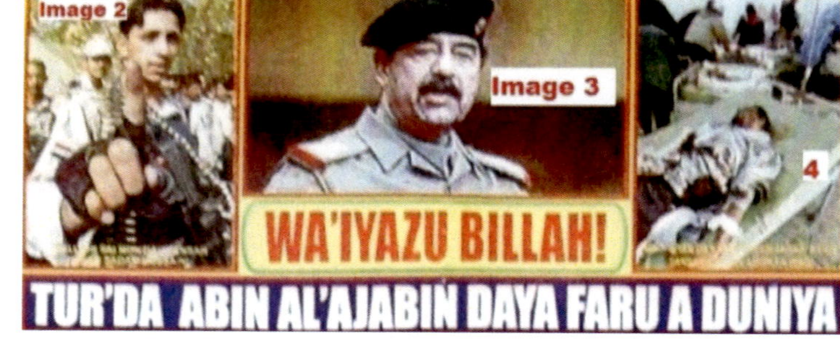


Images 2, 3, and 4 in the same row narrate the story of a military leader who was killed by Americans and how his people promises to avenge his death.

In image 2, a young boy is depicted against a backdrop of busy activities. He is dressed in what looks like a military uniform with machine gun bullets all around his body The Hausa inscription further explains that he is a supporter of Saddam Hussein. The Hausa inscription reads "Wallahi sai mun dau fansar Saddan Hussein" (I swear in the name of Allah, we will avenge the killing of Saddam Hussein) and was deliberately written by the poster producers to domesticate the photograph to appeal to his target audience.

The next photograph in the same row shows Saddam Hussein dressed in Iraqi military uniform. He is so well known and important that no name is needed – the mass media's common practice in relation to the death of celebrities such as Princess Diana and Elvis Presley. Their photograph is their identity – a name would be redundant. The Hausa inscription written in bold capital red and white letters at the bottom of the photograph "wa'iyazu billah – tur da abin al'ajabin daya faru a duniya" (We seek refuge through Allah, to hell with the shameful thing that happened) is shouting at world leaders, particularly the Arab leaders. By displaying the message in Arabic transliteration and Hausa, the poster addresses the Hausa people in a language they understand.

Image 4 shows the corpse of a man with blood all over his shirt against a background full of dead or wounded bodies attended by people giving first aid. Even though the bodies are not identified in the photograph, the written message at the bottom of the photograph in Hausa "Minti biyar da kashe Saddam aka kai hari a sansanin sojojin Amirka a Iraqi" (Five minutes after the execution of Saddam, there was an attack on the American military base in Iraq) suggests that the bodies belong to Americans killed or wounded in retaliation for the killing of Saddam Hussein.

Reading the six pictures from the second row of the poster (image 6, 7, 8, 9, 10 and 11), a visual story is narrated about how Saddam is tried in a court of law and later hanged to death by some people wearing masks. In image 6, Saddam is shown pointing his warning finger at the judge. The message written in Hausa at the bottom of the picture "Ttallah alkali inji sadam Hussein" (Fear Allah, Saddam Hussein warned the judge) confirms this.

Image 7 in the same row depicts Saddam with masked people putting a noose around his neck. Depicting them with masks attempts to persuade the viewer that, even though they hanged Saddam Hussein, they do not want their identity to be disclosed because they are afraid of retaliation from his followers. Image 9 is there to supplement images 6 and 7, while 11 reveals even the time he was hanged. Images 8 and 10 communicate a sense of loyalty not only from his family members, but also from the Iraqi army. The written message in image 8 reads "wasu manyan sojan Iraqi suna taka Bush suna la'antarsa" (some high-ranking Iraqi military men marching on the portrait of President Bush and cursing him) purports to show the extent to which the military in Iraqi is loyal to Saddam even after his death. The written message in the picture further informs the reader who is behind the killing of Saddam Hussein. Image 10 depicts some people kneeling and crying in front of a corpse. The written message tells that these people are members of Saddam Hussein's family and the corpse is that of Saddam Hussein.

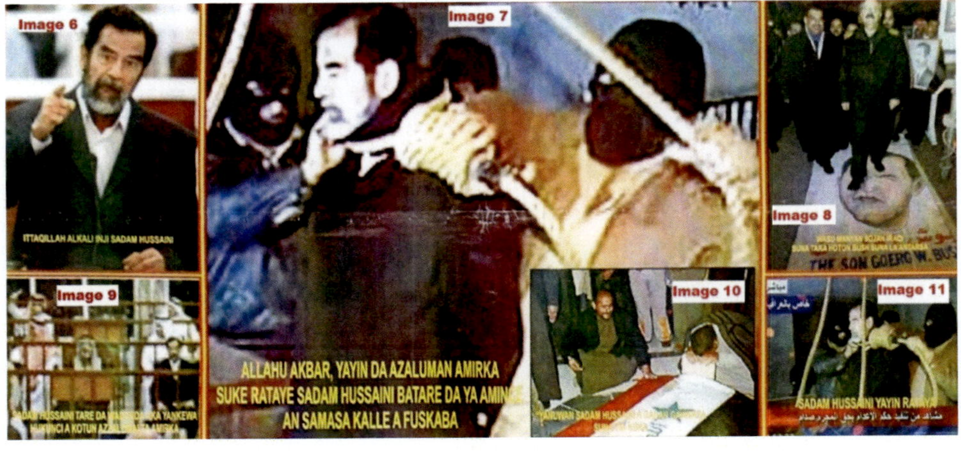


Obviously, the poster is trying to create a sense of sympathy with, loyalty to, and identification with Saddam among the people of Northern Nigeria.

Images 12 and 13 were purposely selected to portray Saddam Hussein as a family man and at the same time as an adherent of Islam. In image 12, he and his sons are shown in an office with an Iraqi flag at their backs. Saddam is portrayed here as a true nationalist who, despite the foreseen danger, involved his sons in the affairs of ruling and

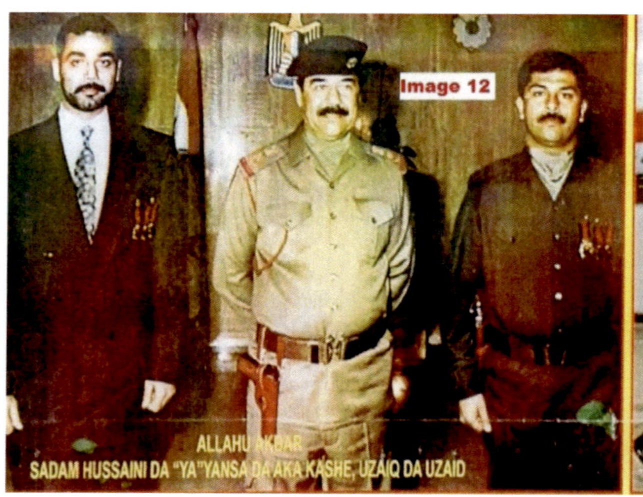


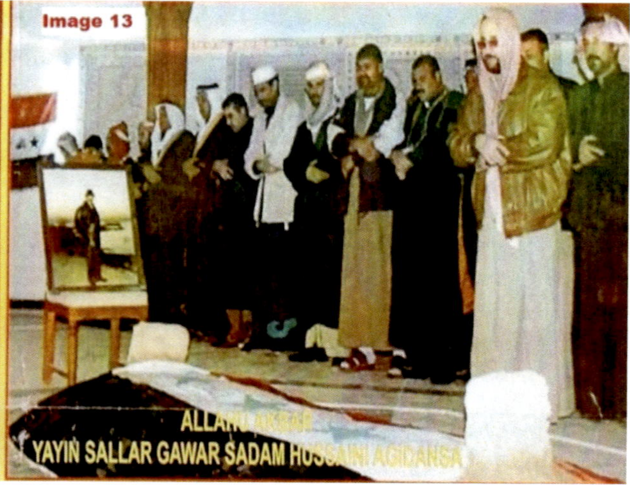


defending Iraq. On the one hand, the depiction of one of his sons wearing Western clothing informs the viewer that he is not in the army, but possessed a Western education and serves his father as a special assistant. On the other hand, the other son in a military uniform portrays Saddam Hussein as a selfless and nationalist leader who recruits not only other people into the army, but even his son.

Image 13 depicts several people praying, standing over a body covered with an Iraqi flag, apparently Saddam Hussein. The environment, which looks like a living room, is decorated with another Iraqi flag. Placing Saddam Hussein's photographic portrait near the Iraqi flag informs the viewer that it is Saddam Hussein's corpse. The written message reads "Allahu Akbar: Yayin Sallar gawar Saddam Hussein a gidansa" (Allah is Greatest: During a funeral prayers over Saddam Hussein's corpse in his house). Thus, the two pictures portray Saddam as a national hero who has sacrificed his life for his country; the presence of an Iraqi flag in his living room and one covering his body attest to this. The manner in which his funeral prayer is depicted also portrays Saddam Hussein as a true Muslim. Carefully reading the montaged photographs in the last row of the poster (images 14 to 21) reveal an retrospective narrative of what took place as a result of hanging Saddam Hussein to death.

Image 14, for instance, depicts several military men carrying Iraqi flags. The message written at the bottom of the picture, "Manyan Sojoji a Bagdad na jimamin abun da ya faru" (senior military men in Bagdad mourning what had happened), communicates that the military in Iraq did not support the court verdict condemning Saddam Hussein to death.

Image 15 shows civilians carrying the portrait of Saddam Hussein and the front page of TIME magazine. Depicting a man dressed in the Arab way with a sword in his hand speaks of his will to fight. The portrait of Saddam Hussein further clarifies the reason for the fight, and the TIME Magazine front page tells against

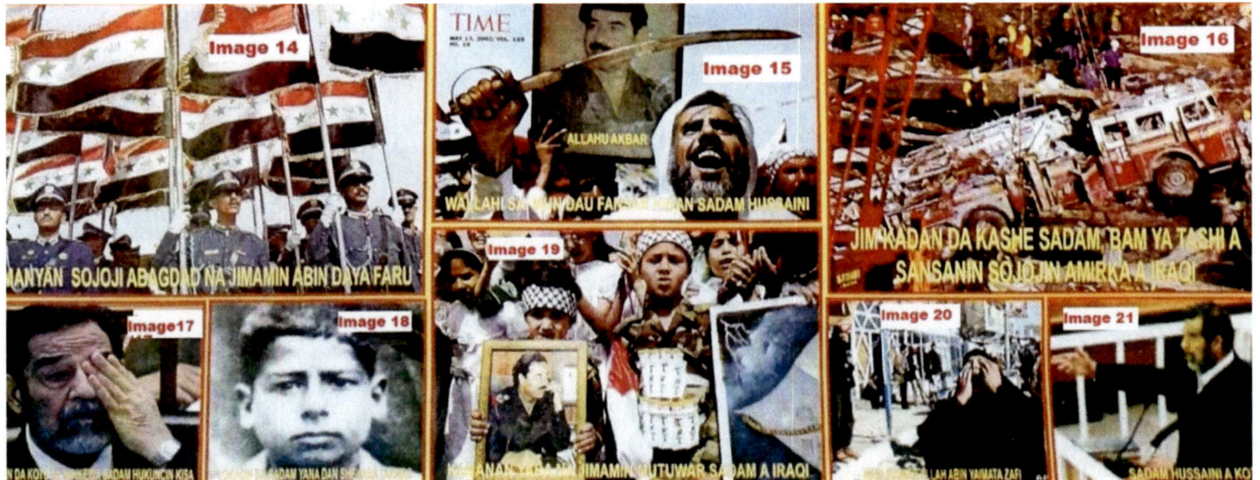


whom the war is intended. The written message reads "Wallahi sai mun dau fansar Saddam Hussein" (we swear by the name of Allah, we will avenge the killing of Saddam Hussein). The image thus contradicts what people saw on international news media like CNN, BBC, etc., which showed people, apparently Shiites, celebrating the downfall of Saddam Hussein in Iraq. The narration continues in image 16, depicting a scene of destruction with some people, apparently first aid workers, trying to help the victims. The written message reads "Jim kadan da kashe Saddam, Bam Ya tashi a sansanin Sojojin Amirica a Iraqi" (shortly after Saddam was killed, a bomb exploded in an American military camp in Iraq) thereby giving the example of an act of revenge.

Image 17 shows Saddam Hussein in court covering his left eye with his hand; the extreme close-up shot reveals his sad, depressed face. "Yayin da kotu ta yankewa Saddam hukuncin kisa" (at the time when the court sentenced Saddam to be hanged to death) reads the written message, further explaining why Saddam looks so sad. Immediately following that picture, in the same row, is the picture of a small boy shown against a lifeless background with the written message "Saddam Hussein yana dan shekara takwas" (Saddam Hussein at the age of eight). This photograph attempts to evoke sympathy in (Hausa) audiences. Image 19 shows many young boys dressed in a military uniform carrying portraits of Saddam Hussein. "Kananan yara na jimamin mutuwar Saddam a Iraqi" (small children mourning the death of Saddam in Iraq) reads the caption, communicating a long-term message of retaliation.

Image 20 shows a woman dressed in black crying. In the background are many people and some buildings. "Wata Baiwar Allah abin yayi mata zafi" (a woman who feels so sad about the incident) reads the written message, affirming that the Iraqi people found themselves in mourning and despair after the demise of Saddam Hussein. The last picture in the poster, image 21, depicts Saddam Hussein in the court dock raising his hand in the judge's direction. The caption reads "Saddam Husseinn a kotu" (Saddam Hussein in the court).

The photographs on the poster were deliberately selected and arranged to narrate in visual form a story of Saddam Hussein's tribulation and humiliation in court. The reader will immediately be struck by its use of saturated tones of red, blue, and yellow. The Hausa text, written in bold red and white at the upper section of the poster, reads: We seek refuge through Allah, to hell with the shameful thing that happened. In addition, some of the photographs and captions depict the trial as an injustice, while others evoke loyalty, love, and commitment. The photographs are designed to convey a sense of sympathy in spite of the bitter situation. Although all the photographs of Saddam Hussein depict him with a sad, depressed face, this sense of sympathy and bitterness is also partly expressed through the short social distance between the represented person and the photographs' viewers. This is achieved through the angle from which most of the photographs were shot. Saddam is depicted at eye level, which forces the reader to look straight at him. According to Kress and Van Leeuwen (1990:40), if a represented participant is depicted at eye level, the implied relationship is equal and symmetrical power between the represented participant and the interactive participant. Since Saddam Hussein was a political leader, one would expect the photographs to be created with a frog's-eye perspective to reflect his status, rather than at eye level, which suggests that he and the viewer have the same status.

The photographs that dominate the poster (Saddam Hussein and sites of destruction) can be classified as "presentational snapshots". According to Kress and Van Leeuwen, this is about doing and happening. In this sense, the poster represents a "conceptual" process in which the represented participant is seen as a leader of a major political movement. The sites of destruction are depicted as revenge for the killing of Saddam Hussein. The depiction of several people praying over Saddam Hussein's body in his own house carries political and religious overtones, to portray him as both very religious and also a nationalist.

Nearly all the lyrical titles accompanying various photographs (textual meta-function) in the poster are written in Hausa. We realize that the poster is all about Saddam Hussein's court ordeals from the time his trial started to the time he was hanged – along with the consequences of his death for the American military camps in Iraq.

The use of Hausa slogans pinpoints the poster as being for local consumption in the studied area. The use of strong red and yellow colors vividly reflects the dominance and primacy of interpersonal meaning over ideational meaning.

Finally, the main intent of the Saddam Hussein poster is to mobilize the Muslim community (Hausa Muslims in the studied area) to regard what happened to Saddam Hussein as injustice not only against him or his people alone, but against the entire Muslim community. Another message vividly displayed in the poster is a picture of a bomb blast, which appears twice in the poster to show the reader that the death of Saddam has promoted acts of terrorism.

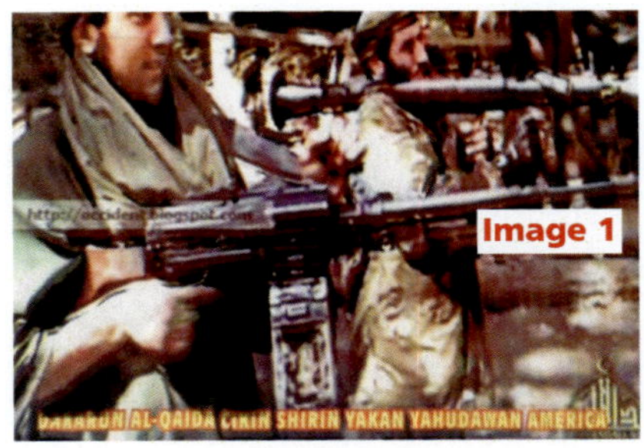

Image 1

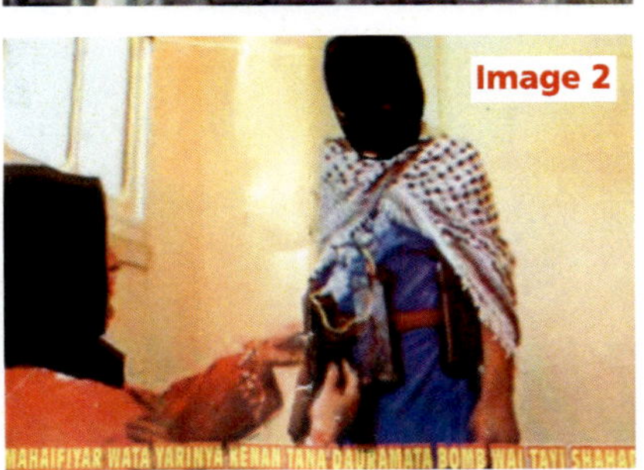

Image 2

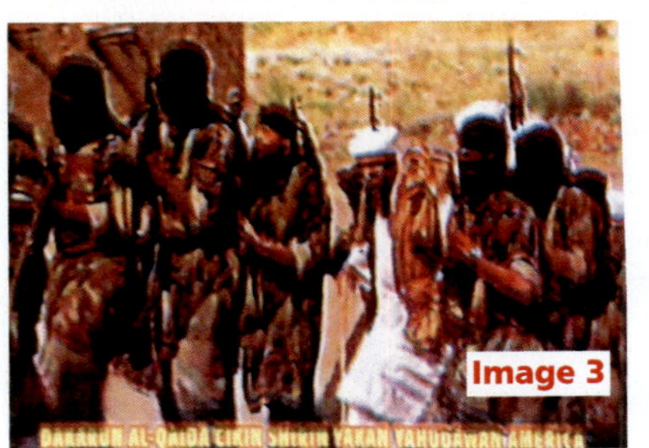
Image 3

## THE OSAMA BIN LADEN POSTER

The second poster that this paper examines centers on Osama Bin Laden. The poster was conceived as a result of the September 11, 2001 bombing of the World Trade Center by what the United States refers to as the terrorist group "Al Qaida", which is believed to be headed and financed by Osama Bin Laden, the Saudi Arabian-born Islamic militant. The poster started appearing in 2002, and since then, in spite of the fact that it was forbidden and confiscated by the police, it has dominated the streets, work environments, living rooms, and many other places in Muslim northern Nigeria.

The images on the poster are logically arranged to portray the principal character and to show that he was not only a freedom fighter, but also someone who had total control over and the support of ordinary people. In images 1, 2, and 3, we notice several young men with sophisticated weapons in a state of preparedness, a woman getting her daughter ready for a suicide mission, and several men dressed in unidentified army uniforms and multi performing exercise.

Judging from the photograph's rhetoric of struggle and the overall color coding of the poster that frames it, we could assume that it is part of a campaign launched by the members of Al Qaida to promote their ideology. In image 2, we are confronted with a picture of a woman, supposedly a mother, preparing her daughter to become a martyr. The contextual background from which the participants emerge accentuates the timelessness and firmness of their intentions. The mask in the face of the subject and the bomb jacket send a signal to the viewer about their states of mind.

The slogan "Dakarun Al-Qaida cikin shirin yakan Yahudawan America" (Al Qaida's warlord ready to fight the American Jews), situated at the bottom

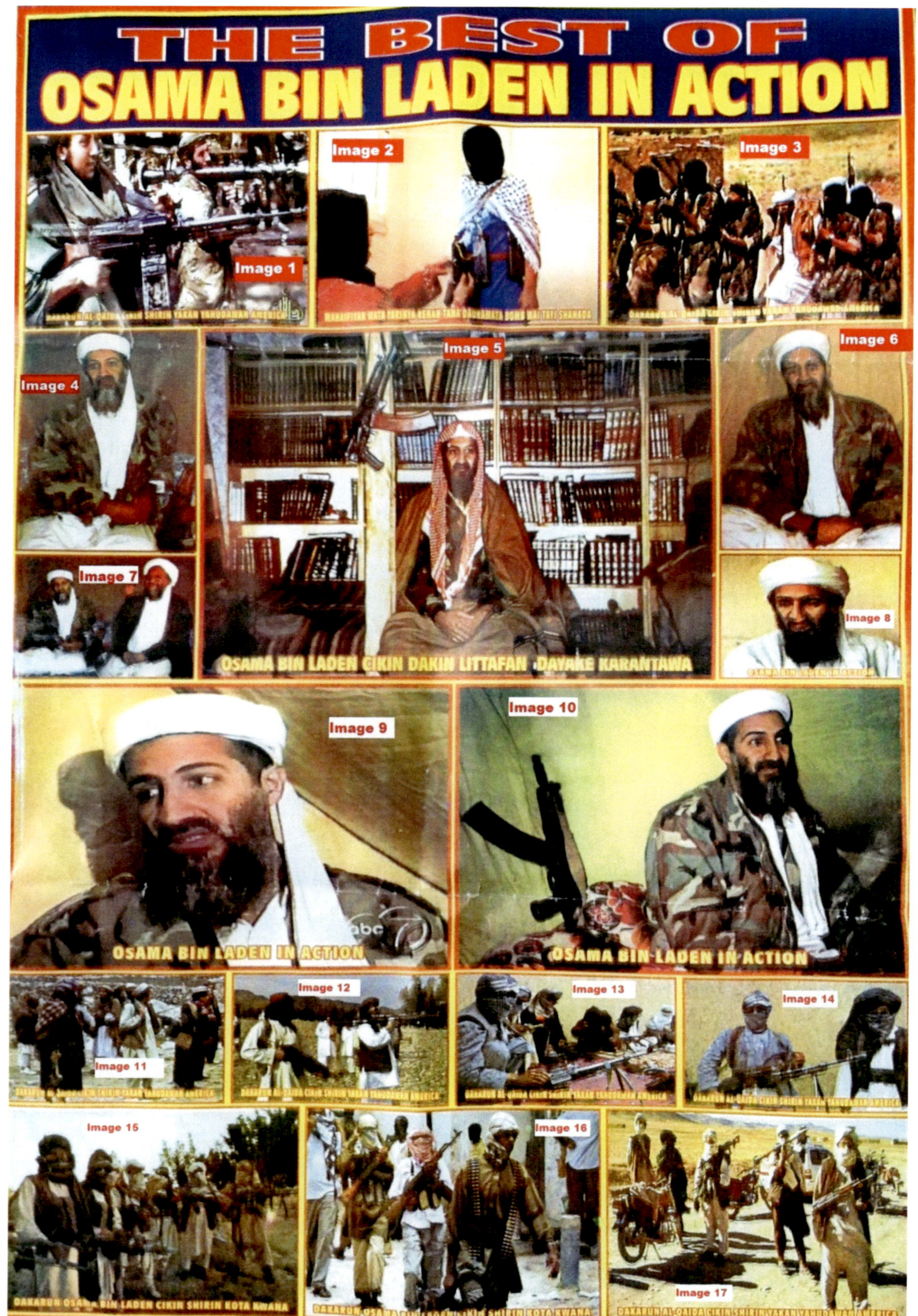


**Osama Bin Laden poster,** obtained from Abubakar Rimi Market, Kano (2007).

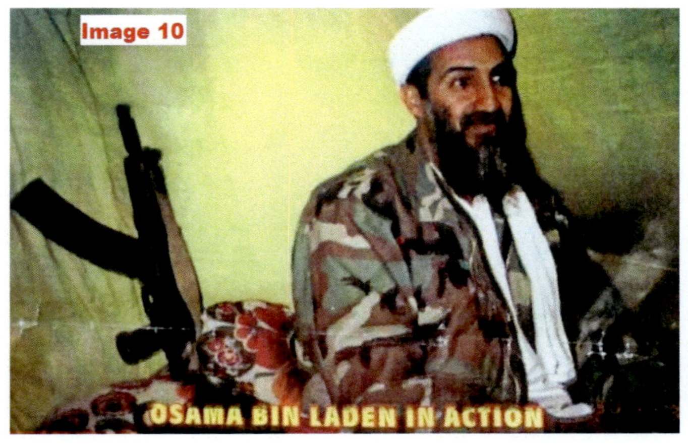


of image 3, further buttresses the above assertion. Here the enemy is identified not as the American government, but as the American Jews, who in northern Nigeria are tenaciously believed to be the brains behind all the American actions in the Arab countries. The background within which the photograph was taken suggests a rural setting or even jungle serving as a training ground. The soldiers in the photograph represent Al Qaida's combatants ready for action.

Unlike the above photographs, the principal character in image 10, Osama bin Laden dressed in an army uniform and wearing a turban, is depicted against a bedroom background with a machine gun by his side. A slogan in English, "Osama Bin laden in Action", is emblazoned in bold yellow letters at the bottom of the photograph. Bin Laden is seen in his bedroom wide awake and fully dressed, which says a lot about his readiness to confront any circumstances that might arise.

Images 11, 12, 13, and 14 also show the level of commitment and seriousness of Al Qaida members. In all the photographs, the Hausa slogan, "Dakarun Al-Qaida cikin shirin yakan Yahudawan America" (Al Qaida's warlord ready to fight the American Jews) keeps reappearing. In image 11, for instance, a group of people, supposedly Al Qaida members, are dressed in Muslim attire with turbans on their heads, standing ready for command. Image 12, next to it, shows the same group with the same attire, practicing with a bazooka against a jungle background. Image 13 shows another group, dressed in the same manner but with their turbans covering the faces, indicating their status as rebel fighters, assembling various kinds of guns. The next photograph shows two of them holding one of the assembled machine guns. The producer deliberately designed images 12 to 14 to show the potential fighting power and the state of preparedness of the Al Qaida members.

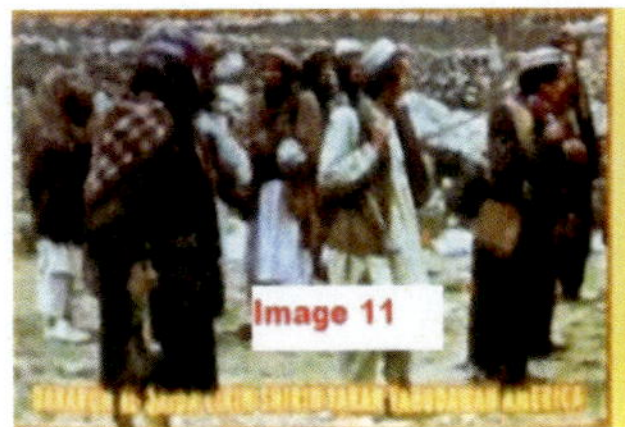


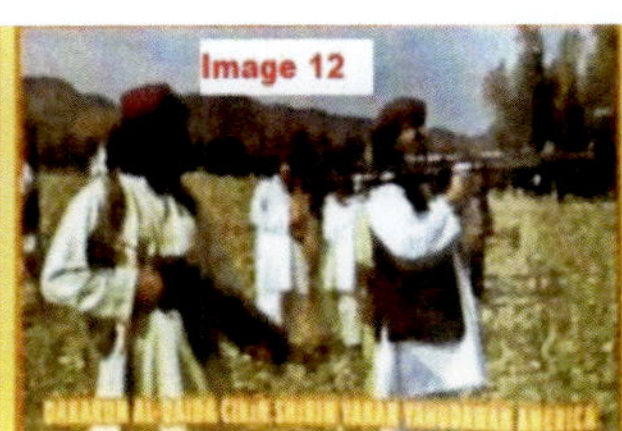


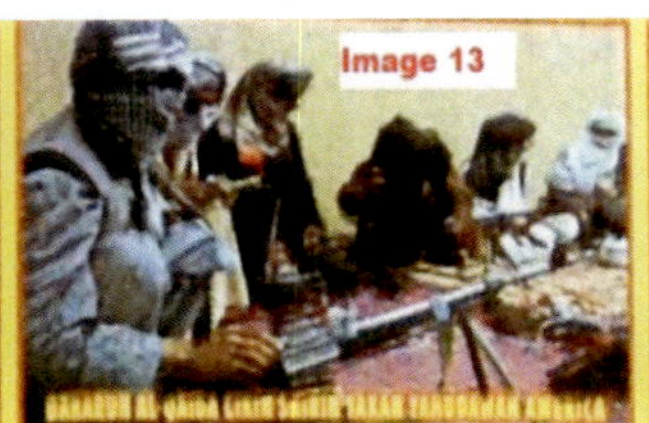


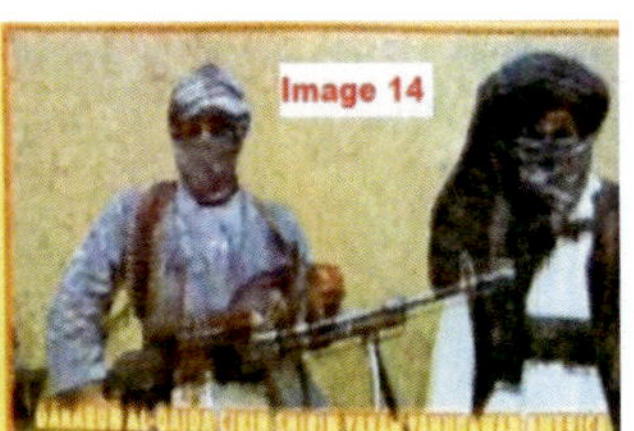

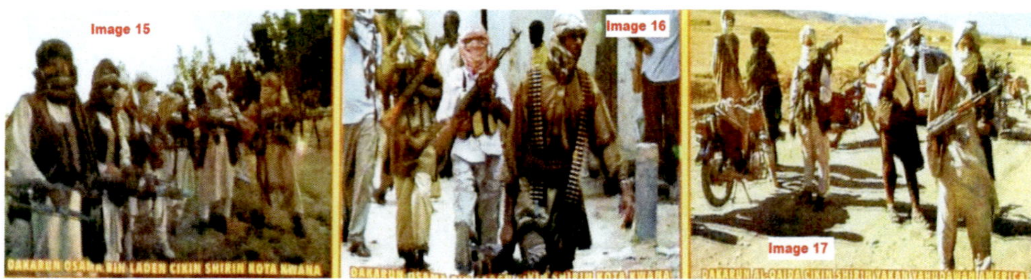


Similarly, images 16, 17, and 18 were also put together to supplement images 11, 12, 13, and 14. In the photographs, fighters in Muslim attire stand defiantly carrying machine guns, their watchful gaze and machine guns directed toward an apparently imminent danger. The elaborate, mountainous background against which they are depicted seems to be somewhere in Afghanistan. The photographic narrative in the poster remediates what the viewers heard, read, or watched in the related news in the mainstream media.

Images 4, 5, 6, 7, and 8 were selected and assembled in the middle of the poster to communicate a feeling of togetherness and humbleness and above all to demonstrate that Osama bin Laden is not only a leader of a rebel group, but also someone who is grounded in Islamic education. Images 4, 6, and 8 portray him against a more neutral background to show that he is able to communicate with the world without exposing his hiding place. In point of historical fact, Osama bin Laden was the Americans' and their allies' most wanted person, but with all their satellite technologies, he remained invincible (for 10 years).

In image 7, Osama bin Laden is montaged with another person to show that he is not alone in the movement and has other people very close to him. An adjunct message is that Osama bin Laden listens to other people's opinions. The image 5 that serves as the focal point of the poster portrays Osama bin Laden as an Islamic scholar. The bookshelf background coupled with the Hausa slogan "Osama bin Laden a cikin littafan da yake karantawa" (Osama bin Laden in his library) written in bold yellow lettering across the bottom of the photograph further displays his scholarly position. The machine gun hanging on the shelf to his right communicates a sense of constant readiness for war (with the Americans and their allies).

Pictures of Osama bin Laden appear in seven strategic places on the poster, dominating it, with the remaining ten pictures supplementing this narrative. The poster's viewer is immediately struck by its use of strong, saturated tones of red and yellow, showing bin Laden dressed in both Muslim attire and in military uniform. The pictures were assembled to narrate the story of Al Qaida's struggles, from the photographs in the upper section of the poster, which show the recruitment processes, to the photographs in the lower section of the poster, which narrate how members are dispersed or assigned responsibilities.

The Osama bin Laden photographs, which dominate the poster as a whole, are clearly designed to convey a sense of sincerity and commitment. Apart from the serious, smiling face with which all seven pictures portray Osama bin Laden, this sense of sincerity and commitment is also expressed by means of the photos' short social distance from the viewer. As in the Saddam poster, this is achieved through the eye level angle from which the photographs were shot. The viewer looks straight at the represented person; this suggests an equal, symmetrical power relationship between them, creating the impression of compassion and shared aims. The subject in the poster is cast in soft light and dry colors, conveying a sense of loyalty and allegiance. Osama bin Laden is also depicted as representing the world Muslim community, thus confirming him as a leader. The backgrounds in the pictures further emphasize his firm resolve to serve the entire Muslim community.

An English text (textual meta-function) is inscribed at the top of the poster in conspicuous, bold red and yellow letters, "The Best of Osama Bin Laden in Action". Going beyond the poster of Saddam, the text and the medium close-up shots of Osama bin Laden thus appeal not only to Hausa readers to identify themselves with the ideology he represents, but address the greater English-speaking world. Finally, the main message that the "Best of Osama Bin Laden in Action" poster carries to the Muslim community and the English-speaking world is the sophistication, power, Islamic knowledge, and technological advancement

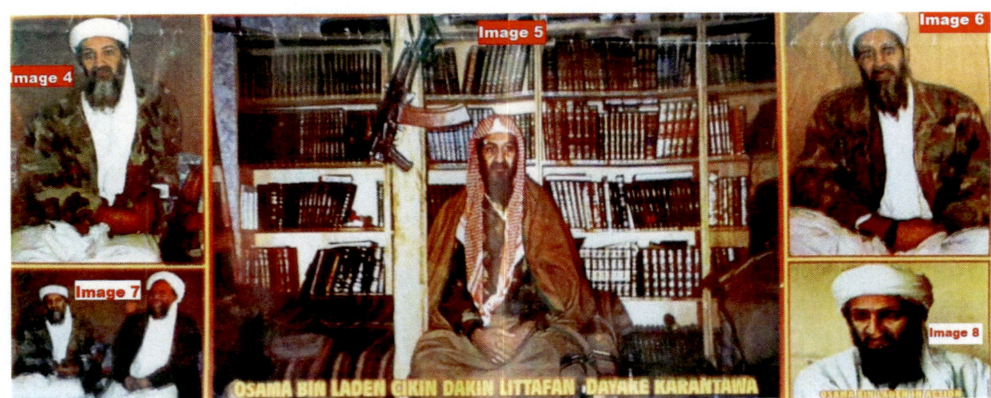

of Al Qaida under the leadership of Osama bin Laden in his fight against the United States and its allies.

## CONCLUSION

Semiotic analysis shows how the two posters in question were able to prompt the dominant popular discourse among the Hausa Muslims in northern Nigeria, who are the direct clients of the posters. The two posters used both functional and emotional appeals to capture the interest of the readers. In the Saddam Hussein poster, the protagonist was presented as a hero who is not afraid of his killers – the judge and the Americans. In the Osama bin Laden poster, the image-makers depicted him as someone who is well grounded in Islamic education and who at the same time is fighting America and the West for the sake of his people. Among the various categories of posters produced in Kano (film, musical, political, sports, war, religious posters, etc.), the American War on Terror posters are the most sensitive and problematic. The Kano state censorship board and the police arrested and detained most, if not all, of the producers of American War on Terror posters. An interview with the members of the poster producers' association revealed that the state censorship board and the police have banned the production of all posters that relate to the American War on Terror on the grounds that their images and texts might fuel existing religious tension in the state.

## REFERENCES


Arrieta-Walden, Michael, "Searing Images. Paper Weighs Conflicting Values in Publishing Photos of Iraqi Prisoners". In: *The Oregonian*, 23 May 2004, pp. 13-16.

Back, Irit, "Muslims and Christians in Nigeria: Attitudes towards the United States from a Post-September 11th Perspective". In: *Comparative Studies of South Asia, Africa and the Middle East* 24/1 (2004), pp. 211-218.

Bestley, Russell and Noble, Ian, *Up Against the Wall: International Poster Design*. Mies: Rotovision 2002.

Chiluwa, Innocent, "Religious Vehicles Stickers in Nigeria: A Discourse of Identity, Faith and Social Vision". In: *Discourse & Communication* 2/4 (2008), pp. 371-387.

Ellis, Stephen and Killingray, David, "Africa after 11 September 2001". In: *African Affairs* 101 (2002), pp. 5-8.

Etter, Jean-François and Laszlo, Evelyne, "Evaluation of a poster campaign against passive smoking for world No-Tobacco day". In: *Patient Education & Counselling* 57/2 (2005), pp. 190-198.

Davis, Murray, "Review of 'Frame Analysis: An Essay on the Organization of Experience' by Erving Goffman". In: *Contemporary Sociology* 4/6 (1975), pp. 509-603.

Gitlin, Todd, *The Whole World is Watching: Mass Media in the Making and Unmaking of the New Left*. Berkeley: University of California Press 1980.

Gomaa, I., "The image of Islam and Muslims in the Western Press after 9/11. An analytical study of American, French, and German newspapers (in Arabic)". In: *Annual Scientific Convention of the Faculty of Communication, Cairo University* (2002), pp. 221-266.

Hodge, Bob and Kress, Günther R., *Social Semiotics*. Ithaca N.Y.: Cornell University Press 1988.

Howarth, David R., *Discourse*. Buckingham: Open University Press 2000.

Kerr, Jaqueline, et al., "The influence of poster prompts on stair use: the effects of setting, poster size and content". In: *British Journal of Health Psychology* 6/4 (2001), pp. 397-407.

Khatib, Lina, "Communicating Islamic Fundamentalism as Global Citizenship". In: *Journal of Communication Inquiry* 27/4 (2003), pp. 389-409.

Kress, Günther R., Van Leeuwen, Theo et al., Reading Images: Sociocultural Aspects of Language and Education. Geelong: Deakin University 1990.

Maher, T. Michael, "Framing: An Emerging Paradigm or a Phase of Agenda Setting". In: Reese, Stephen, et al. (Eds.). *Framing Public Life: Perspectives on Media and our Understanding of the Social World*. Mahwah: Lawrence Erlbaum Associates 2001.

Van de Bulck, Jan, "Estimating the Success of Political Communication Strategies: The Case of Political Poster Impact in Belgian Election". In: *European Journal of Communication* 8 (1993), pp. 471-481.

Griffin, M. (2004) 'Picturing America's 'War on Terrorism' in Afghanistan and Iraq. Photographic motives as news frames', in Journalism, Vol. 5(4): 381-402.

Zelizer, B. (2004) 'When war is reduced to a photograph', in Allan, S. and Zelizer, B. Reporting War. Journalism in Wartime. London and New York: Routledge, pp. 115-135.

**ONLINE**

Folkenflik, David, "Iraqi Prison Story Tough to Hold off on, CBS Says" (2004). http://www. Baltimoresun.com/news/ accessed May 2004.

Gadsby, Jane, "Looking at the Writing on the Wall: A Critical Review and Taxonomy of Graffiti Texts" (1995). www.graffiti.org/faq/critical.review.html accessed January 06, 2015.

Homepage "Truman Library": Harry, Truman, "Mobilizing for War: Poster Art of World War 11". http://www.trumanlibrary.org/muesum/posters/, accessed December 10, 2007.

Inbaraj, Sunny, "Media: Post-Sep. 11 reportage adds to Divisions, Stereotypes" (2002). In: *Global Policy Forum*, http://www.globalpolicy.org/empire/media/2002/0701australia accessed March 14, 2007.

Nisbet, Matt, "Media Coverage After The Attack: Reason and Deliberative Democracy Put To The Test" (2001). http://www.csicop.org/genx/terrorattack/ accessed June 2, 2007.

Wittmann, Kelly, "Soviet propaganda posters" (2002). http://www.essortment.com/soviet-propaganda-posters-37362.html accessed January 05, 2015.

Yousuf, S. (2004, April 23rd). Sarai Fellowship 2004. Retrieved from [Reader-list] Popular religious art of the Muslims: http://mail.sarai.net/pipermail/reader-list_mail.sarai.net/2004-April/003642.html

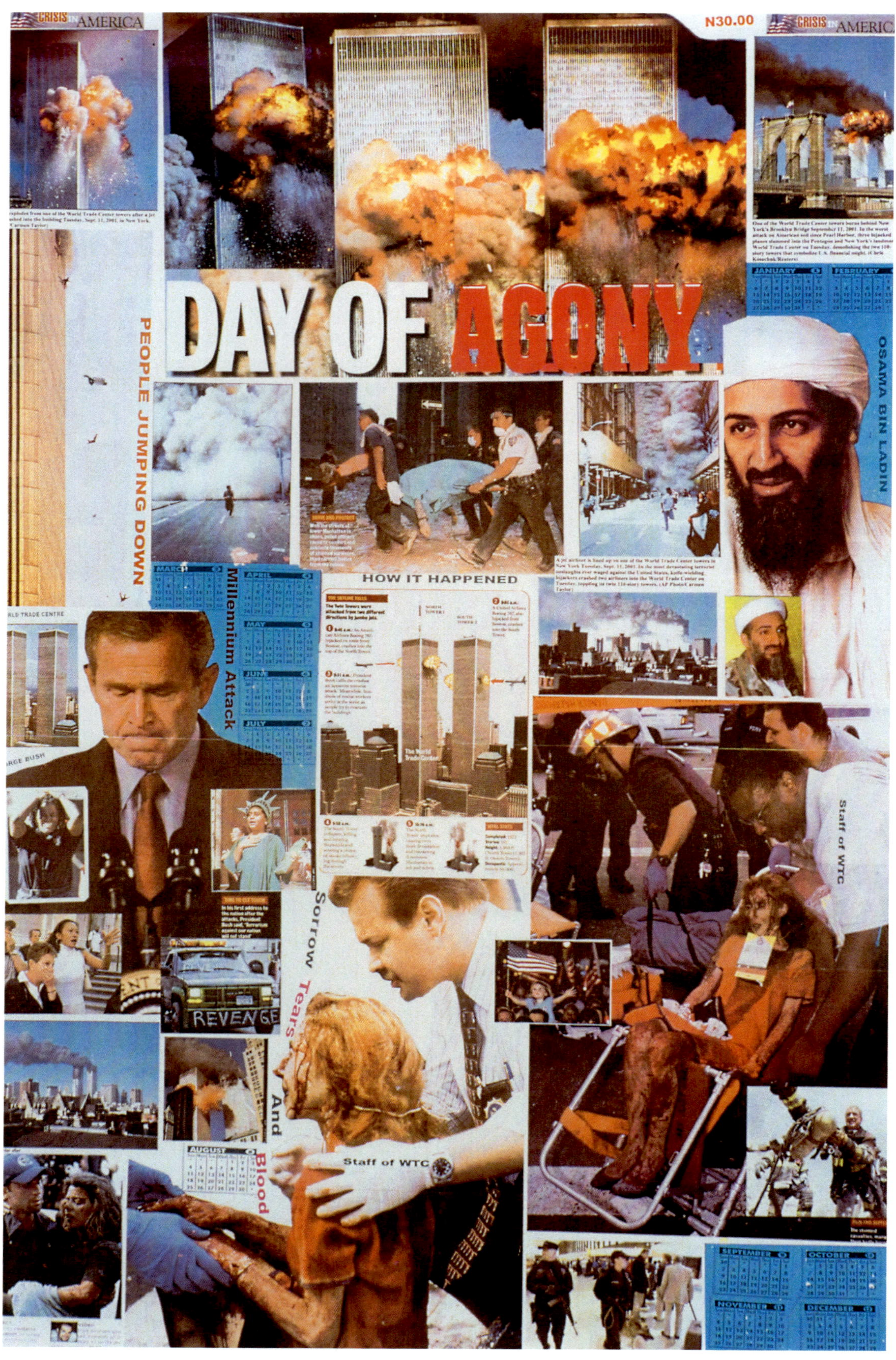


**„Day of Agony" Poster,** Nigeria, 2002 (collection Behrend)

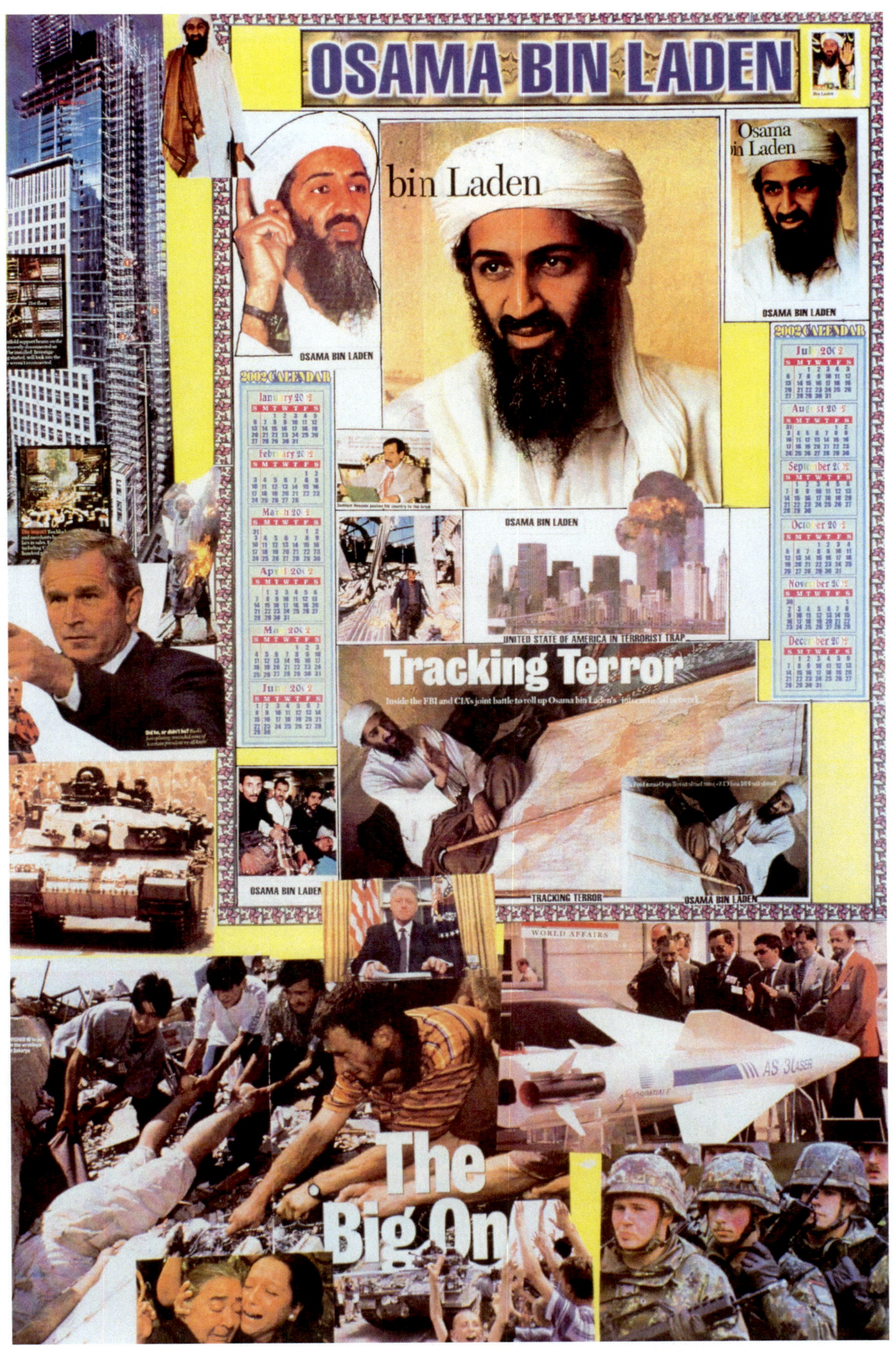


**Osama bin Laden Poster,** Nigeria, 2002 (collection Behrend)

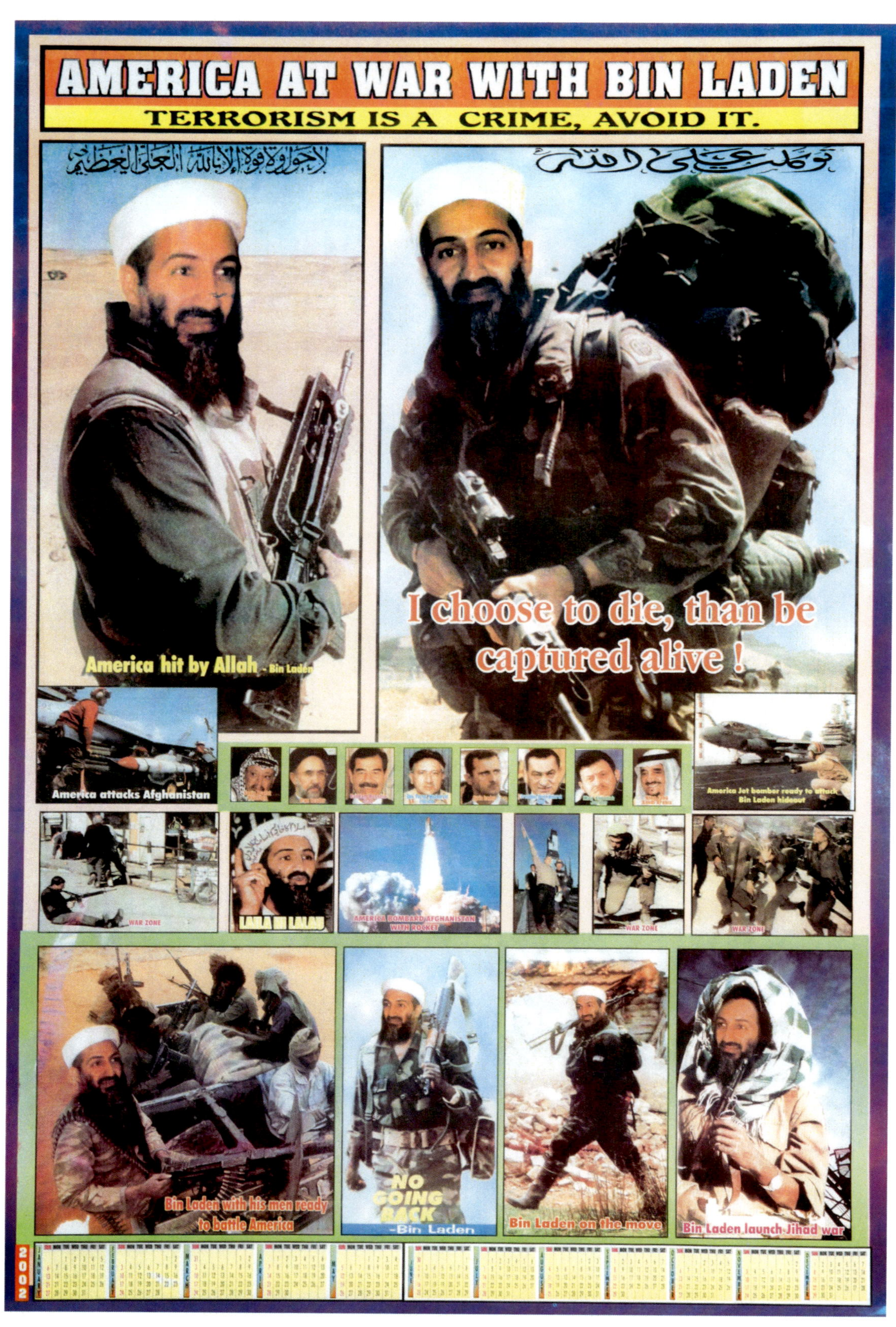


**Osama bin Laden Poster,** Nigeria 2001/2,
National Museum of World Culture, coll. no. TM 6014-1, The Netherlands

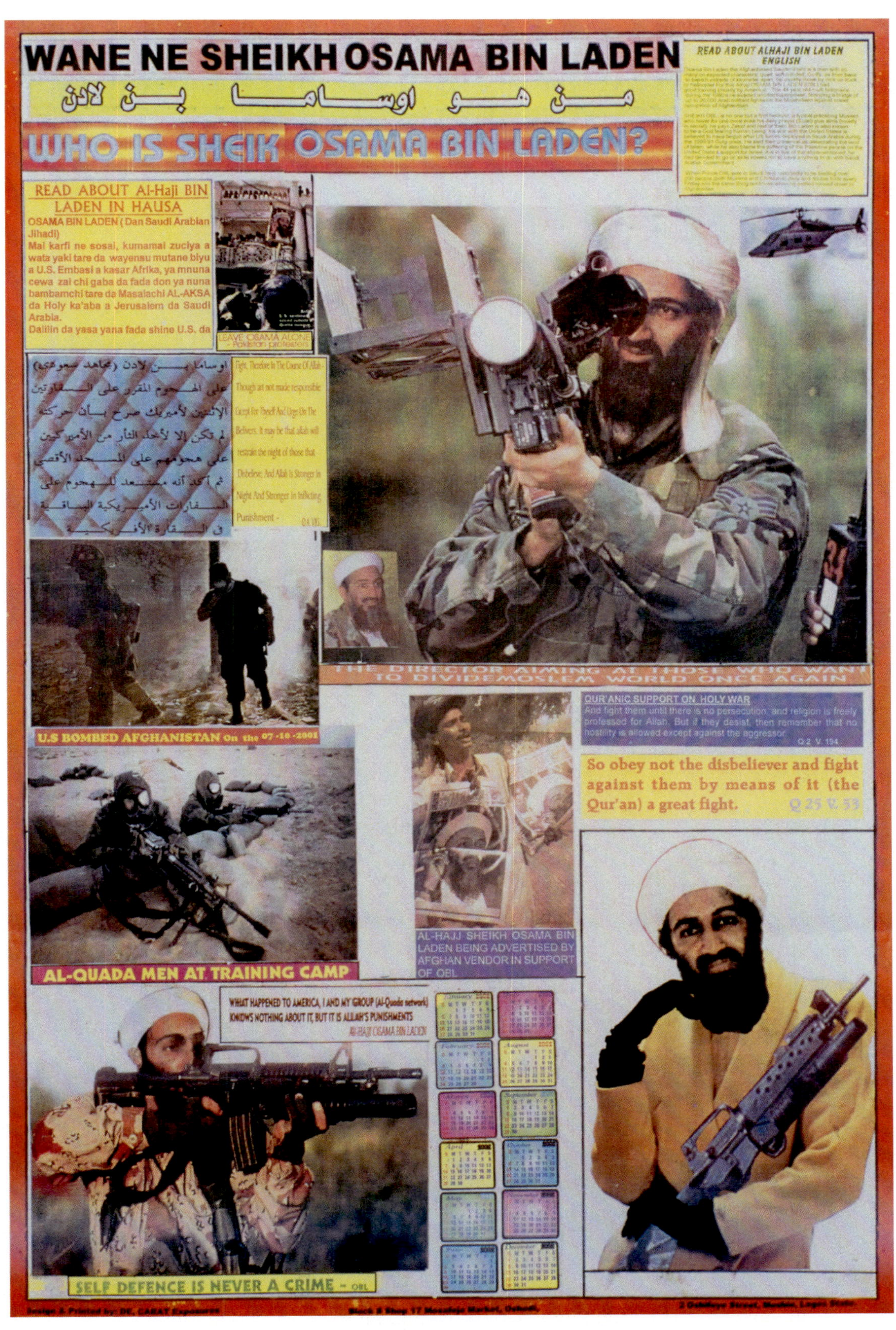


**Osama bin Laden Poster,** Nigeria, 2002 (collection Behrend)

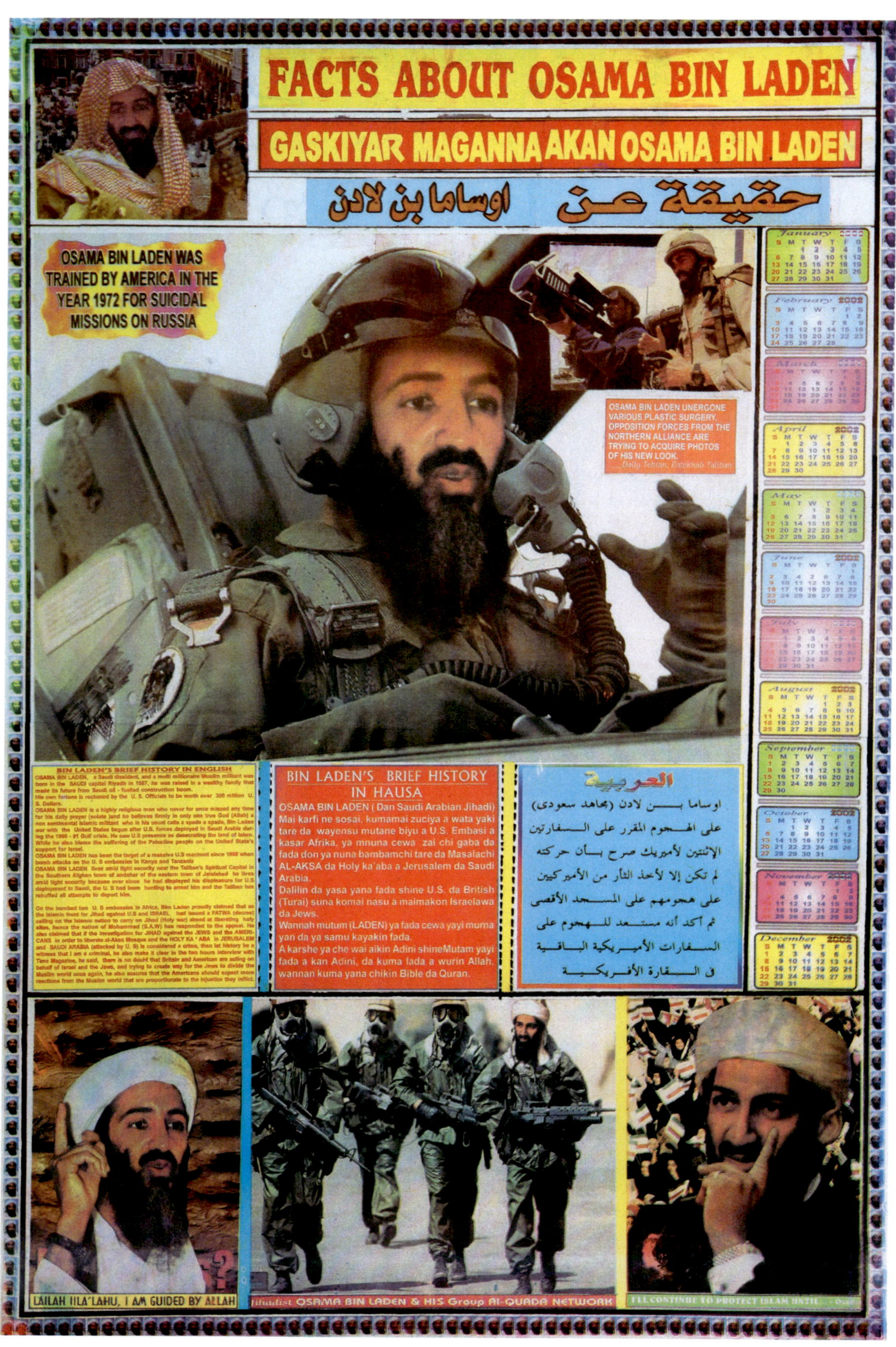


**Osama bin Laden Poster,** Nigeria ca 2002,
National Museum of World Cultures, coll.no.TM 6014-3, The Netherlands

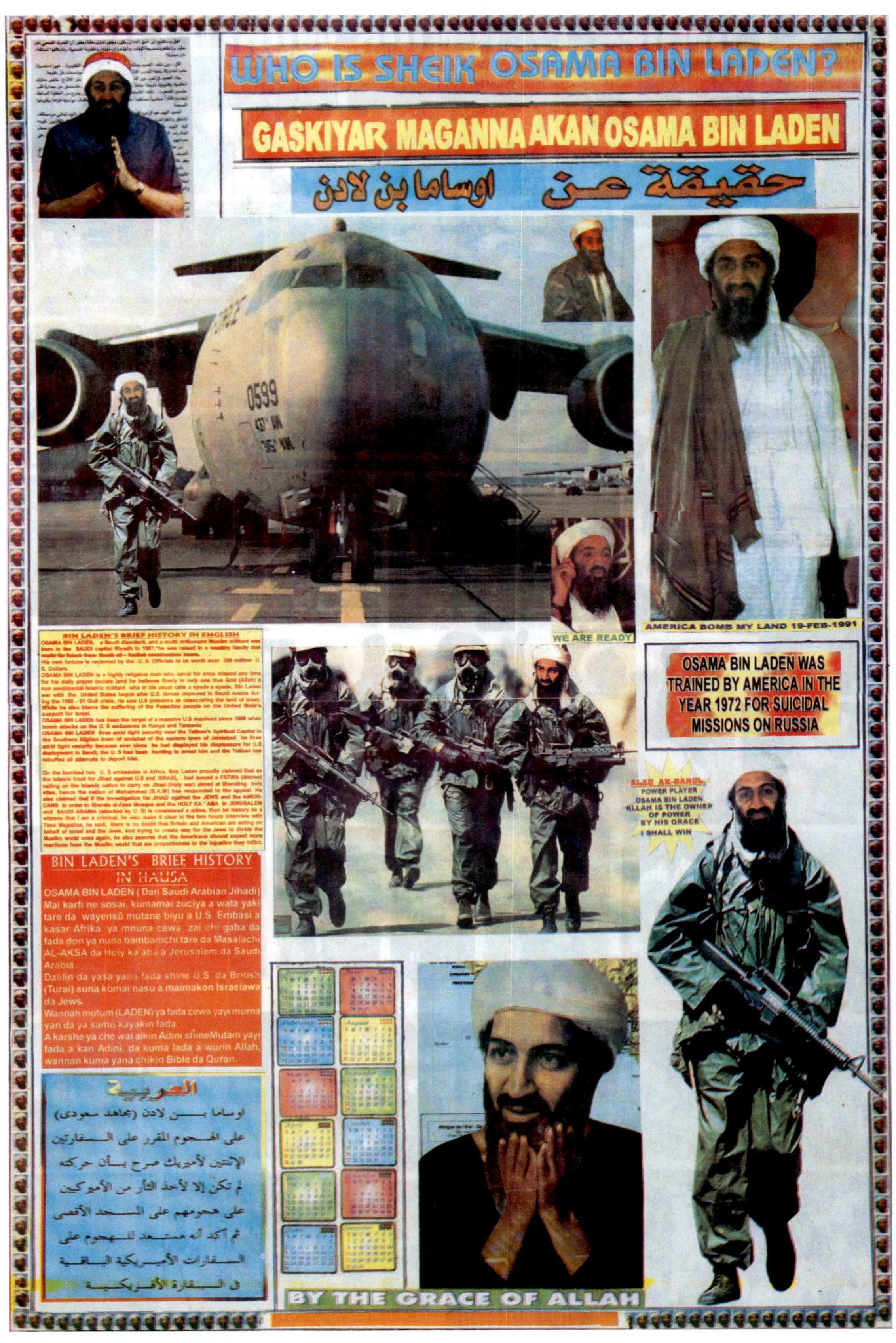


**Osama bin Laden Poster,** Nigeria 2002,
National Museum of World Cultures, coll.no. TM 6014-2, The Netherlands

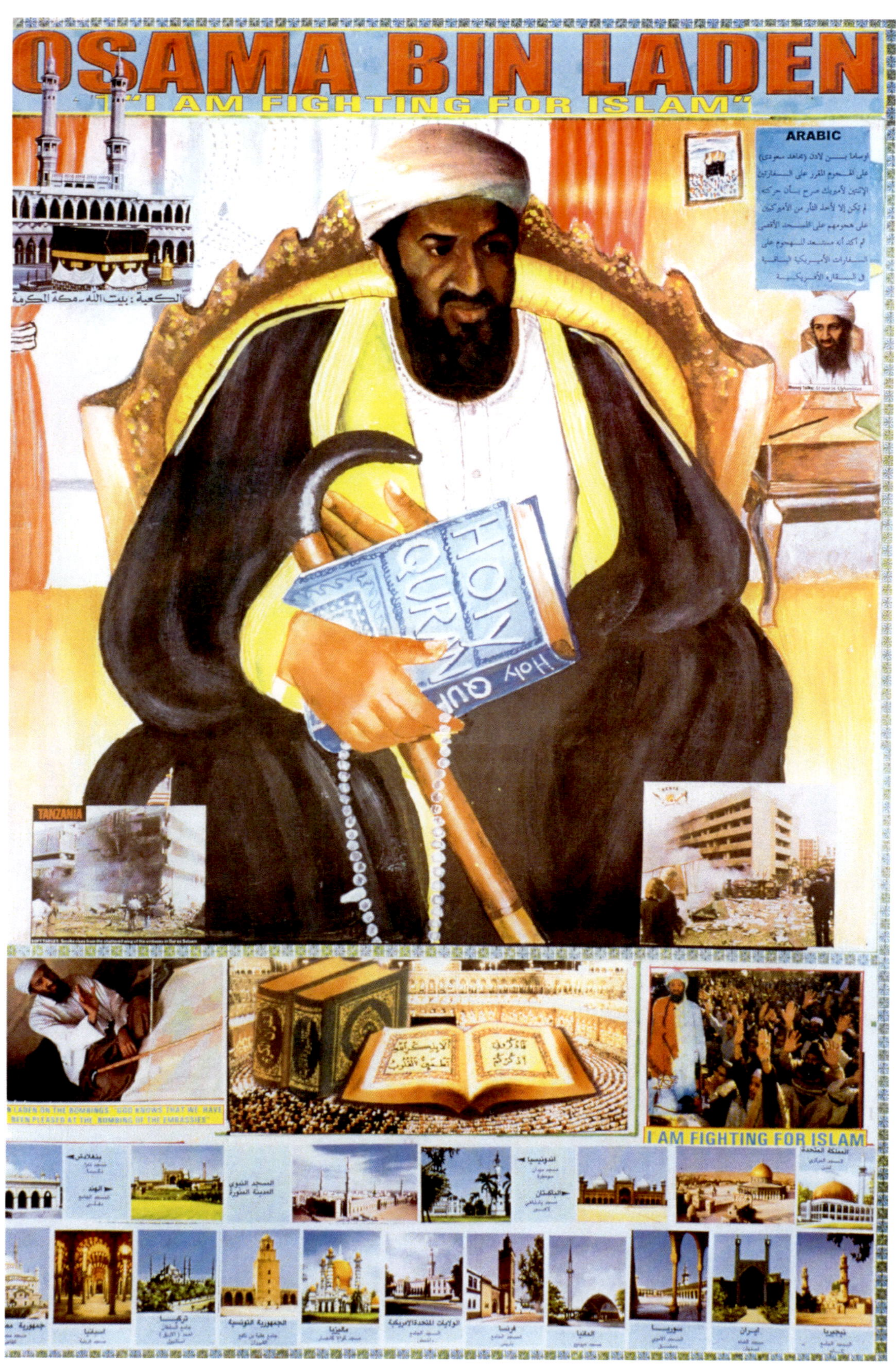


**Osama bin Laden Poster,** Nigeria 2002,
National Museum of World Culture, coll. no. TM6014-3, The Netherlands

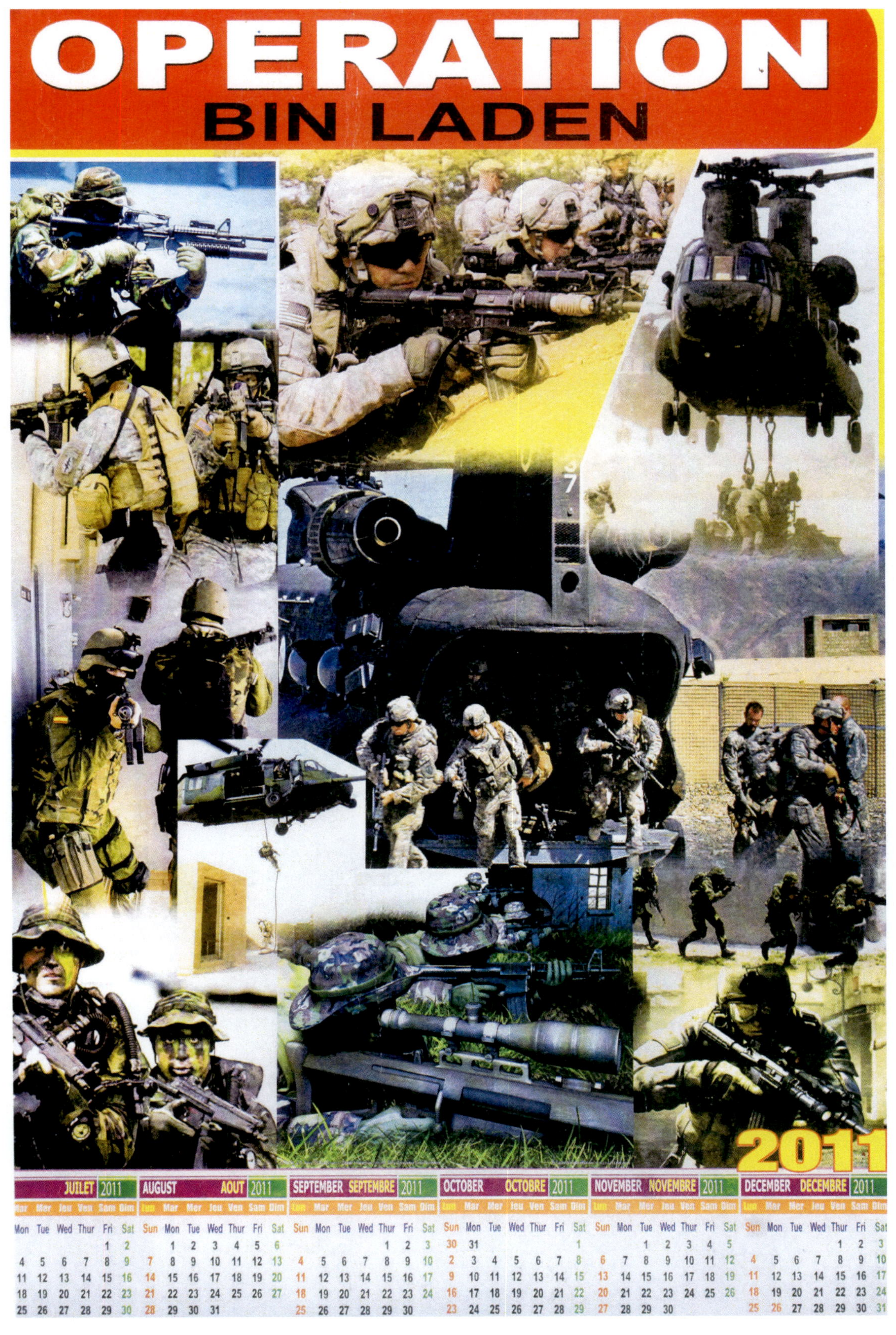


**"Operation bin Laden"** Poster, Nigeria 2011 (collection Behrend)

Duncan Omanga

# (RE) MAKING ENEMIES:

## REPRESENTATIONS OF THE TERRORISTS IN PRE- AND POST-9/11 EDITORIAL CARTOONS IN KENYA

As I have shown elsewhere (Omanga 2014), the editorial cartoon in Africa has moved beyond the previously limiting and constrained focus of lampooning the local political class to a more complex text that is often saturated with multiple meanings. These meanings may be imbued with ideologies, values, fears, culture and the aspirations of a group of people concerned with a particular issue, be it political, economic, social or cultural, that is germane to a particular time and space. The cartoon as a concrete medium is unlike a news report, as it is a discursive product reflecting on an earlier event. As commentaries, editorial cartoons are largely condensed distillations of public opinion beyond mere social commentary. "They go beyond a preoccupation with mere laughter and humor, sometimes assumed as the main weapon in the cartoonist's armory, and are more a site through which 'culture' in its varied forms is reproduced, maintained, and reaffirmed." (Omanga 2014:17). More importantly, editorial cartoons' potency resides in their ability to capture latent feelings on an issue and provide indices of identity construction by constantly defining and revealing peoples' values, fears and struggles, their images of enemies and friends and their hopes and aspirations. At the same time, it provides a mirror of the tensions and contests in a particular society in shaping and defining interpretations of a particular issue, thus evincing a characteristic power dimension. Structurally, the logic underlying editorial cartoons (in which oppositional pairing works to foreground the ideologies, stereotypes, values, hopes and fears of a particular group) gives the reader an active and discursive role of meaning making, in which he is positioned to identify with one side (DeSousa 1984). Thus, the editorial cartoon draws on public knowledge to reproduce aspects of the world and, as such, reconstructs meaning and knowledge of events such as a terror attack or other issues of social-political prominence (Walker 2003, Greenberg 2002). Nyamjoh (2009:97) argues that, in Africa, the editorial cartoon emerged from a context of political control, draconian press laws, selective communication and downright misinformation by the state. Here editorial cartoons were strategies for sneaking past stringent editorial controls and a way of speaking back to power (Mbembe 2001). Most scholars on the subject of editorial cartoons in Kenya view cartoons as a comic intervention in socio-political issues (Musila 2007, Obonyo 2011, Lent 2009, FES 2004). Such perceptions have helped to furnish widespread but obviously erroneous assumptions that the editorial cartoon is most effective through its humorous ridicule of those who wield political power.

In the following sections, I will show how editorial cartoons in two Kenyan newspapers were used to construct "the enemy" after both the "embassy attacks" and the 9/11 attacks. I argue that, even in the absence of claims or responsibilities by known terror groups or the lack of a clearly defined perpetrator, editorial cartoons have a way of constructing labels through which the public is able to imagine the enemy. The paper also shows that after 9/11, the imaginings of this enemy mutated from a local proximate one into a universalised enemy. Notably, with the passage of time and with mixed outcomes from the war on terror, the constructions of the enemy shifted ambiguously. In the editorial cartoons, the assumed finality of the killing of bin Laden in Abbottabad revealed the extent to which terrorism continues to be a contested concept. As previously argued, analysis of 9/11 representations in Kenya are best understood through the prism of how the "embassy attacks" of 1998 were framed.

## INVENTING THE ENEMY: THE 7 AUGUST 1998 EMBASSY ATTACKS AS SEEN IN EDITORIAL CARTOONS IN KENYA

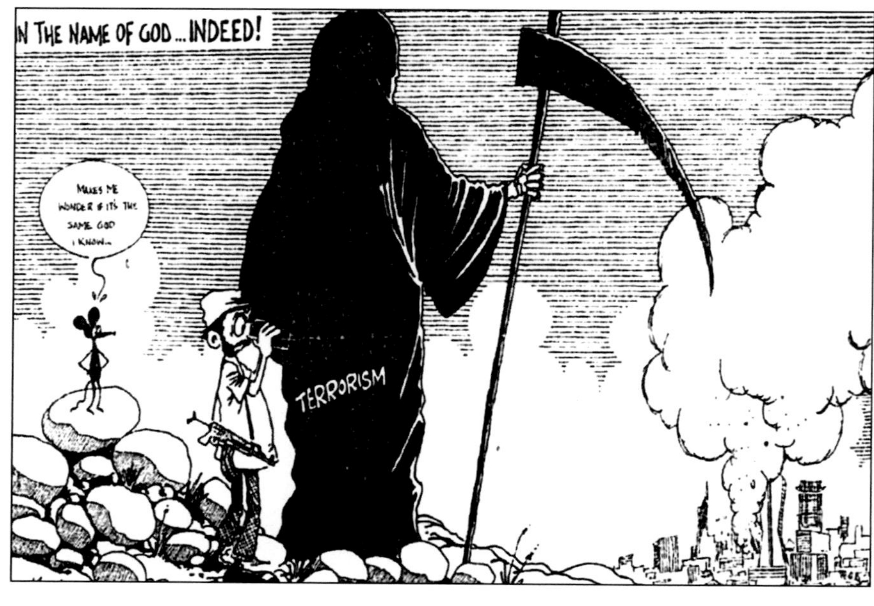


Fig. 1
The Standard,
11 August 1998.
Reprinted with permission

Soon after the embassy attacks, there was a strong media bias towards apportioning responsibility and telling audiences who the perpetrators were. Later, responsibility was claimed by members of the Egyptian Islamic Jihad, a group closely associated with Ayman al Zawahiri, the Egyptian physician who later succeeded Osama bin Laden to become Al Qaida's leader. On 11 August, The Standard newspaper published the cartoon above (figure 1). The cartoon prominently constructs the enemy as it attempts to imagine who was behind the attacks. The inscription "in the name of god...indeed!" hints at a religious ideology motivating the attacks. Dressed in a deathly black flowing gown inscribed with the word terrorism on it, the scythe-armed hooded figure appropriates the historical Grim Reaper, a Western representation of death. The *glocalisation* of this symbol from the global to the local can be traced to the 1980s, when it became the standard symbol for the HIV/AIDS pandemic. Due to its strong connotations and the fear of stigmatising HIV/AIDs patients, the figure of death was abandoned as a symbol of the disease, but re-emerged in

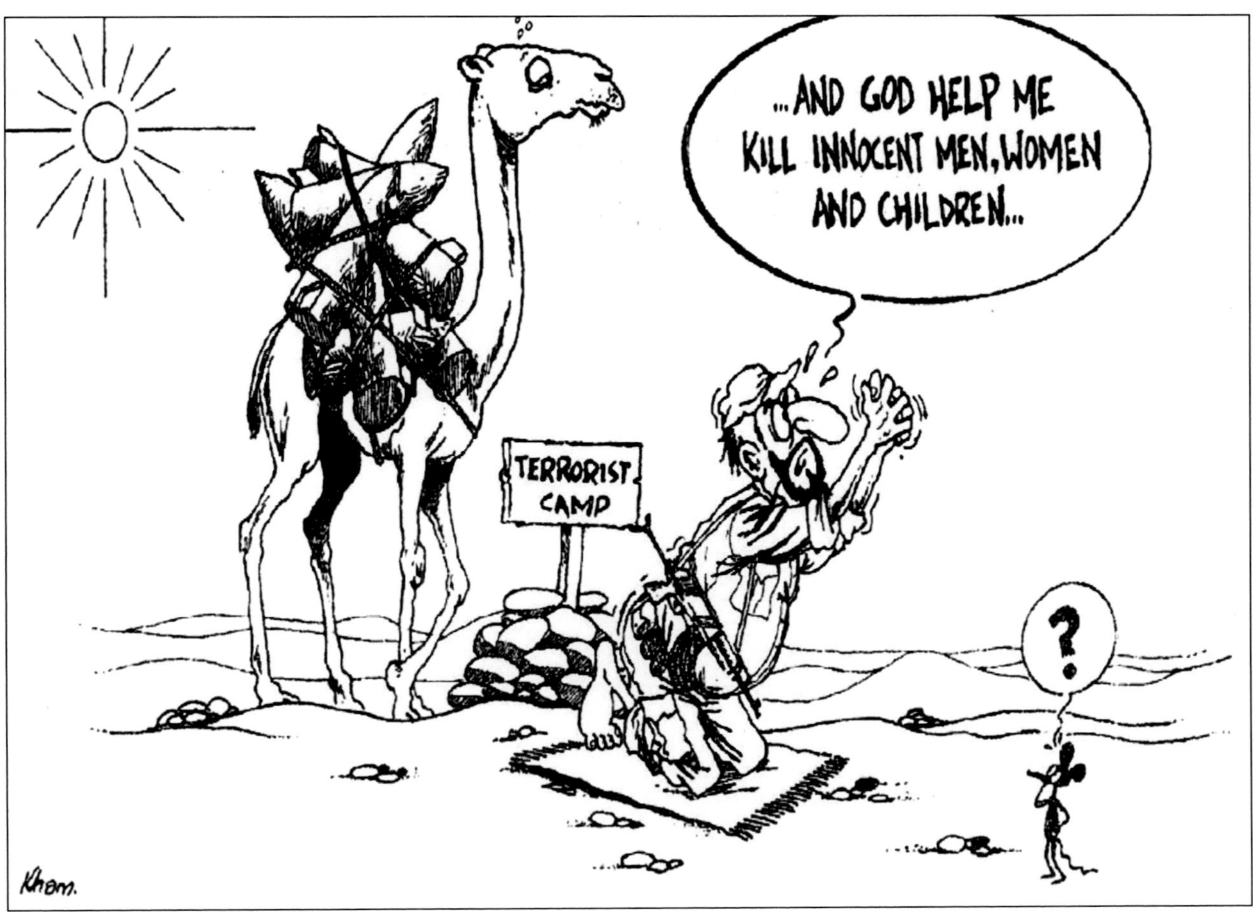


Fig. 2
The Standard,
12 August 1998.
Reprinted with permission

the late 1990s as a way of picturing terrorism and terrorists. Also, the cartoon taps into our conception of evil to graphically portray the enemy as such.

The public space was inundated with discussions about Islam and terror. The attack happened when Kenya was growing increasingly uneasy with the rising numbers of refugees from neighbouring Somalia, most of them Muslims and perceived to be sympathetic to the attackers. In an editorial cartoon appearing only a day later, the dominant discourses at the time were captured in graphic form. As seen below, the cartoonist has wide latitude in framing his message, in ways that few if any journalistic writing can achieve. Still, as a result of the charged global and local politics after 9/11, it is unlikely that this cartoon would have been published in the post-9/11 context.

This cartoon shows a camel laden with explosives under a scorching sun while standing next to a man of Arabic appearance. The man is performing Islamic prayers and seeks divine help to kill innocent women and children. Since the cartoon attempts to construct the enemy as one who subscribes to the Islamic faith, it met with "controlled" outrage and sharp reactions from Muslims in Kenya. Sheikh Ali Shee, then head of Islamic preachers in Kenya, and Sheikh Khalif, an official of the Supreme Council of Kenya Muslims (SUPKEM), protested

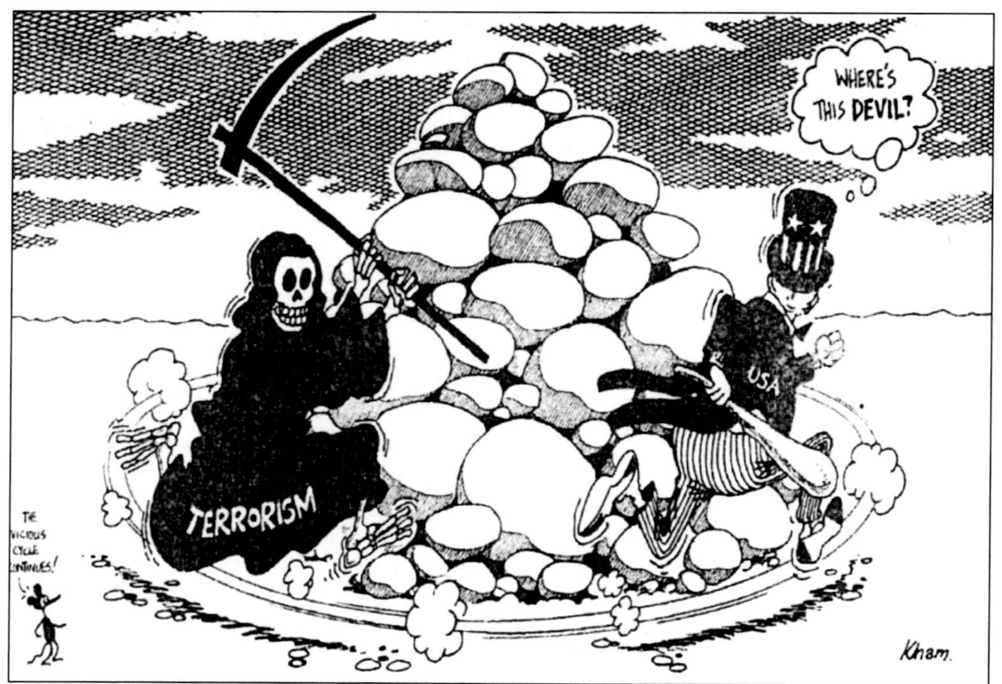


Fig. 3
The Standard,
30 August 1998.
Reprinted with permission

against these representations and claimed that the media had already tried, prosecuted and judged Islam as the perpetrators of the attacks They called for sensitivity in how terror is mediated and how claims of responsibilities should be interpreted. Their objections may have made way to representing terror as a cunning devil as seen below.

The media later imagined terrorism and terrorism in images of greater political and ideological neutrality. This construction seeks to represent terrorists as criminals, clearly mirroring the public discourse that called for perpetrators of terror to be seen and treated as isolated criminals. Echoing the definition of terrorism provided by the United Nations, the US Federal Bureau of Investigations and the Kenya government, the cartoon below emphasises the idea of terrorism as an unlawful act. This construction allows a dispassionate commentary on terrorism, since it emphasises the criminality and not its controversial ideological background.

Fig. 4
The Daily Nation,
9 August 1998.
Reprinted with permission

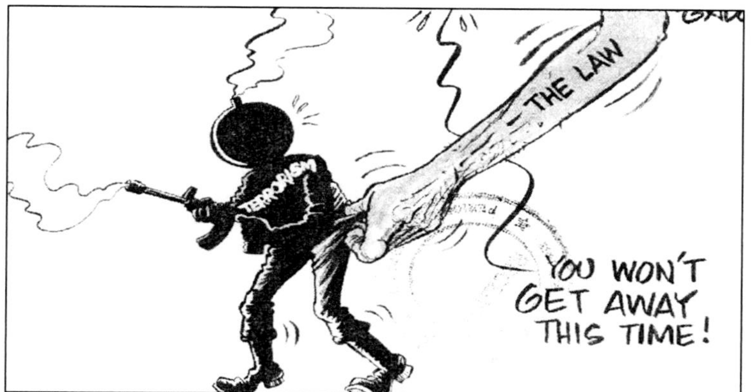


The cartoon obviously draws heavily from the interface of crime and accountability in Kenya. In informal Kenya law enforcement procedures, grabbing somebody by the back of the waist as shown in fig. 4 always signifies low-level crime (mostly at the level of a misdemeanour, such as pickpocketing or trespass). However, crime is a quotidian experience,

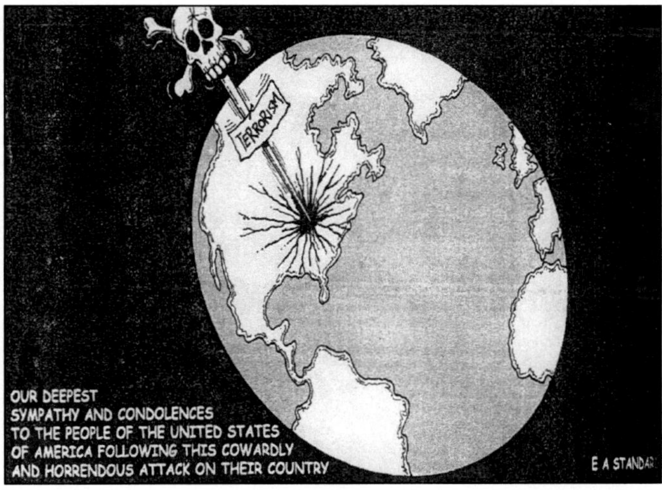


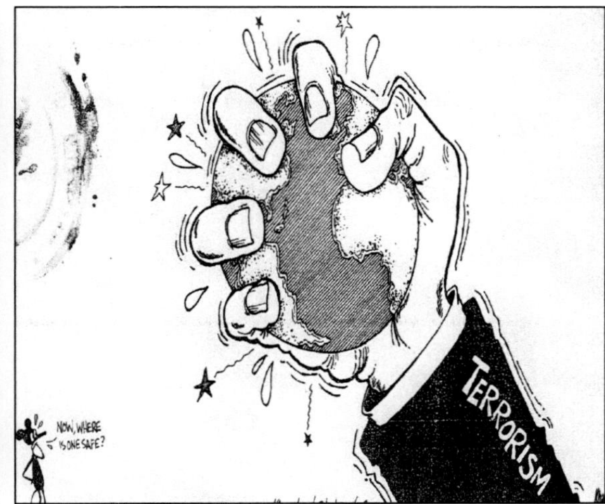


Fig. 5
The Standard,
13 September 2001.
Reprinted with permission

Fig. 6
The Standard,
14 September 2001.
Reprinted with permission

especially in Nairobi; the reduction of the embassy attacks to crime largely sought to minimise potentially harmful ideological interpretations of the event.

## REVEALING THE ENEMY: THE 9/11 ATTACKS IN EDITORIAL CARTOONS IN THE KENYAN PRESS

In the first few days after the 9/11 attacks, the editorial cartoons from Kenya's two leading newspapers revealed different views of the embassy attacks. The 9/11 attacks were primarily universalised as a global attack. While the embassy attack was a local tragedy, the discursive construction of 9/11 as a global tragedy of unprecedented proportions in scale, target and tactic meant that editorial cartoons, too, used this universalising language. Shortly after the 9/11 attacks, The Standard published an editorial cartoon meant to both express sympathy and imagine the enemy behind the attacks. The editorial cartoon (fig. 5) shows the image of the globe on a darkened background, pierced by what appears to be a sharp rod. Atop the rod is the skull and crossbones symbol. The graphic presentation of the earth in outer space stands as a symbol of humanity and at the same time as an iconic sign of the planet itself. In this view of 9/11, the enemy was carefully constructed as a global enemy who attacks a locale, the heart of the USA.

By deploying the globe, a clear condensation of all humanity, an implicit "we" is assumed in which all humanity is seen as affected by the attacks. At the same time, the attackers are no longer personalized, but instead disappear behind their deadly actions.

The cartoon (fig. 6) shows a big hand with the word "terrorism" on its wrist, tightening its grip on earth, symbolising humanity, as if to crush it. Terrorism is seen not only as universalised, but also as an omnipresent danger.[1] A construction of heightened fear emerges from this editorial cartoon, effectively representing

[1] From today's vantage point, the problem of universalized terrorism does not seem unrealistic, especially with the trans-nationalisation of the flows of violence through such militant groups as Al Shabaab (Somalia), Boko Haram (Nigeria) and Islamic State (Syria & Iraq).

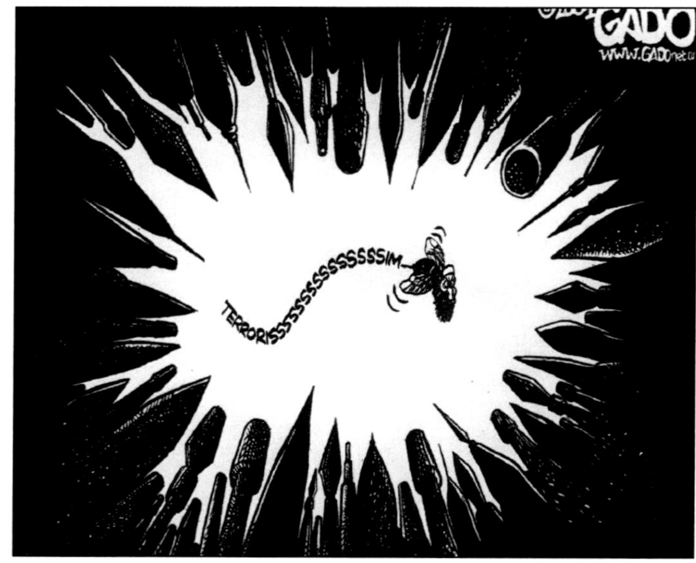


the (invisible) enemy. More importantly, 9/11 was constructed much more in the idiom of war than the embassy attacks were. Although the attacks were said to be under his direct command, bin Laden initially denied responsibility, but congratulated the attackers for what he termed successful strikes at the enemy. However, this did not prevent talk that bin Laden had raised the curtain on another war. The caution needed in fighting the "enemy" in such a war was shaped more clearly in the following cartoon (fig. 7), which attempted to give form to the enemy.

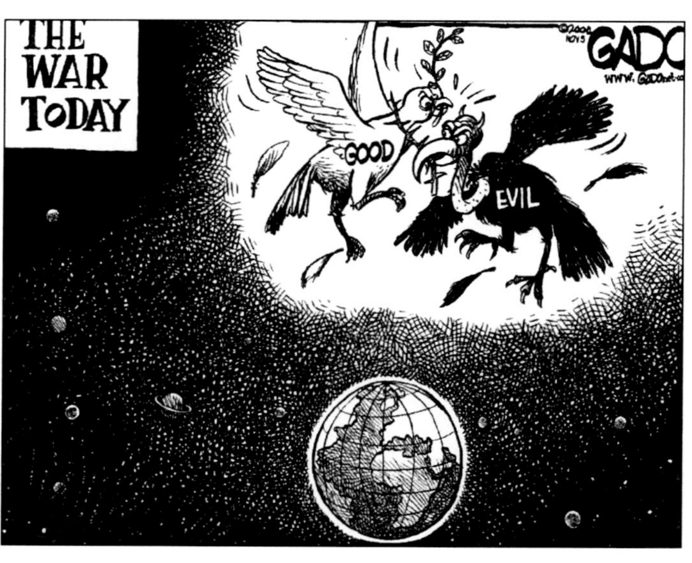


Using the process of *physiognomizing* (Gombrich 1985) or what El Refaie (2003) calls homospatiality, in which two distinct images are merged into a single image without effacing the separate components, the face of bin Laden, the man believed to be behind the 9/11 attacks, appears. Presented in part-human and part-animal form, an insect with a human face is foregrounded and cast as a focal point upon whom military hardware of various types and capabilities is aimed. More importantly, this cartoon highlights the oddity of using military might to fight terrorism by questioning the disproportionate relationship between the "verminised" bin Laden and the enormous stock of weaponry pointed at him. Still, like the embassy attacks, the September 11 attacks were presented in terms of the oppositional pair of good and evil, but with greater emphasis (fig. 8). Religious language defined the post-9/11 discourse and editorial cartoons in this trend. As Keen observes, the effectiveness of labelling our enemies evil serves to smoothen the path for their destruction, for we believe that as devil, demon, or myrmidon of evil, the enemy is possessed by an alien power. He fights not of his own will, but because he has been taken over by an alien spirit and is compelled by an illusion. Any warrior who kills such an enemy strikes a blow for truth and goodness and need have no remorse (Keen 1986:41).

Fig. 7
The Daily Nation, 26 September 2001.
Reprinted with permission

Fig. 8
The Daily Nation, 23 October 2001.
Reprinted with permission

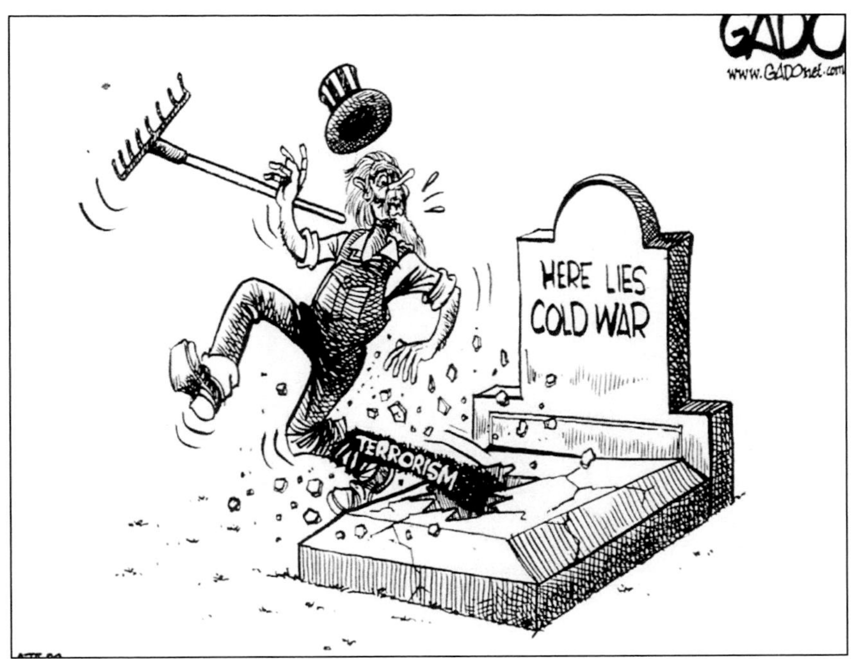


Fig. 9
29 September 2001.
Reprinted with permission

As seen below, it was not long before editorial cartoons in Kenya began tapping into the good/evil dichotomy to construct and identify the enemy. Instructively, these constructions not only remediated transnational codes, but also commented on fractious relations among religious groups in Kenya.

The cartoon suggests a transcendental interpretation as the outstretched heavens host the fight of good versus evil. The cartoon clearly draws on a Judeo-Christian interpretation in which the dove symbolizes the essence of godliness and God's presence – the very gentleness of the Holy Spirit. In contrast, the horned head of the vulture is an obvious exaggeration accentuating the visual monstrosity of some devilish creature. The thorny twig, deliberately hurled at the dove's neck, apportions the blame to the vulture, which is seen as the unprovoked evil aggressor. Again, black, often a sign of evil, is contrasted to white, a sign embodied by the "good" dove. Editorial cartoons nonetheless questioned their own assumptions about the "enemy" and occasionally sought to challenge the commonly held constructions of terrorism as a brute concept. Was it not possible that the villain was also, historically speaking, the victim? Is it simply a situation of victim and villain swapping fluid positions?

The representation of 9/11 (fig. 9) as the unfinished business of the Cold War briefly disrupted the concept of an enemy who was alone responsible for the attacks. These images were reflections of counter-discourses that post-9/11 terror stemmed from the lack of a proper closure to the Cold War. This is seen again in the cartoon (fig. 10), which once more builds on the Cold War template. Worth noting is that, although bin Laden, the alleged mastermind of the attacks, is represented with a hooked nose to accentuate the oriental "other" as the perpetrator of "new terrorism",[2] there is limited visual monstrosity, verminisation or negative exaggerations. The Afghan jihad had devoured its creator.

[2] "New terrorism" is a term used to differentiate the mostly religiously motivated and indiscriminate use of violence for political aims as opposed to "old terrorism", in which violence was used proportionately for clear aims such as independence struggles, for example in the revolutionary wars of the 1960s in Africa and Latin America.

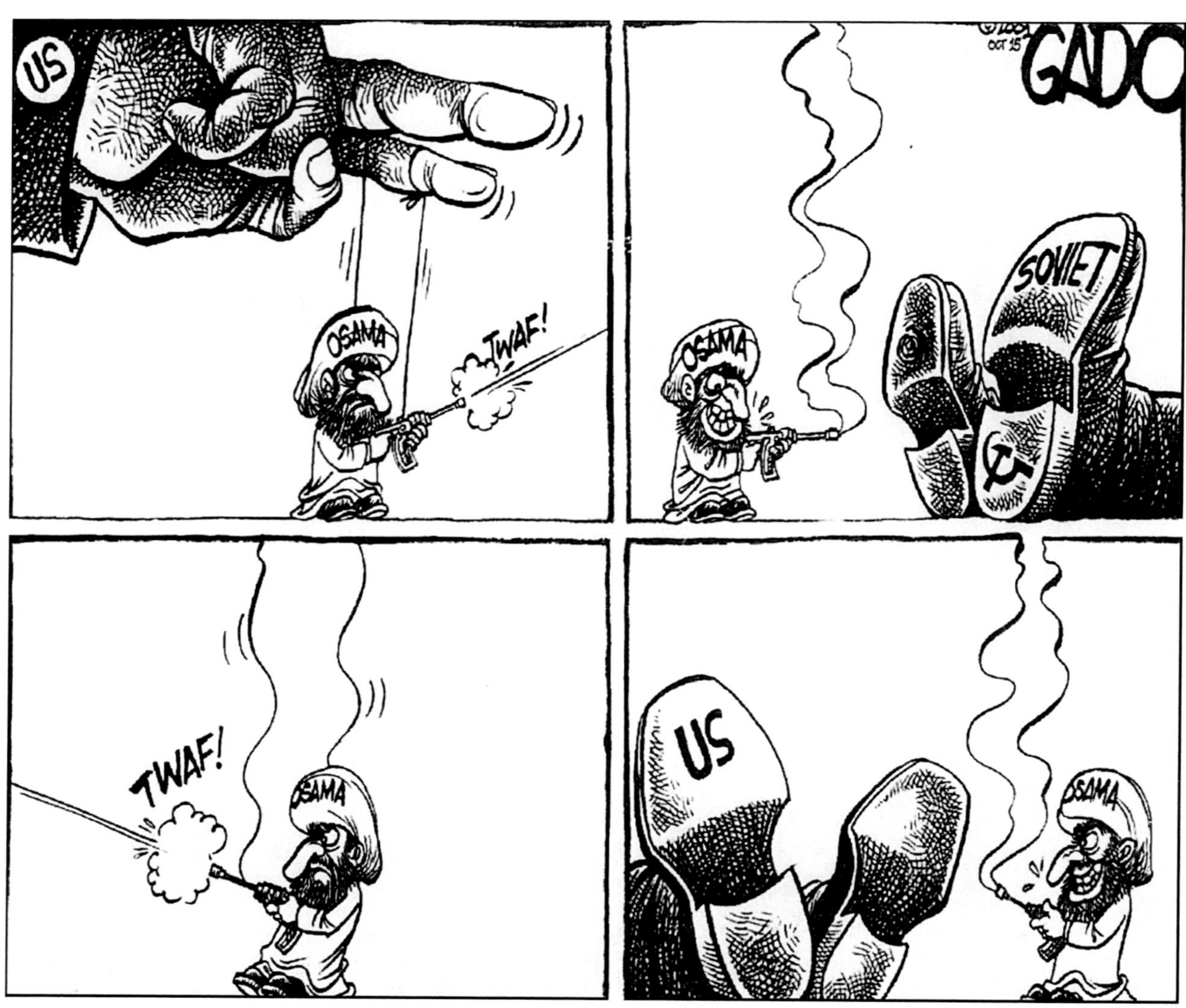


Fig. 10
15 October 2001.
Reprinted with permission

**KILLING THE ENEMY: (DE)CONSTRUCTING THE ENEMY**

The War on Terror proved a big disappointment. Terrorists were still running roughshod over "humanity" and most of the leading terror suspects, like bin Laden, were still alive. The military onslaught only served to furnish images of an invincible terrorist. Thus, there emerged a construction of terrorism as an overwhelming geopolitical condition with Al Qaida and its leader bin Laden featuring prominently. The image of the invincible terrorist emerged out of the debris of bombed-out buildings in Afghanistan and the increasing number of innocent civilian casualties.

Fig.11
Daily Nation,
22 October 2001.
Reprinted with permission

The cartoon (fig. 11) gives an overall negative appraisal of the war effort. In a typical David-versus-Goliath binarism common in constructing editorial cartoons, the legitimacy of the war on terror is questioned on the basis of the enormous firepower and the many victims resulting from fighting it. Osama bin Laden, shown sitting atop the bomb, begins to look more and more like a good guy. As Al Qaida continued to carry out more attacks and bin Laden continued to avoid capture, his image as an invincible and powerful man grew. According to the cartoon below (fig. 12), bin Laden was on top of the world (as well as the apex of his career).

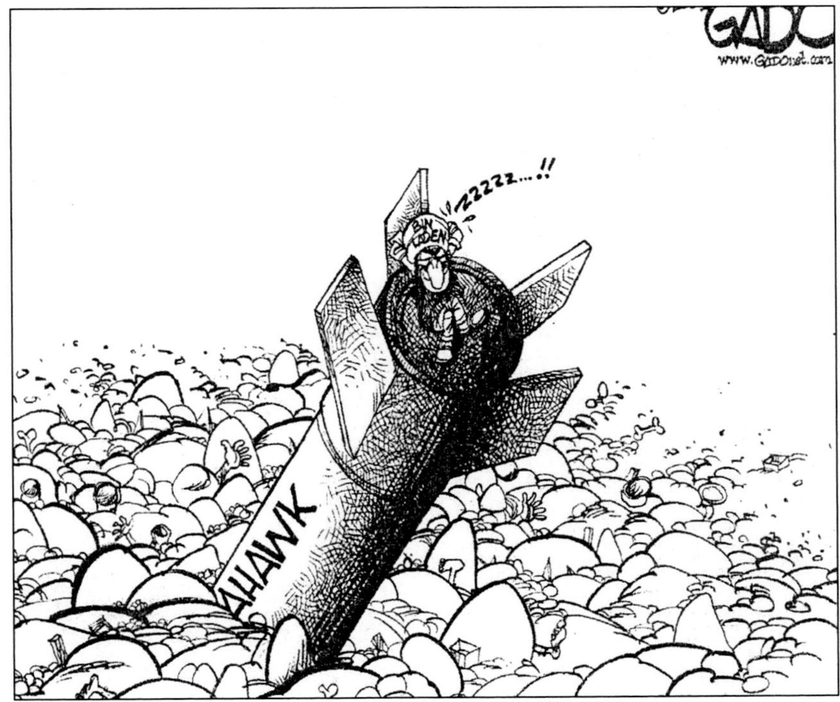


This cartoon depicts a world under siege, a world that is slowly becoming the playground of terrorists, primarily through the handiwork of a single man – bin Laden. To drive this point home, the perplexed mouse trembles in fear, muttering, "How can one guy hold the entire world ransom." This is of course very similar to the cartoon below (fig. 13), which was published after the London tube attacks. The visuals show a gigantic bin Laden, constructed almost in the proportions of a deity, with frightened people scampering away from this omnipresent terror.

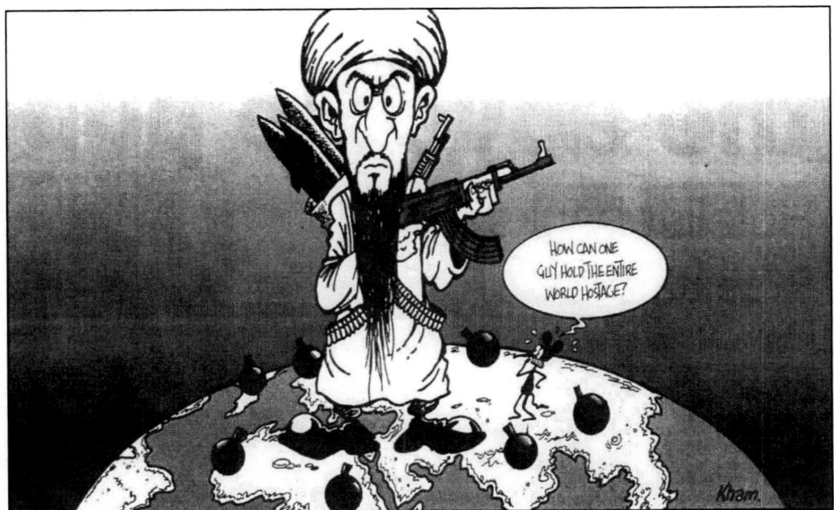


Fig. 12
The Standard,
1 December 2002.
Reprinted with permission

But even more powerful was the construction of bin Laden as the equal of and just as powerful as other world leaders, such as George Bush (fig. 14).

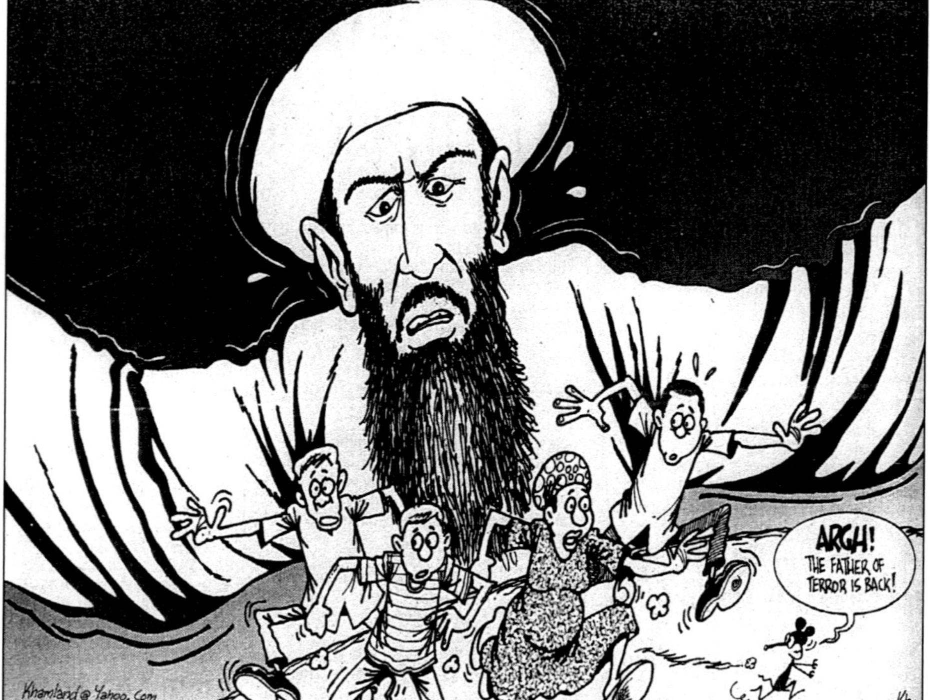


Fig. 13
The Standard,
11 July 2005.
Reprinted with permission

This and many other constructions of equivalence reproduced imaginations of the enemy as extremely powerful, and at the same time gave the erroneous impression that the on-going war on the suspected terror masterminds was proportionate. From a hunted vermin, a bug whirring hopelessly about to be swatted and a fugitive hiding away in a cold cave, bin Laden now comes "face to face" with his foe, in which both are humanized and bin Laden stands just as colossal as his foe, the US President. He towers metaphorically at a height similar to that of the Twin Towers he brought down. And with this "feat", he is cast as a worthy opponent in a war against the most sophisticated and advanced war machinery in the history of man.

After several years on the run, bin Laden was killed in a raid on his compound in May 2011. The killing in Pakistan of the most wanted fugitive showed just how much ambiguity terrorism evinced even in the editorial cartoons. Basically, two different interpretations emerged. On the one hand, the implied end of terrorism; and on the other, the beginning or rather the continuation of more terror. On 2 May, the editorial cartoon (fig. 15) that appeared in The Standard suggested closure in the reign of terror that had kept the globe in fear for the past decade. The image of a gravestone lying on the bed of the sea engraved with the words "Here lies Osama bin Laden the father of terror, 1957-2011" summarised the event. The picture strongly implies that this may be the end of terrorism as we know it. Dead and buried at the bottom of the sea, with no visible grave to pay homage to, no mourners to grieve and no dirges to be sung, the culturally loaded message that he was "lost" and gone for good could not have been conveyed more clearly.

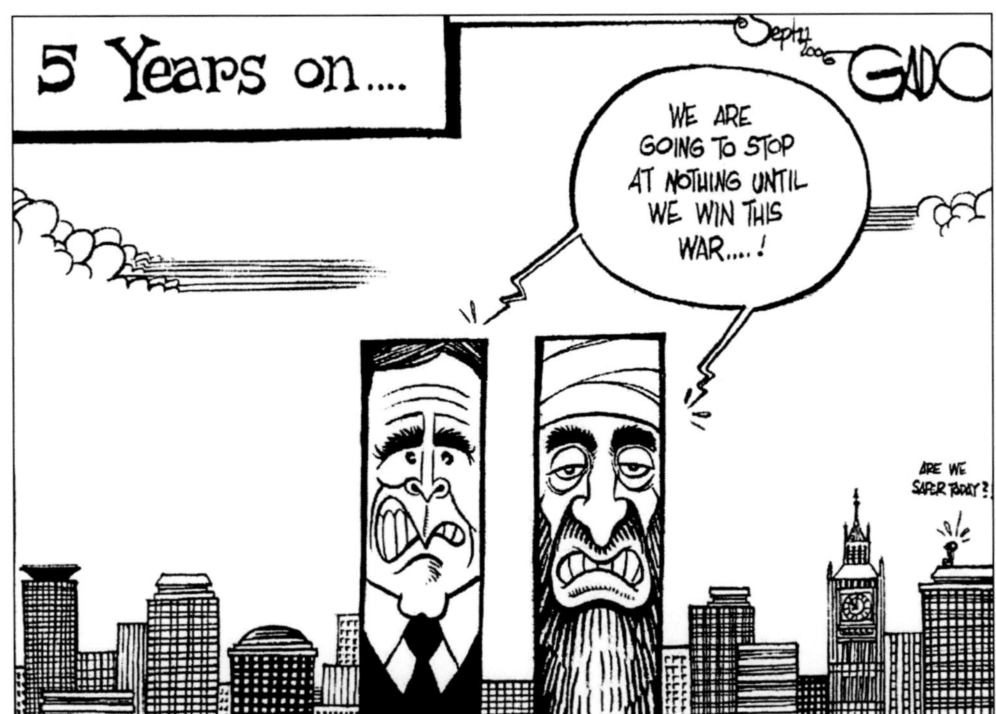


Fig. 14
The Daily Nation,
11 September 2006.
Reprinted with permission

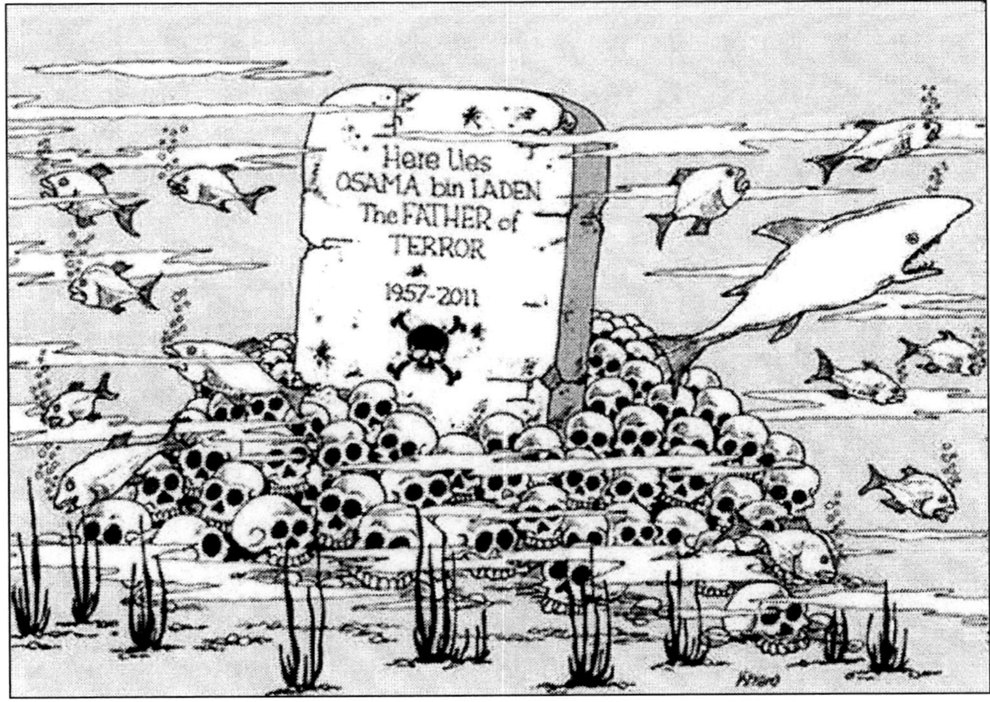


Fig. 15
The Standard,
2 May 2011.
Reprinted with permission

On the same day, perhaps a much more accurate depiction of bin Laden's death and its ramifications appeared on the pages of The Nation (fig. 16). Coming shortly before a heated debate on whether to release the pictures of the dead bin Laden, the following editorial cartoon may have momentarily suppressed

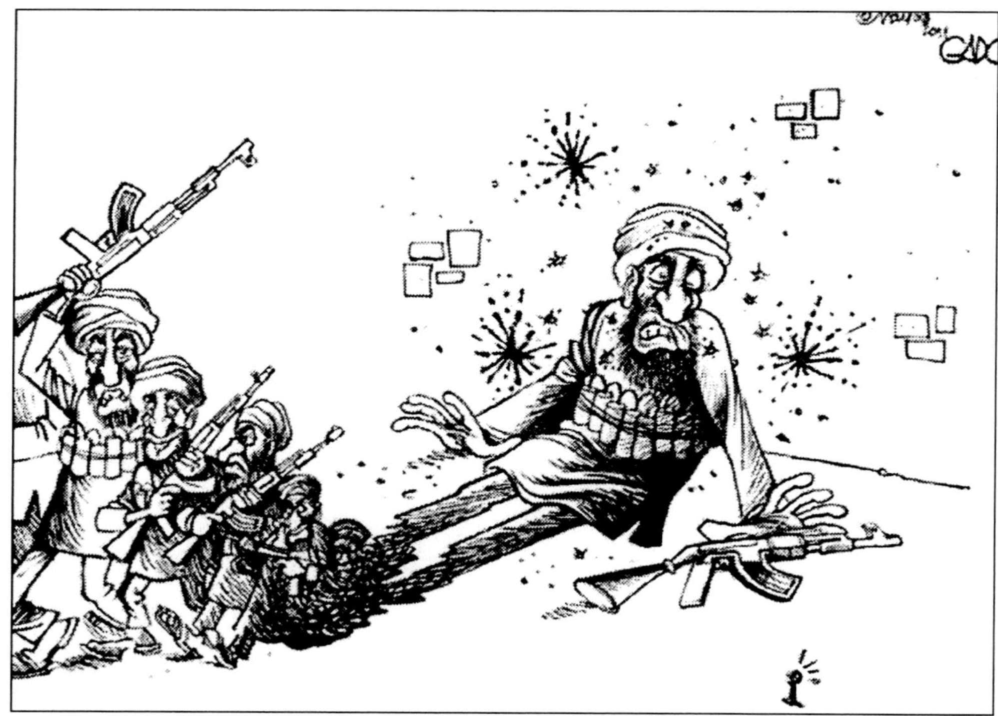

Fig. 16
The Daily Nation, 2 May 2011.
Reprinted with permission

the visual appetites of those who wanted to see the image of the slain Al Qaida chief. The cartoon shows bin Laden just moments after his death, as evidenced by the bloodied walls. His "belt of death" still intact, he lies supine, loosening his grip on his ever-present rifle. Below his feet, however, what looks like miniature Osamalets mutate from the dead "progenitor", almost analogous to a resurrection of the man himself.

The image suggests that even with the killing of bin Laden, the world's most feared man was still alive in several ways. The image of this almighty terrorist had taken years to create and the simple elimination of the man behind the lionized image will equally take longer to die. Possibly with this in mind, the US administration launched the propaganda war on the more potentially lasting, and also potentially more galvanizing foe: the symbolic Osama bin Laden. In addition, and rather unlike the previous editorial cartoon that appeared in The Standard, this cartoon suggests that eliminating the Al Qaida leader did not mean the end of terrorism. In fact, the re-emerging quartet, armed with rifles and strapped with bombs, connotes multiplied risk in the pipeline, as opposed to the danger posed by the previous "lone" terrorist. Aside from the multiplied risk, the spectre of more defiance and resistance is implied by the shift in the position of the rifle, which one "Osamalet" holds under his arms, the next raises to his chest, the third shoulders and the fourth finally provocatively raises and waves above his head. The editorial cartoons suggest that, while the "father of terror" had indeed become seafood, terrorism might outlive its pallbearers.

## CONCLUSION

The pre-9/11 representations of terrorism and terrorists were mostly blunt depictions insofar as religion is concerned. Terrorism was mostly seen as a local problem, especially in countries like Kenya, to the extent that it could be pinned on a specific religion or sanitized as normal crime. However, things changed in the post-9/11 period, when terrorists were seen as global enemies and the 9/11 event as a universal problem. Still, over time, and with little success in the so-called war on terror, images of the terrorist in editorial cartoons moved from mere verminisation to more complex forms. This was especially so when terror was personalised in the image of bin Laden.

### LITERATURE


DeSousa, Michael A., "Symbolic Action and Pretended Insight: The Ayatolla Khomeini in U.S. Editorial Cartoons". In: Medhurst, Martin J. and Benson, Thomas W. (Eds.), *Rhetorical Dimensions in Media: A Critical Casebook*. Dubuque/Iwoa: Kendall/Hunt 1984. pp. 216-243.

El Refaie, Elisabeth, "Understanding visual metaphor: The example of newspaper cartoons". *Visual Communication* 2/1 (2003), pp. 75-96.

FES (Friedrich Ebert Stiftung) (Ed.), *Drawing the Line: The History and Impact of Political Cartooning in Kenya*. Nairobi: Friedrich Ebert Stiftung 2004.

Greenberg, Josh, "Framing and Temporality in Political Cartoons: A Critical Analysis of Visual News Discourse". *Canadian Review of Sociology and Anthropology*, 39/2 (2002), pp. 181-219.

Gombrich, Ernst H., *Meditations on a Hobby Horse, and other Essays on the Theory of Art.* Oxford: Phaidon 1963.

Keen, Sam, *Faces of the Enemy: Reflections of the Hostile Imagination*. San Francisco: Harper Row 1986.

Lent, John A. (Ed.), *Cartooning in Africa*. Cresskill, NJ: Hampton Press 2009.

Mbembe, Achille, *On the Postcolony*. Berkely: University of California Press 2001.

Musila, Grace A., "Democrazy: Laughter in GADO's Editorial Cartoons 1992-1999". In: Ogude, James and Nyairo, Joyce (Eds.), *Urban Legends, Colonial Myths: Popular Culture and Literature in East Africa*. Trenton, NJ: Africa World Press 2007. pp. 97–124.

Nyamnjoh, Francis B., "Press Cartoons and Politics: The Case of Cameroon". In: Lent, John A. (Ed.), *Cartooning in Africa*, Cresskill, NJ: Hampton Press 2009. pp. 97-110.

Obonyo, Levi, "Talking Health: HIV/AIDS in Kenyan Toons". *African Communication Research* 4/2 (2011), pp. 243–368.

Omanga, Duncan, "Raid at Abottabad: Editorial cartoons and the terrorist almighty in the Kenyan Press". *The Journal of African Cultural Studies* 26/1 (2014), pp. 15-32.

Heike Behrend

# 9/11 IN A PHOTO STUDIO:

## THE LIKONI PHOTOGRAPHERS AT THE "STEIRISCHER HERBST" IN GRAZ, AUSTRIA[1]

As mentioned in the introduction, never before has an event been mediated so often in pictures (and sounds), and for the first time in "real time", as 9/11 (Paul 2011:137). In fact, the proliferation of new media and the creation of technical images allowed people all over the world to participate in 9/11 and to develop a sense of personal affiliation with this catastrophic event. Though 9/11 happened in the USA, it created highly diverse responses also in parts of the world that were not directly involved in the War on Terror, and it inscribed itself in many different ways into national, regional, and local conflicts.

Yet, in spite of the sheer quantity of images of 9/11 and the fantastic global extent of their circulation, only a few images gained the status of "icons". For example, Thomas E. Franklin's photograph of the three firefighters raising a flag at Ground Zero was quickly turned into an object of veneration and emotional response. It was reproduced and reworked widely and placed prominently in both private and public settings. Echoing the earlier iconic photograph of the flag raising on Iwo Jima of World War II, this photograph was modeled visually for a national audience, affirming patriotic citizenship in the face of disaster, destruction, and death. It acquired its own history of appropriation, reworking, and commentary in various media (Hariman and Lucaites 2007:128ff).

While the photograph of the three firefighters addressed primarily a national audience, photographs of the destruction of the World Trade Center's Twin Towers entered deeply into the popular imaginary also outside the USA. Images of the Twin Towers' annihilation were remediated in various ways in other parts of the world and operated as a powerful resource within various publics. They became a kind of "composite icon" that unfolded performative spaces open to continued and varied articulations. In the following, I will deal with a group of popular migrant studio photographers, the so-called Likoni photographers of Mombasa in Kenya, and explore the aesthetic practices with which they related to 9/11. In this contribution, I will explore the remediation of 9/11 in the genre of studio photography. This implies reflection on transnational movement, travel, and censorship, because the photographers dared to relate to 9/11 only in the "protected" realm of an art festival in Europe that had invited them to attend and address a European audience.

[1] This is a revised version of chapter 6 of my book *Contesting Visibility* (2013). For more detailed information on the Likoni photographers, their history and photographic practices, and their aesthetics, see Behrend 2000 and 2003.

## THE LIKONI PHOTOGRAPHERS

The Likoni photographers emerged at the beginning of the 1990s as a group of young street photographers in Mombasa who originated in the central and western provinces of Kenya. The "Golden Age" of studio photography had already declined; and mobile, highly adventurous photographers were on the rebound. In Mombasa, they occupied a steep bluff directly on the shore of the mainland, an area called Likoni, where the ferry connects the mainland with the island of Mombasa. Here, as squatters, they started to set up small kiosks, more or less ambulant studios with little equipment and without electricity, appropriate lamps, or running water. They catered primarily to (local) African tourists and other migrant workers.

The Likoni photographers defined themselves as *jua kali*, "hot sun" or "sharp sun" in Kiswahili, a term that designates people who work in the so-called informal sector. In fact, the informal and illegal status of the space the Likoni photographers occupied has contributed substantially to the particular aesthetic of these studios. The postcolonial state rigidly prohibited street photographers who worked on public squares from creatively altering these sites. As one street photographer put it, these sites must remain "natural". But the Likoni photographers were not subject to this degree of state restriction and sanctions. Their existence was repeatedly threatened; they had to fear eviction and finally were evicted in 2006. Yet, for a while, their studios enjoyed "artistic freedom". In postcolonial Kenya, they were able to occupy a space that eluded the state authorities.

In their studios, the photographers created a splendid realm out of heterogeneous elements from various parts of the world, including tapestries from Turkey that reached Mombasa via Dubai, balloons, plastic flowers, and the glittery decorations from Bombay that adorn Mombasa's Hindu temple during religious festivities. Moreover, they asked the painter Samuel Chakua Masada to provide fancy backdrops to attract customers. Together, the Likoni photographers invented a unique photographic style nowadays well known as the "Likoni style" that has spread to other areas along the coast, to the hinterland, to Nairobi, and even to Tanzania. As one of the photographers told me, what was staged in the studio was generally not mundane, but constructed in opposition to everyday life. The scenarios the photographers created in their studios praised, above all, the absent, the foreign, and the global that they gave presence to. The decor of the Likoni studios embodied an aesthetic of bricolage, pastiche, plenitude, luxury, and festivity. The pictures – and the depicted individuals, so I was told – should look shiny, glamorous, bright, and colorful. In fact, the Likoni photographers consciously made use of color photography and did their best to turn their studios into a site where colors exploded. As Sammy Njuguna explained, the photos not only created a festive mood, they

Fig. 1
**"Desert Storm",**
Anyole Photo Studio,
Mombasa 1998
(collection Behrend)

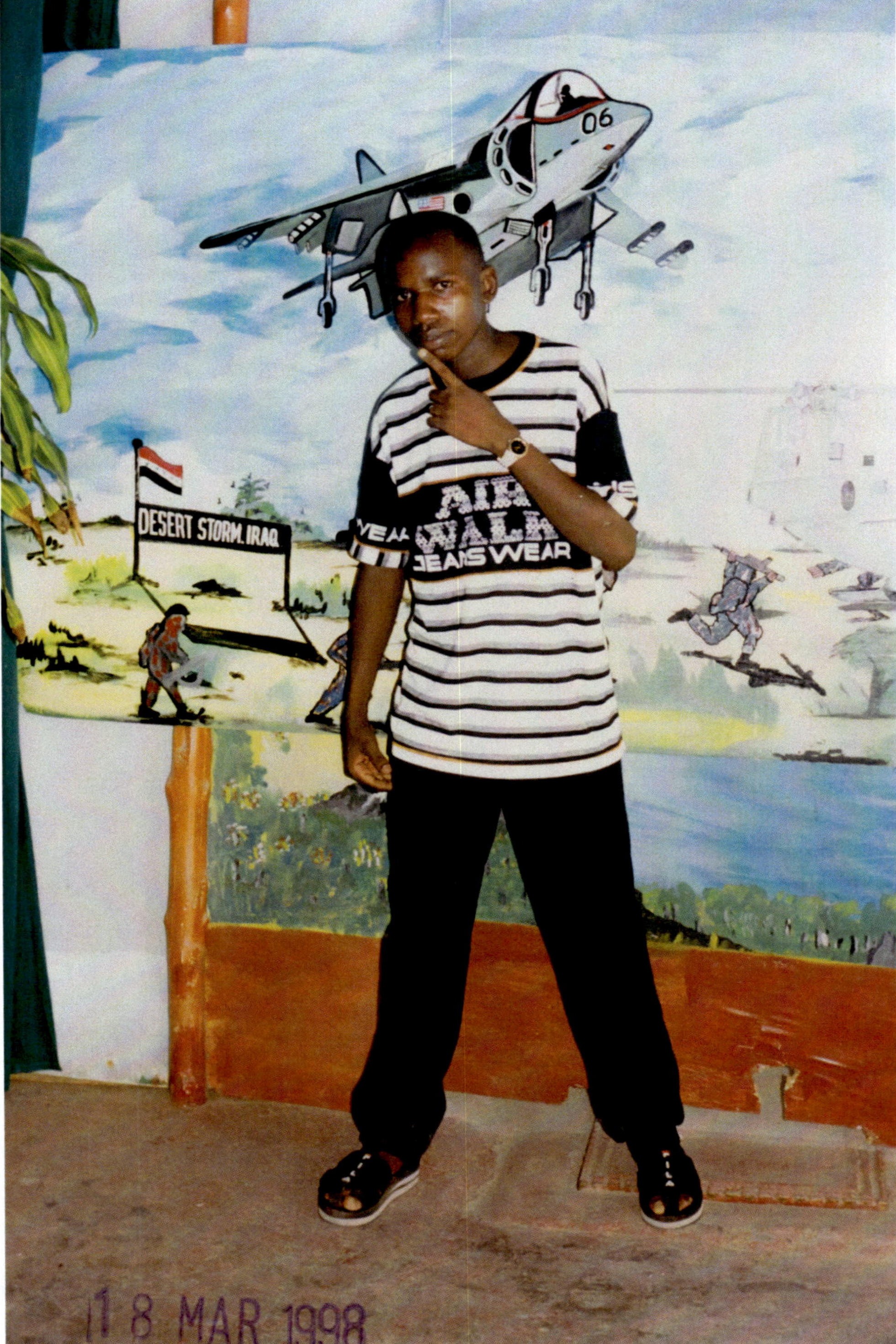


were themselves part of the festivity. "We crown the celebration with a photo," he said. Against the background of poverty, financial hardship, migration, and discrimination that the photographers and most of their customers experienced, the studios were wish-fulfillment machines, visions of spectacle, and an instant utopia. It is as if the photos were employed to create the illusion that a richer, cosmopolitan world was at one's disposal.

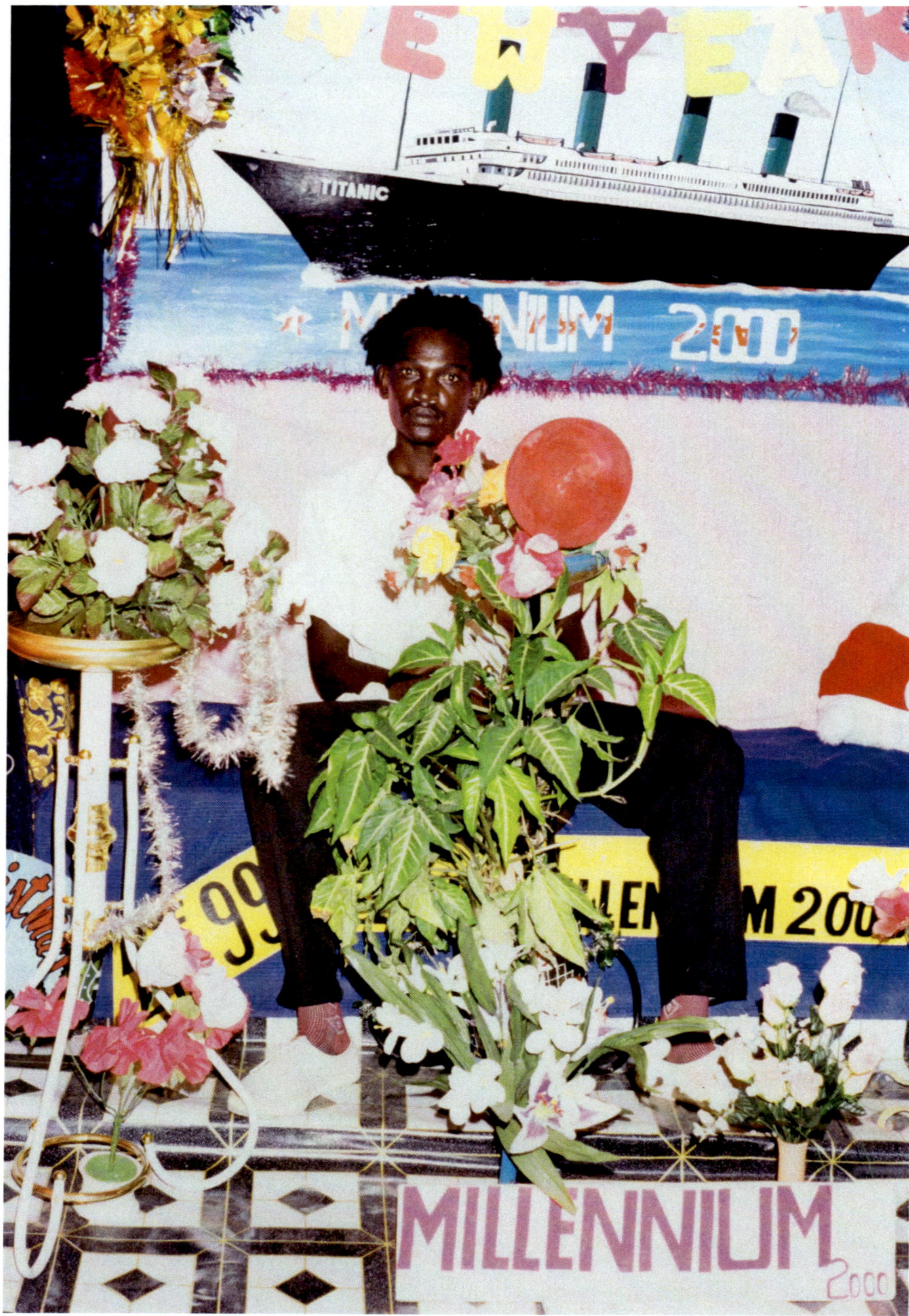


Fig. 2
**"Titanic" backdrop,**
Omalla Studio,
Likoni 2000
(collection Behrend)

As photographers and customers told me, many customers had their pictures taken in order to send home and convey to those at home where and how they lived. At home, relatives displayed the portraits in the sitting room or mounted them in a photo album, to be shown to visitors and to members of the family. Thus, photos were used to connect with and to compensate for the absence of the migrant workers by giving them a photographic presence.

Photographs not only reminded the ones at home of their migrant and absent relatives or friends, they also depicted social status and economic success and thereby gave evidence of the social pressure to be successful to which migrant workers were strongly exposed. Often, people at home funded the migrants' travel and then waited for the migrant to repay this debt. In a way, these photographs then substantially shaped translocal subjectivities by producing an idealized, successful photographic person who anticipated in the photograph what might not be attained in real life.

The Likoni photographers created not only their own unique and fanciful "Likoni style", they also followed the logic of capitalistic competition and the law of accelerated innovation. They "always offered the latest thing" and changed backdrops and equipment frequently. Long before 9/11, they started to take up, relate to, and rework events that troubled the world; for example, one of the studios took up the Gulf War and the campaign that US military titled "Operation Desert Storm" (fig. 1). And when James Cameron's blockbuster film "Titanic" was released and shown successfully in Kenyan cinemas and video halls, painted backdrops appeared in the photographers' studios that displayed a ship named the Titanic.[2] This backdrop allowed their customers to stage a personal affiliation with the steamer and the movie that remediated the catastrophic event of 1912 resulting from Western technological hubris (fig. 2).

## THE LIKONI PHOTOGRAPHERS AND 9/11

A few weeks after 9/11, in October 2001, two Likoni photographers, Bonifaz Wandera and Sammy Njuguna, and the artist Samuel Chakua Masada, who had painted most of their backdrops, were invited to attend the international art festival "Steirischer Herbst" in Graz, Austria.[3] This festival was founded in 1968 and is one of the oldest avant-garde events in Europe. It strives to connect theater, painting, film, literature, dance, music, and architecture with new media and theoretical debates. The festival became notorious for its "scandals": The works of Bill Fontana provoked aggression and controversies, and Hans Haacke's "reworked" monument titled "Victory Column" was destroyed in an iconoclastic arson attack by neo-Nazis (Gamboni 1997:169).

In Graz, the curators of the "Steirischer Herbst" asked the three Kenyans to build a studio in the "Likoni style" and to offer their services to the visitors. Thus, the curators created an ambiguous space where the production of art, the performative act of taking pictures, was exhibited, rather than the photographs as such, as artworks. In this space, the photographs of the Likoni photographers

[2] The trope of the Titanic has powerfully entered the popular imaginary in Africa and elsewhere; see Behrend 2011 and Hüwelmeier 2015.

[3] After Tobias Wendl, Kerstin Pinther, Henrike Grohs, and I had curated the exhibition "Snap me One" and published a catalogue (Wendl and Behrend 1998) with photographs by the Likoni photographers, the curator of the Steirischer Herbst contacted me and then invited the three Kenyans to participate in the art festival. With the kind assistance of Henrike Grohs, they made it to Graz. Unfortunately, I was not able to participate in the exhibition. However, back in Mombasa in 2005, 2007, and 2011, I had the chance to talk to Sammy Njuguna, Bonifaz Wandera, and the painter Masada about their experiences in Graz.

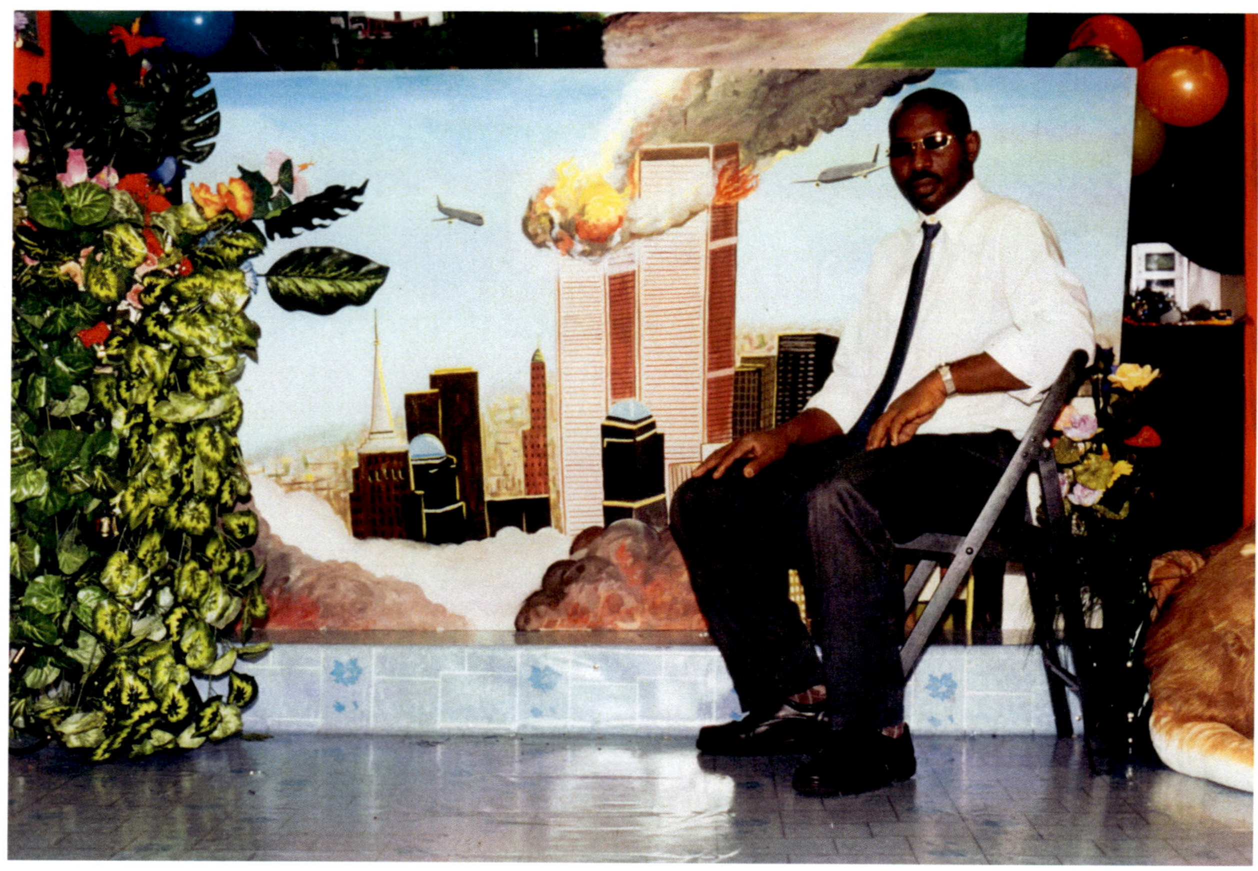

Fig. 3
**Portrait of photographer Sammy Njuguna,** photographed by Boniface Wandera, Graz 2001 (collection Behrend)

– although part of an art exhibition – were not clearly given the status of art. They were redefined as popular commodities that could be bought "as if in a studio". In this ambiguous space, the photographers established their studio and were allowed to freely interact with their "customers". Integrated into the art world, the photographers were at the same time excluded and their status problematized.

Since "the day that shook the world" had happened only a month before, Sammy Njuguna, Bonifaz Wandera, and Samuel Chakua Masada decided to make this event the subject matter of their studio backdrop. Sammy Njuguna told me that during the flight with Swiss Air to Europe, the idea of representing the destruction of the World Trade Center had entered his mind, especially since two Kenyans who had lived in New York had been among the victims. In addition, 9/11 had a strong emotional impact on the three Kenyans because they took it as a repetition of the Embassy Bombing in 1998 that had injured or killed thousands of people in Nairobi.

When Masada painted the backdrop of the World Trade Center in Graz, he reformulated 9/11 and its global mediation in the images produced by mass media, translating it into a painted backdrop (fig. 3). He reduced the complex event (9/11 consisted of four coordinated attacks with four passenger airliners,

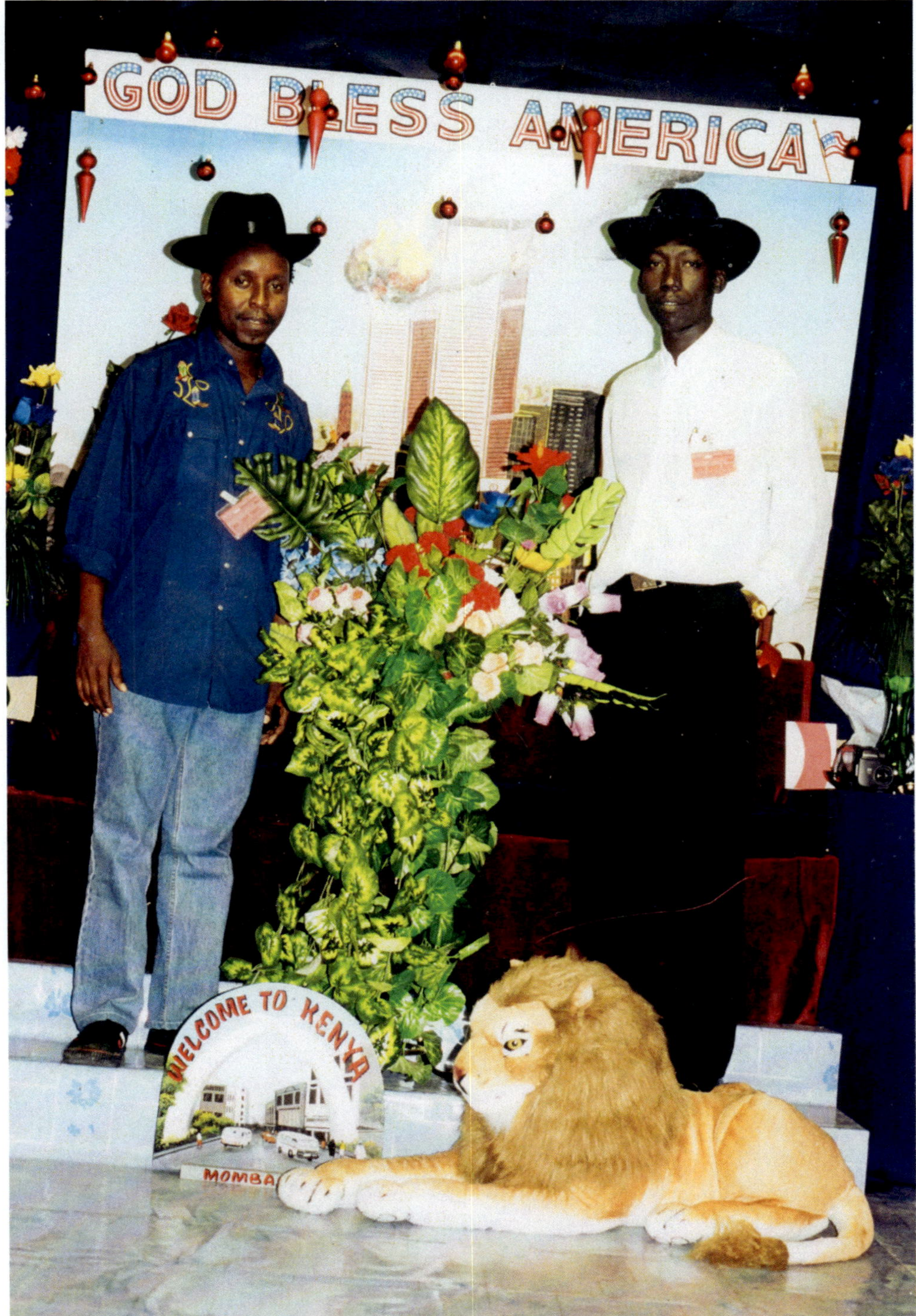


Fig. 4
**Portrait of painter Masada and photographer Boniface Wandera,** photographed by Sammy Njuguna, Graz 2001 (collection Behrend)

two destroying the World Trade Center, the third partially destroying the Pentagon, and the fourth targeting Washington, D.C. and crashing into a field near Shanksville, Pennsylvania) to the destruction of the Twin Towers, thereby focusing on those images that had already gained an iconic status. He also tapped into the specific traumatic power of the (original) iconoclastic act, turning the disaster image into a distinctive screen to provide an aesthetic mediation of anxieties.

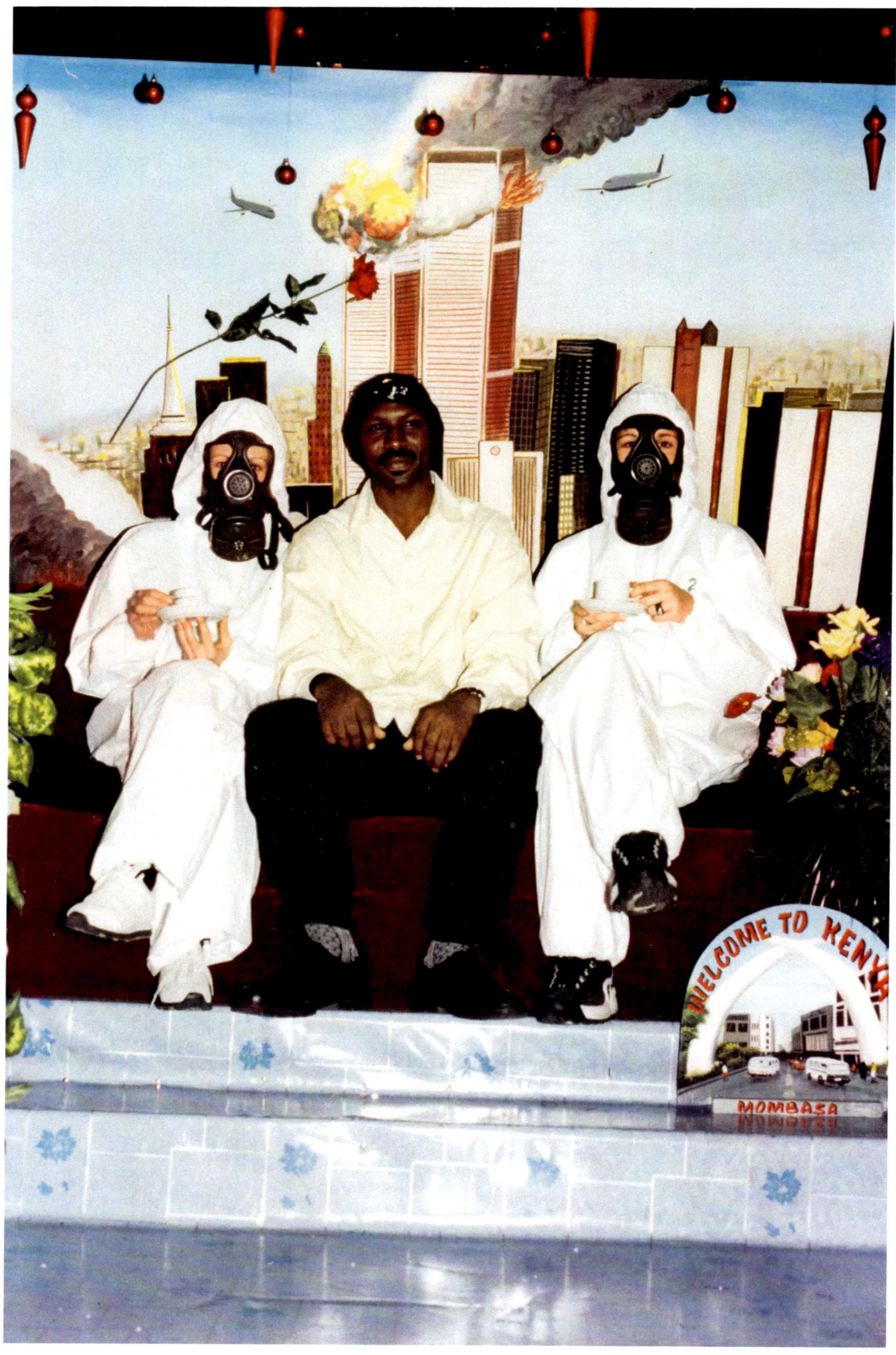
WELCOME TO KENYA
MOMBASA

Fig. 5
**Portrait of photographer Sammy Njuguna and two customers,** photographed by Boniface Wandera, Graz 2001 (collection Behrend)

By painting the image of the already burning Twin Towers and the two (sic) still arriving planes, he set up a narrative structure that juxtaposed the approach of the two aircrafts and the final result of their attack, the burning Twin Towers, thereby transforming the chronology of the event into simultaneity. In the painted backdrop, he distanced himself from the photographic model and its "realism" and took the risk of collapsing photographic space and time. By remediating the photographic icon into a painted backdrop, the "original" image was "unmade", loosing the hold of indexicality..

To create a festive atmosphere in the "Likoni style", the three Kenyans decorated the backdrop with various plastic flowers, Christmas tree decorations, and a huge stuffed lion. In addition, a signboard with the message "God bless America" was placed above the backdrop, decorated with red plastic roses. A second signboard "Welcome to Kenya" was put on the ground to invite Western visitors to Kenya, as Sammy Njuguna explained (fig. 4).

In the photographic practice of the Likoni photographers, signboards had already played an important part. The photographed sites were often marked with signboards and thereby actually doubled. It is as if the indexicality of the photographs needed the written texts to additionally authenticate space and time. Sammy Njuguna explained: "The signboard is the message." The representation of the burning Twin Towers in the studio and the resulting aesthetic impulse or shock was thus anchored in the dominant message "God Bless America". Moreover, the photographers set up a soundscape in the studio by playing Gospel music in Kiswahili on a ghetto blaster that, as Sammy Njuguna suggested, made them feel at home.

Through the studio's backdrop, the three Kenyans participated in the "war of images" that ushered in a New World Order defined by terrorism. Yet, they submitted this remediated icon, as well, to their specific studio aesthetics. As part of the Likoni style, the backdrop functioned as a window or screen giving a view onto the burning WTC and the two arriving airplanes while the customers would sit in front on a chair or sofa as if in a nicely decorated sitting room. In their studio, the photographers offered their European customers the possibility to participate in 9/11 as a spectacle for touristic and/or artistic consumption. While on the one hand connecting to the disaster and bringing it close, on the other hand the studio provided a distanced, "safe" space, a kind of homey sitting room whose backdrop was the only "window" providing access to the catastrophe unfolding behind the backs of the photographed persons.

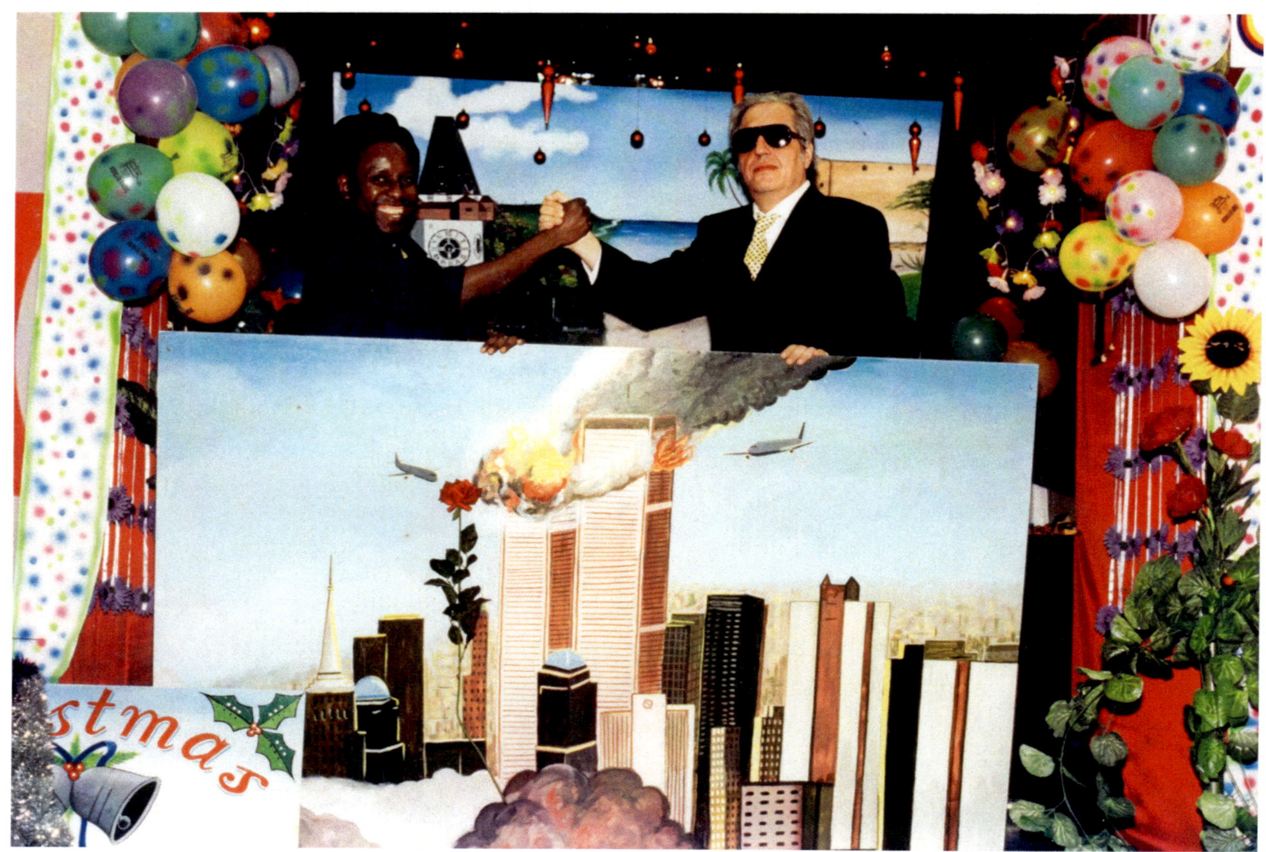


Fig. 6
**Painter Masada and customer**, photographed by Sammy Njuguna, Graz 2001 (collection Behrend)

After they had finished constructing and decorating the studio, the director of the Steirischer Herbst arrived, extremely upset. He felt alarmed because he feared the studio and its props could be (mis)understood as a gesture of anti-Americanism. In spite of or perhaps even because of the festival's iconoclastic reputation, he was afraid of creating a scandal. But the Likoni photographers assured him of their allegiance to unmistakable support for the USA; and this is why he backed off from any sort of censorship.

The Likoni photographers and their studio were very successful. Visitors had to line up to have their pictures taken in various poses and arrangements in front of the burning Twin Towers (fig. 5). Not only photographs, but also backdrops painted by Masada were in high demand. Masada had to hurry to replenish the ones he sold, his main patron being an Italian gallery owner (fig. 6).

The reasons for the photographers' success seem to be highly ambiguous and clearly do not coincide with their own intentions and the meaning they themselves attributed to the scenario in their studio. Many visitors, so I was told, took the studio as a popular site where the catastrophe of 9/11 was transformed into an exotic space of downright popular commercial entertainment and a kind of disaster tourism. The customers continued the processes of commodification, museumization, and trivialization of 9/11 that took place in various media in many parts of the world, particularly in the United States (Heller 2005).

## 9/11 REMEDIATED IN A PHOTO STUDIO

As has been repeated rather often, in Europe already in the 1840s, the institution of the photo studio evolved as a hybrid space out of different media such as theater, painting, drawing, writing, and photography. In addition, studios formed interfaces of mediation between various public media, newspapers, journals, cinema, TV, and radio. They provided a space where the public and the private interacted in complex ways. And they offered a site of transformation and experimentation that enticed customers to exploit the illusionist and fantastic potential of photography, its possibilities to fulfill dreams. Within the studio space, backdrops, props, and costumes lost their indexical certainty and became detached from origins and available for play. Studios allowed people to physically enter the space of fantasies and bring them home as private property, materialized within an image (Strassler 2010:77ff).

In Graz, embedded in the art festival, the Likoni studio allowed visitors to relate in a playful, more or less trivial way to a catastrophic event that changed the world. Instead of providing the spectacle of a beautiful landscape or a luxurious interior, the studio space permitted customers – pro- or anti-American – to insert themselves into disaster and into the war of images that followed 9/11 with unprecedented force. Customers projected themselves "into the picture" of scenes of a catastrophe remediated from national and global media. In fact, the studio portraits bridged the gap between the distant and as yet unrealized "elsewheres" and the intimate spheres of personal memory and self-representation (Strassler 2010:79). At the same time, the numerous acts of photography turned also into performances mediating the traumatic potential of 9/11 and the customers' (and the photographers') anxieties and lack of control over the potentially catastrophic technologies necessary for modern life.

From the perspective of the European visitors, this was not only the translation of a global iconic image into a more private and personal studio photograph, but also into something else, an exotic form provided by African photographers transcending the limits of the here and now by bringing in an "elsewhere", the perspective of others. The studio and its props thereby brought to the fore the moral implication of social, cultural, and geographic distance. Artists and visitors were confronted with their (reflexive and reflective) responses and with the ways they resonated with others and were asked to contemplate the possibility of complicity (Spivak 2004:87).

In a way, the Likoni photographers repeated the paradoxical act that turned

Al Qaida's original iconoclastic gesture into a flow of secondary images of defacement or annihilation for local consumption in the Western art world (Mitchell 2005:18). Their studio in Graz became a controversial space in which series of photographs with often overlapping, diverging interpretations of 9/11 were produced that mediated between widely shared iconic images, different visual logics, and more intimate concerns. Against the background of a history of exclusion and discrepant globalization, the studio space allowed the photographers (and their customers) to articulate their specific response to a global event in a wider public sphere. And it allowed some of the visitors to express a critical perspective on American politics (in opposition to the photographers) that otherwise would have remained silent.

## BACK IN MOMBASA

By selling the photographs and backdrops, the photographers and the painter made a substantial amount of money that allowed them to establish a more secure living back in Mombasa. Sammy Njuguna and Bonifaz Wandera diversified their business by buying a video camera. They are now offering not only photographs but also videos. And they started using digital photography.

Back in Mombasa, I asked Sammy Njuguna whether he planned to relate to 9/11 in his studio in Mombasa, as well. He explained that he could not do so because it would be too dangerous. In Kenya, the "Embassy Bombing", 9/11, and the War on Terror have aggravated local tensions between Christians and Muslims. Many Muslims in Kenya sided with Al Qaida and regarded 9/11 as a "victory" in the larger political struggle against the United States (though not as openly as, for example, the Muslims in northern Nigeria did). But most Kenyan Christians, among them the "saved" Likoni photographers, saw themselves more as allies of the USA, the (Christian) West, and the (Christian) central government of Kenya. Although popular photographers in Mombasa have always tried to keep up with the latest events, because of the increasing tensions between local Muslims and Christian migrant workers, they did not dare to make 9/11 a show and topic in their studios. In fact, there was no debate about the content and materials of representation or the permissibility of depiction and reproduction of 9/11. On the coast, 9/11 created a visual void among the Likoni photographers, who are "outsiders within". This negative attitude and restraint poses significant questions about the fate of images in situations of political and religious turmoil, about the power of images and the ethics, the politics and polemics of the visual in an era of mass media. Interestingly, in this case it was Christian migrant photographers who – as a minority on the coast – refrained from depicting

9/11 in their studios, to avoid offending and provoking the majority of Muslims with whom they attempt to live in peace. While in editorial cartoons in the newspapers circulating in Kenya's national publics, 9/11 was made an important topic (see the contribution of Dan Omanga in this volume), Christian migrants along the coast felt too vulnerable to challenge the efforts of containment and censorship, as well as the invisible borders policing the limits of public space and what is and what is not allowed to be shown.

**LITERATURE**


Behrend, Heike, "Feeling Global: The Likoni Ferry Photographers in Mombasa, Kenya". *African Arts*, 33/3, (2000), pp. 70-77.

Behrend, Heike, "Imagined Journeys. The Likoni Ferry Photographers in Mombasa/ Kenya". In: Pinney, Chris and Peterson, Nicolas (Eds.), *Photography's Other Histories*. Durham and London: Duke University Press 2003. pp. 221-239.

Behrend, Heike, "The Titanic in Kano: Video, Gender, and Islam in Northern Nigeria". In: Badran, Margot (Ed.), *Gender and Islam in Africa: Rights, Sexuality and Law*. Stanford: Stanford University Press 2011.

Behrend, Heike, *Contesting Visibility. Photographic Practices on the East African Coast*. Bielefeld: Transcript 2013.

Gamboni, Dario, *The Destruction of Art. Iconoclasm and Vandalism since the French Revolution*. New Haven: Yale University Press 1997.

Hariman, Robert and Lucaites, John Louis, *No caption needed. Iconic Photographs, Public Culture, and Liberal Democracy*. Chicago: University of Chicago Press 2007.

Heller, Dana A. (Ed.), *The Selling of 9/11. How a National Tragedy Became a Commodity*. New York: Palgrave Macmillan 2005.

Hüwelmeier, Gertrud, "New Media and Travelling Spirits: Pentecostals in the Vietnamese Diaspora and the Disaster of the Titanic". In: Behrend, Heike; Dreschke, Anja and Zillinger, Martin (Eds.), *Trance Mediums and New Media. Spirit Possession in the Age of Technical Reproduction*. New York: Fordham University Press 2015. pp. 100-115.

Mitchell, W.J.T., *What Do Pictures Want? The Lives and Loves of Images*. Chicago: University of Chicago Press 2005.

Paul, Gerhard, "The Image as an Act and the New Wars of Images". In: Hoffmann, Felix (Ed.), *Unheimlich Vertraut. Bilder vom Terror*. Köln: König 2011. pp. 143-169.

Spivak, Gayatri Chakravorty, "Terror. A Speech After 9/11". In: *boundary 2*, 31/2 (2004), pp. 81-111.

Spyer, Patricia and Steedly, Mary Margaret (Eds.), *Images That Move*. Santa Fe: SAR Press 2013.

Strassler, Karen, *Refracted Visions. Popular Photography and National Modernity in Java*, Durham: Duke University Press 2010.

Wendl, Tobias and Behrend, Heike, *Snap me One! Studiofotografien in Afrika*. München and New York: Prestel 1998.

Tobias Wendl

# 9/11 IN THE VISUAL ARTS OF AFRICA AND BEYOND

## INTRODUCTION

In September 2005, the distinguished New York-based philosopher of the arts, Arthur C. Danto, curated an exhibition titled "The Art of 9/11", which was hosted at the non-profit Apex Art Gallery in Lower Manhattan. Danto conceived his show as a "public mourning ritual" and as an "act of piety". For a period of four years, he had surveyed his artist friends in New York City – trying to find out how they had responded to the event, directly or indirectly. The artworks on display showed a striking absence of the major 9/11 icons: crashing airplanes, burning buildings, and other apocalyptic imagery. Instead, there was a bewildering and disparate array of consternation and dismay. "The artists," Danto (2005) wrote in the press release, "could not have done better than the many anonymous shrine-makers who – all over the city – spontaneously had erected small memorial sites in honor of the victims." Next to Cindy Sherman's "Clown" self-portrait ("cheery on the outside but horrific underneath"), Danto presented a Sunday-painterly watercolor by Audrey Fleck with fishing boats in Montauk harbor and a cheesy shrine installation piece titled "Prayer for the New Ancestors" by Leslie King-Hammond (fig.1). The works on display were concerned with the artists' affective responses and did not attempt to convey a critical reflection of the event and its transmissions. The lack of curatorial rigor and artistic coherence in favor of diffuse consternation, piety, and subliminal patriotism made Danto's exhibit a dubious endeavor. The separation of 9/11 trauma, loss, and grief from the unfolding events – the subsequent crusades against Osama Bin Laden and Al Qaida, the invasion of Afghanistan and Iraq,

Fig. 1
**"Prayer for the New Ancestors"** by Leslie King-Hammond 2005. Courtesy the artist.

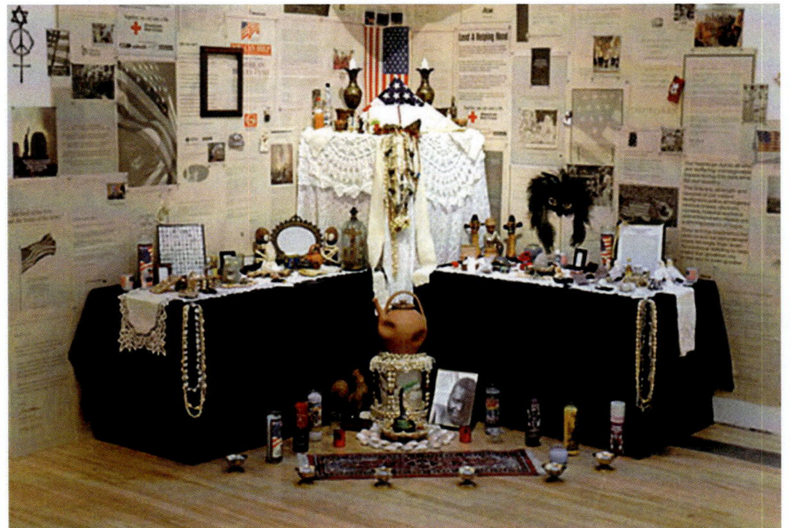

From the artist's statement:
"This altar installation was my response to the devastation and trauma of September 11, 2001. (...) I was consumed with shock, the wounded bodies, traumatized survivors, heroes, soldiers, citizens, and the tremendous loss of human life. (...) *Prayers for the New Ancestors* became means for me to create a site of peace for the recently departed spirits. (...) The walls of the shrine are lined with the public prayers from the newspapers. The altar is dressed with lace and doilies, an American flag, the Bible, and photos of departed loved ones gathered from my community." (See http://www.apexart.org/images/danto/artiststatements.pdf)

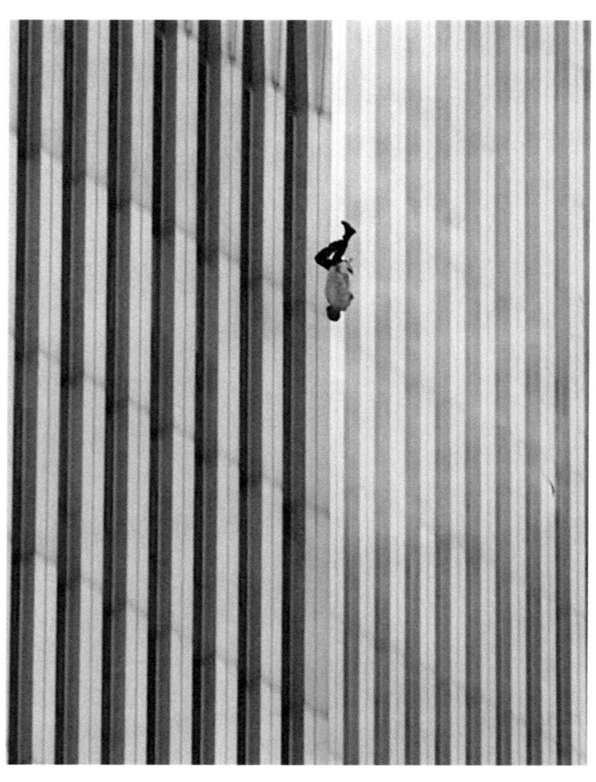

the re-election of born-again George W. Bush, and the tortures of Abu Ghraib – was not obvious at all. In addition, the show completely obscured the critical attitude of many other New York artists toward US post-9/11 politics and the new war against terrorism.

Although it is beyond the scope of this essay, it is worth remaining for a moment on Ground Zero in September 2001. Already in the immediate aftermath of the attacks and their spectacular re-mediation, ethical concerns emerged and certain images, especially those of persons jumping from the towers to their deaths, became taboo. Richard Drew's iconic photograph "Falling Man" was published in the New York Times and a few other dailies before it disappeared in the archives. The papers were accused of taking advantage of the victims' tragedy and thereby causing pain to their families and relatives. The formal beauty of the pose and the perfection of the composition were not considered appropriate for the event, but distasteful, exploitative, and voyeuristic (Becker 2013:251ff). Similar reactions occurred when Eric Fischl presented his bronze sculpture "Tumbling Woman" at the Rockefeller Center on the first anniversary of 9/11 in September 2002. The statue, meant to commemorate those leaping to their death, was criticized as lacking respect and piety. It was abruptly draped in cloth and removed after only one week on display (Lang 2011:21ff).

Fig. 2
**Richard Drew, The Falling Man,** photograph 2001 for Associated Press.

Fig. 3
**Eric Fischl, Tumbling Woman,** bronze sculpture (94 x 188 x 127 cm) 2002. Courtesy the artist.

The pictures of falling persons, blown out of the towers or jumping to their deaths in despair, aroused feelings of both uncanniness and fear – probably because of their resonances with the Christian imaginary of the descent to hell. And the issue whether the jumpers had chosen suicide rather than accepted their fate at the hand of God created further unease in an atmosphere already heavily imbued with religious fervor. Tabooing these pictures provided a means to reduce the ambivalence and to pave the way for a more patriotic Wagnerian iconography with fearless rescuers and firemen raising the flag on the devastated "Ground Zero land", which soon turned into a venue of disaster tourism.

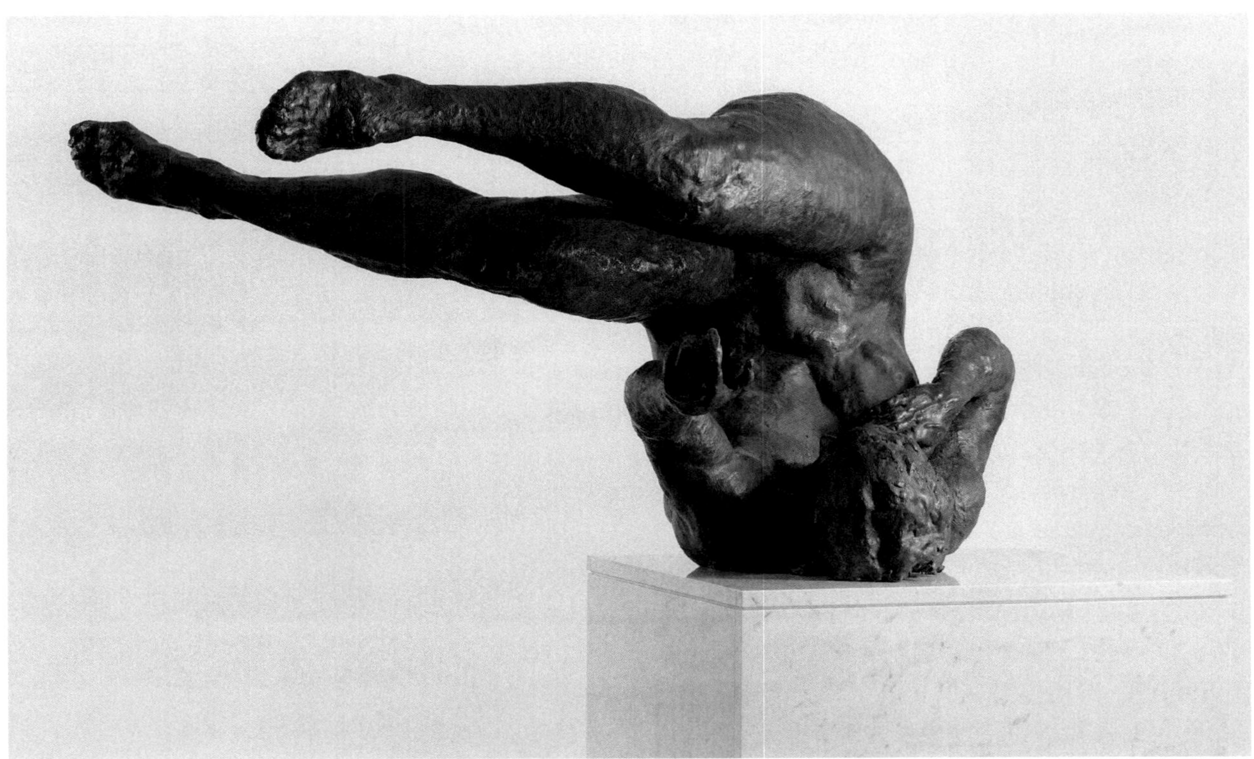

[1] See online: Stockhausen, Karlheinz, Interview with Norddeutscher Rundfunk, September 16, 2001: http://web.archive.org/web/20060829003224/http://www.dansk-musiktidsskrift.dk/doku/stockhausen-16sep2001.mp3 accessed January 05, 2015.

[2] See: Kiefer, Anselm, Genet, Nietzsche, Oussama, Lecture at the College de France, Paris 2011. http://www.college-de-france.fr/site/anselm-kiefer/course-2011-01-24-16h00.htm accessed January 05, 2015.

Sophisticated artistic responses to the immediate emotions triggered by 9/11 (such as fear, rage, patriotism, and the desire for revenge) were virtually absent. Artists found themselves in the difficult situation that the sublimity of the destruction was too overwhelming. Referring to the attack as the "greatest work of art imaginable", the composer Karlheinz Stockhausen expressed the envy many artists experienced while watching what Edmund Burke and Immanuel Kant had conceived of as the sublime[1]. Boris Groys subsequently identified Osama bin Laden and other terrorists as "video artists" who made use of the TV networks to immortalize their terrifying deeds (Groys 2008:122); and Anselm Kiefer, who referred to the crumbling Twin Towers in his "Ex-Voto" drawing from 2004, characterized the media images of the terror attacks as the most perfect images after Neil Armstrong's first steps on the moon[2]. Richard Schechner witnessed the attacks from the terrace of his Lower Manhattan apartment and provided an intriguing account of his own reactions: "I saw the plane slice into the south tower as smoothly as a hot knife into butter. Not a sound. A silent movie in full color. A great ball of orange flame and black smoke. It was terrifying; it was sublime; it was horrible; it was beautiful." Although Schechner clearly admits his fascination with the terrifying splendor of the moment, he remains skeptical that 9/11 could be better understood by labeling it art – especially since the Al Qaida terrorists themselves never conceived it as such, but as the very wrath of God (2009:1820ff).

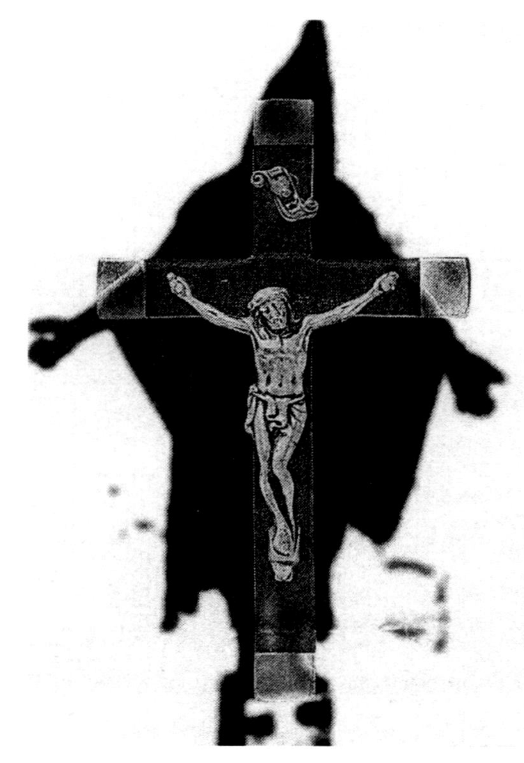

Soon after 9/11, it became obvious that the real aggression was perceived above all as an aggression against a symbol; and as a result, the demand for symbolic comfort items, above all Bibles and American flags, shot up enormously. "Old Glory," Michael Taussig writes, "suggests the flag is venerable in the same way as a person. It is more than a symbol. It is animate and becomes more so in times of war; a state of iconic hypertrophy." (2002:82). The Bush administration started to counteract in the domain of the symbolic by crusading against an enemy who could not be localized. The aggressive "dead or alive" statements issued by the White House and the bombing raids on Tora Bora in December 2001 did not result in capturing the new Public Enemy No.1, but triggered myriads of jokes, cartoons, and web-based patriotic or subversive animations. Matthias Wähner researched the Internet and compiled the reactions in the virtual world in a sarcastic media installation of found images titled "war shots" (2006:161). The announced "war on terror" was a rhetorical trope, and everybody knew that it was impossible to win such a war (reminiscent of other metaphoric wars – such as the wars against poverty or cancer). The subsequent invasion of Iraq on the pretext of taking out the bad guys met with growing international concern and protest in 2003. But the decisive turning point was not marked until April 2004, when the scandalizing photographs of the tortures and atrocities in the Abu Ghraib prisons were released. The iconic hooded Iraqi prisoner with his outstretching arms, reminiscent of Christ on the cross, quickly turned into a martyr figure for all the Iraqi prisoners abused and tortured by American soldiers.

As W. J. T. Mitchell has argued, the iconicity of this image also resulted from the stillness and the equilibrium of the man, which resonate with the Christ figure keeping cool under stress and forgiving his tormentors despite his humiliation (Mitchell 2004; 2011:195). There is also an evocation of the Ku Klux Klan members' costumes and their notorious lynchings, as the graffiti artist Salaheddin Sallat underlined in his famous Bagdad mural.[3] The cartoonist Dennis Draughton merged it with another iconic history image, Nick Ut's famous photograph of the "Napalm girl" Kim Phuc (1972), one of the most haunting images of the war in Vietnam. In his "Abu Ghraib Nam" cartoon, the napalm victim is echoed in the torture victim, suggesting that the U.S. continues to repeat its history, rather than having learned from it.

[3] See the picture of the mural online: http://www.middle-east-online.com/meopictures/big/_10129_abuse-paint-1-6-2004.jpg accessed January 06, 2015.

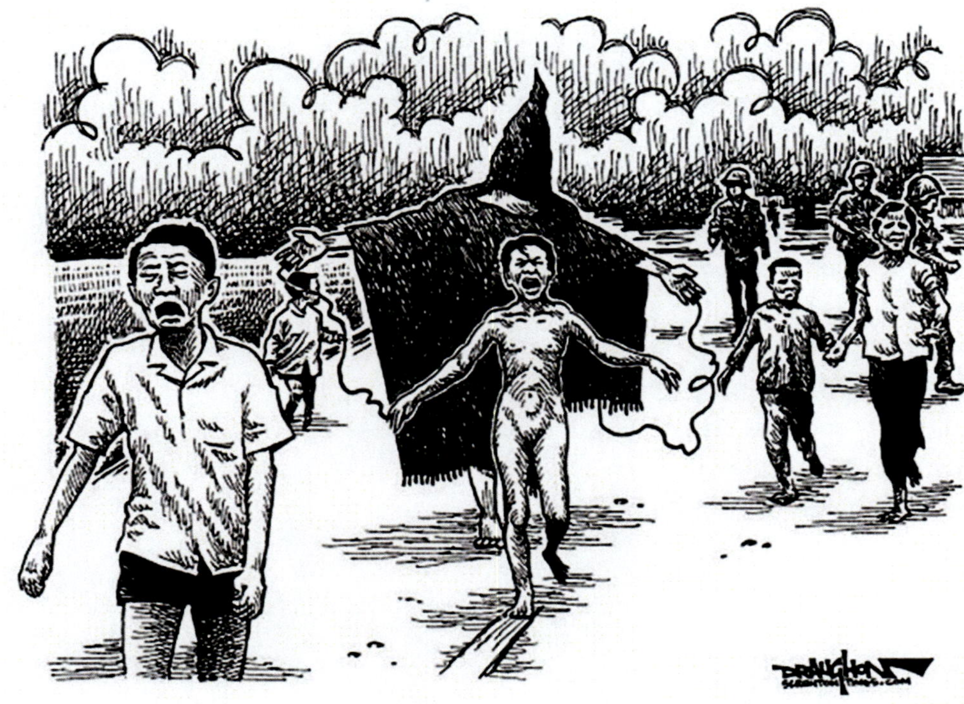

Fig. 4
**Echoes of a Christian Symbol,**
photomontage. Chicago Tribune, June 27, 2004.

Fig. 5
**Dennis Draughton, Abu Ghraib Nam,**
cartoon. Scranton Times, May 12, 2004.

In 2004, Richard Serra, who is best known for his raw metal sculptural projects in public spaces, joined the protest movement against the Republican reelection campaign in 2004 and designed a poster titled "Stop Bush" for the anti-war organization "United for Peace and Justice". The poster's iconography is based again on the hooded Abu Ghraib torture picture. He made his poster available for free download at "www.pleasevote.com", as he did with his Heartfieldian montage, based on Goya's "Saturn devouring his Children", in which George W. Bush has replaced the greedy Saturn (ZEIT 2004).

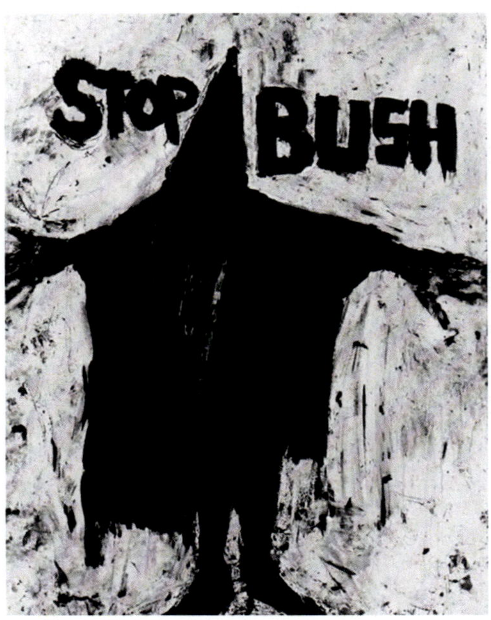


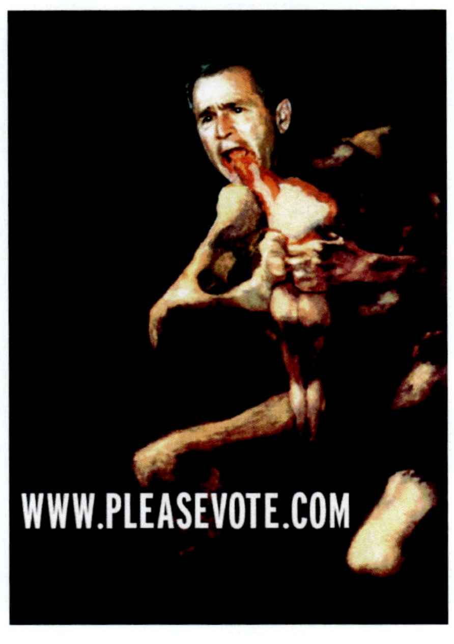


Fig. 6
**Richard Serra, Stop Bush,**
poster. VG Bildkunst, Bonn 2004.

Fig. 7
**Richard Serra,**
photomontage. VG Bildkunst, Bonn 2004

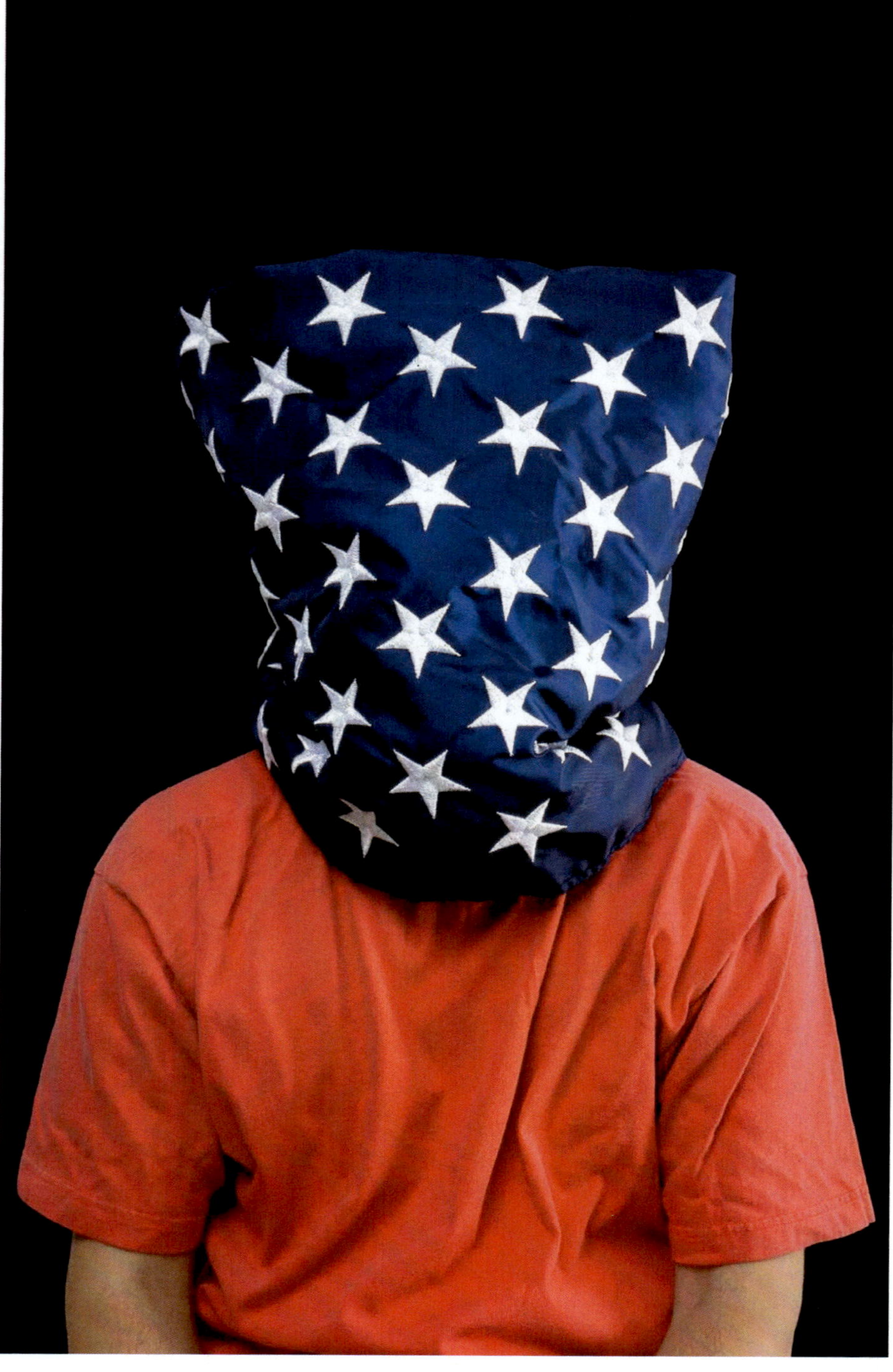

The picture of the Abu Ghraib prisons scandal was quickly integrated in the global image flow of mass culture and subsequently appropriated and re-mediated by contemporary artists. One of the most remarkable re-mediations is Hans Haacke's photomontage "Star Gazing – Times Square", which was first presented at Haacke's solo exhibition "State of the Union" at Paula Cooper's gallery in Chelsea in 2005. It is a fictional artistic intervention on Times Square, featuring among its five vertically aligned neon billboards a strange half-figure of a man whose face is hidden behind a sack featuring the star spangled banner. It refers to the hooded torture victims of Abu Ghraib as well as to vernacular gestures of shame and discomfort, common in US sports when the supporters of a losing team put bags over their heads to become anonymous and conceal their disappointment. Here, the hood as a means to reduce the torture victims to faceless anonymous war trophies and as a means to express shame is merged with the emblem of American sovereignty, summarizing the Bush administration's invasion and occupation of Iraq as a dubious and shameful venture. Haacke's work creates a space for critical contemplation. His "Stargazing Americans" seem to have been blinded by

Fig. 8
**Hans Haacke, Star Gazing,**
C-print 2004.
Courtesy the artist.

their desire for revenge and to have preferred to ignore the consequences and disasters of the attempt to achieve a new military hegemony on the pretext of waging "war on terror".[4]

## PREFIGURATIONS OF 9/11 IN POPULAR CULTURE AND VISUAL ART

Before I shift to Africa, I want to briefly discuss some of the more general relations, links, and overlaps between "popular culture" and "visual art" in the case of 9/11. The concept of "popular culture" is very fuzzy and disputed. Authors such as Johannes Fabian and Karin Barber have advocated it as a means of resistance and subversion, enabling ordinary people to enjoy "moments of freedom" against the backdrop of the elite's "high culture" (Fabian 1998 and Barber 1997). Others – in the tradition of the Frankfurt school – have emphasized its power to seduce to mass consumerism and political agony (Horkheimer and Adorno 1947). The two aspects seem like reverse sides of the same coin, and the crucial question remains: under which historical and political circumstances does popular culture become a means of resistance or a means of domination? Visual art, on the other hand, is much more an elitist commodity, although it often takes its inspirations from popular culture. Its commercial character is usually obscured by pointing to its presumed autonomy and by the postulate that art is able to trigger a reflective space beyond mere consumption.

In his book "The City's End: Two Centuries of Fantasies, Fears, and Premonitions of New York's Destruction" (2008), the US historian Max Page has lucidly demonstrated that the power of destruction belongs to the narrative framework of New York City, which has never been merely a city only, but also – and above all – a powerful symbol and icon. In American popular culture, the destruction of the New York icon has been a leitmotif for nearly two centuries. In novels, paintings, cinema, advertisements, and more recently video and computer games, New York has been destroyed over and over again – by fire and by bombing, by earthquakes, and by battles, by floods, and – of course – by monsters. Whether in *Planet of the Apes* or in *Godzilla* – whether in *Deep Impact or in Superman* – the city has always served as a privileged target of aggression, but it has always witnessed its rebirth in the end. As Max Page writes:

"Visions of New York's destruction resonated with some of the most longstanding themes in American history: the ambivalence towards cities, the troubled reaction to immigrants and racial diversity, the fear of technology's impact, and the apocalyptic strain in American religious life. Furthermore, these visions of the city's end have paralleled the city's economic, political, racial, and physical

[4] For an overview of artistic responses to 9/11 in the US, see (Kröner) 2008.

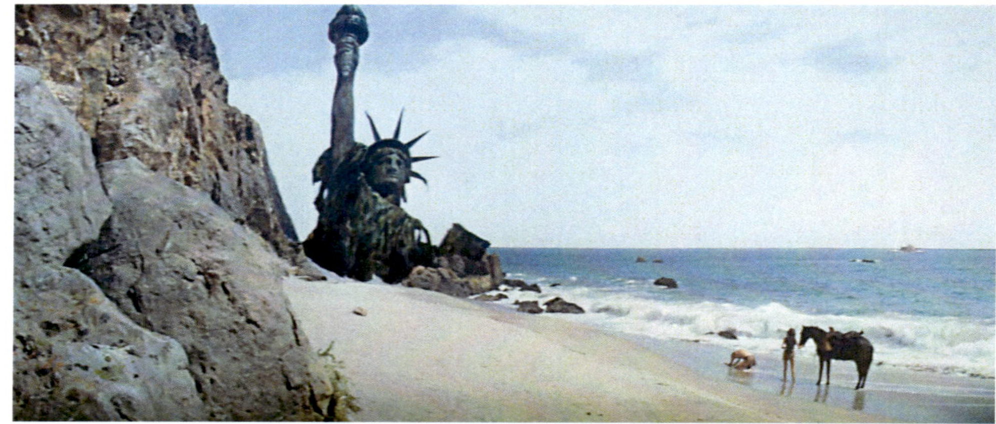

Fig. 9
**Film still, Planet of the Apes**
(USA 1968).

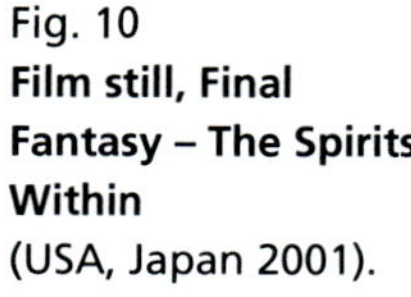

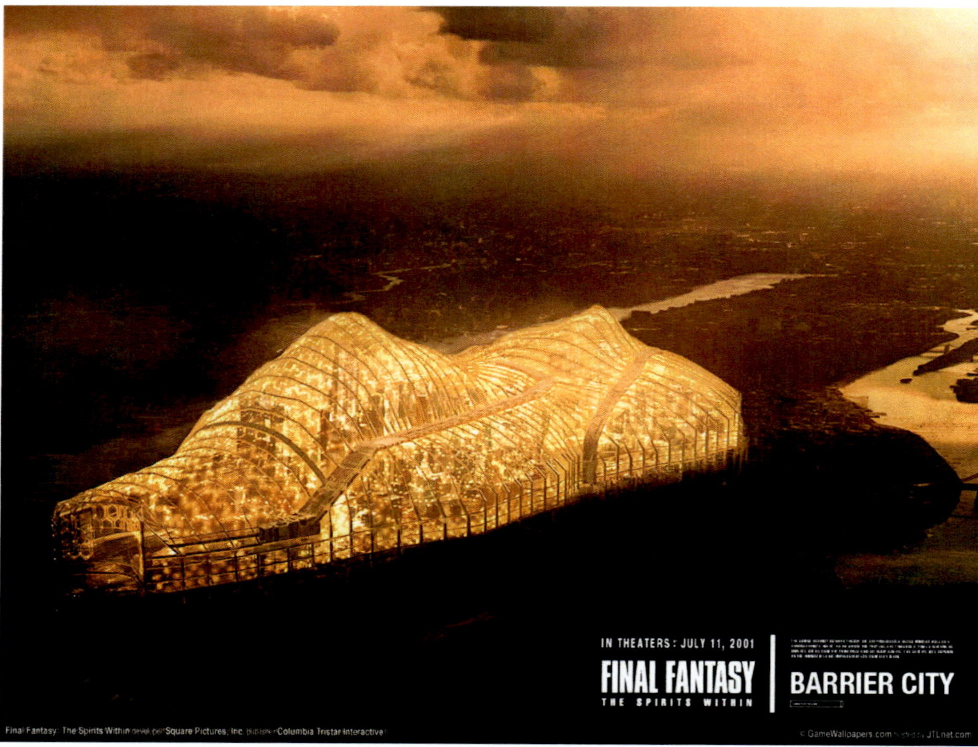



Fig. 10
**Film still, Final Fantasy – The Spirits Within**
(USA, Japan 2001).

transformations. Projections of the city's end reflected and refracted the dominant social issues. Each era in New York's modern history has produced its own apocalyptic imagery that explores, exploits, and seeks to resolve contemporary cultural tensions and fears". (Page 2008:7f).

Against this backdrop, the real 9/11 aggression against the World Trade Center fits perfectly into the long series of older "imaginative experiments" of destroying the New York stone colossus. Prior to the construction of the Twin Towers in 1973, other icons, such as the Empire State Building and the Statue of Liberty, had served as symbolic targets. At the very end of the 1968 Fox production Planet of the Apes, we see the fragments of *Lady Liberty*, half-submerged in the shore (fig. 9); and in the 2001 Japanese-American computer-generated science

Fig. 11
**Charles Gaines, Airplane Crash Clock,** mixed media & electronics (396 x 152 x 274 cm) 1997. Courtesy the artist.

fiction thriller *Final Fantasy – The Spirits within*, officially released three months before the real destruction of the World Trade Center, the whole of Lower Manhattan is covered by a huge protective shield to prevent this part of the city from spiritual attacks by alien creatures who have already devastated Times Square and Midtown (fig. 10).

If we look into the domain of the visual arts, we do not find a proper parallel to the destructive appetite and the anticipation of 9/11 in popular culture. What we encounter, however, are a few striking examples of mixed-media installations and object artworks that reveal a certain affinity, relatedness, and even presentiment. In his 1997 work "Airplane Crash Clock" (fig. 11), African-American artist Charles Gaines staged an airplane crash in an urban area, which is repeated every 60 seconds. Above an architectural model of a fictional metropolis with iconic buildings from different cities, a toy airplane on top of a long pole descends at regular intervals to crash into a trap door on the ground. Each crash is accompanied by screams until the door flips open and reveals the aircraft wreck. Whereas the automated crash clock arrangement could initially be understood as a hint at the statistically unavoidable, generic disaster scenario, in the aftermath of 9/11 the arrangement started to trigger new associations evoking the endlessly repeated media footage of planes crashing into the World Trade Center due to deliberate sabotage and with the strategic intent of unleashing terror (Storr 2007:106f). Another, even much earlier work from 1965 is by the Argentinian artist Léon Ferrari (1920-2013). It is titled "La civilización occidental y cris-

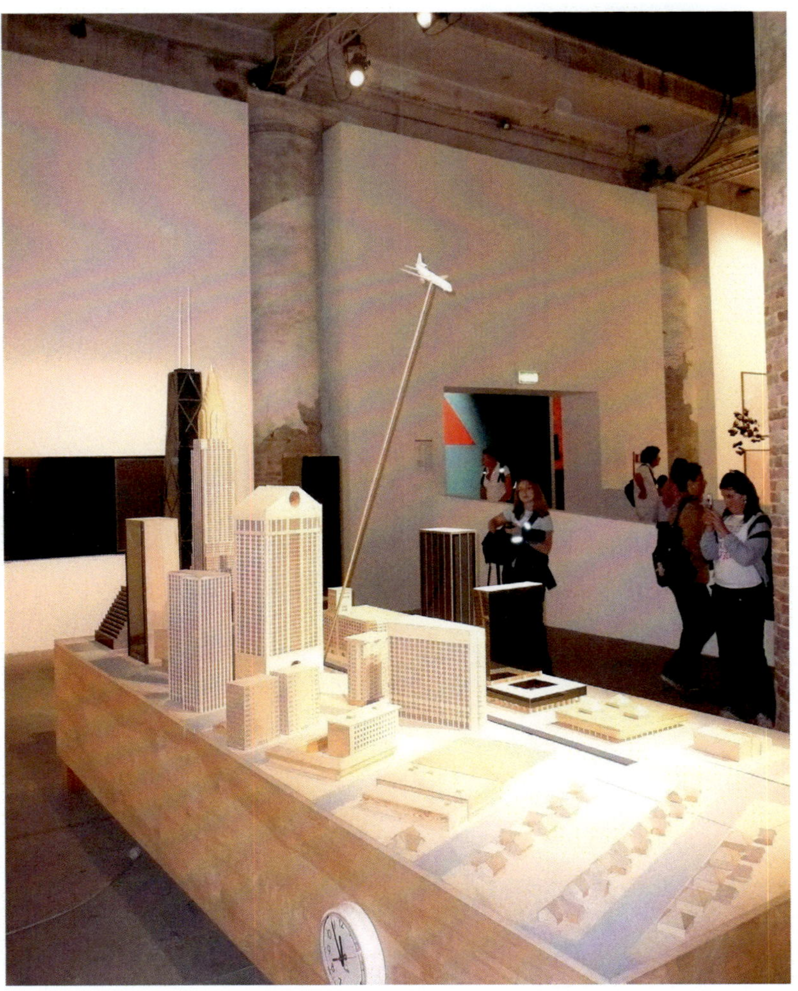

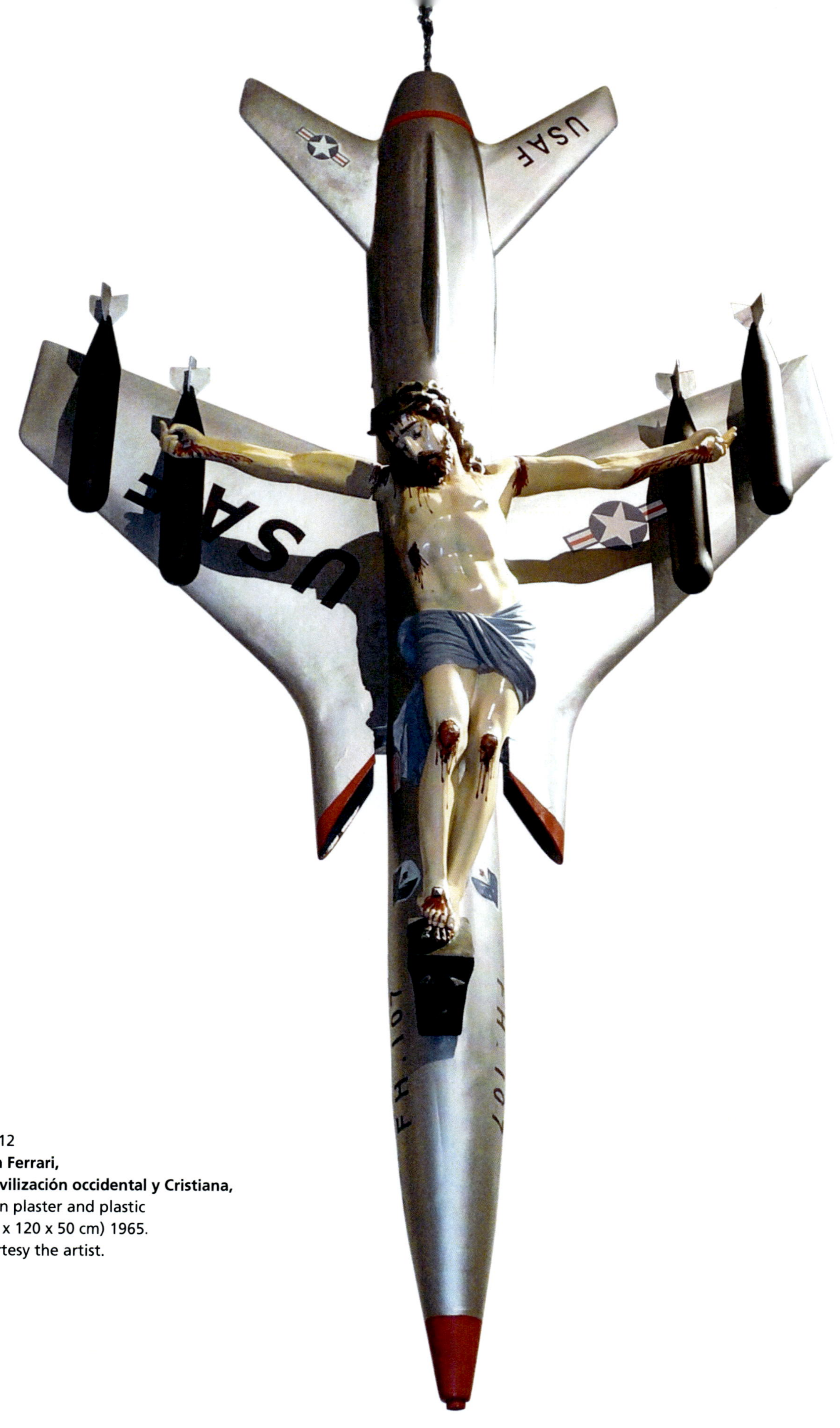


Fig. 12
**Léon Ferrari,**
**La civilización occidental y Cristiana,**
oil on plaster and plastic
(200 x 120 x 50 cm) 1965.
Courtesy the artist.

tiana" and presents a wooden, store-bought devotional Christ figure crucified on a US fighter plane (fig. 12). Originally, Ferrari made this object as an artistic statement against the war in Vietnam, highlighting the hypocrisy of Christianity and the explosive blend of religious ideology, military technology, and violence. The work, originally produced for the Instituto Di Tella Award in Buenos Aires, was rejected as blasphemous and not exhibited until 1998. In the aftermath of 9/11, it triggered new readings and turned into a powerful artistic icon for suicide bombing, martyrdom, and the unfolding of religious furor worldwide (Storr 2007:94f).

The airplane attack was a new form of iconoclasm, anticipated in popular culture (and to a lesser degree in visual art) for a long time. In his essay *The Spirit of Terrorism* (2001), Jean Baudrillard has termed 9/11 an "absolute event", "the mother of events, the pure event which is the essence of all the events that never happened. Not only are all history and power plays disrupted, but so are the conditions of analysis." Baudrillard has stressed the symbolic nature and singularity with which supporters of an anti-globalization ideology successfully made use of the means of globalization (airplanes, media, Internet) to destroy the very icon of globalization and advanced capitalism. According to his reading, the genuine horror of the event did not result from the number of victims, but from the power of the images that reached their worldwide audience within a few minutes and that has allowed the world to participate in a hitherto unknown, real-time media spectacle of destruction. Compared with the attack on the Pentagon, the attacks on the Twin Towers did not have any strategic military significance. They were purely symbolic. For the terrorists, the death of thousands of civilians was deplorable collateral damage, conceded in order to send a message to America. As W.J.T. Mitchell has put it: "The real target was a globally recognizable icon, and the aim was not merely to destroy it, but to stage it as a media spectacle. Iconoclasm in this instance was rendered as an icon in its own right, an image of horror that has imprinted itself in the memory of the entire world" (Mitchell 2005:13f). 9/11 fostered the proliferation of a new "geography of anger" (Appadurai 2006), deepened the gap between the Muslim and the Christian worlds and left its marks in seemingly distant areas in Africa that were only marginally affected by the subsequent war on terror.

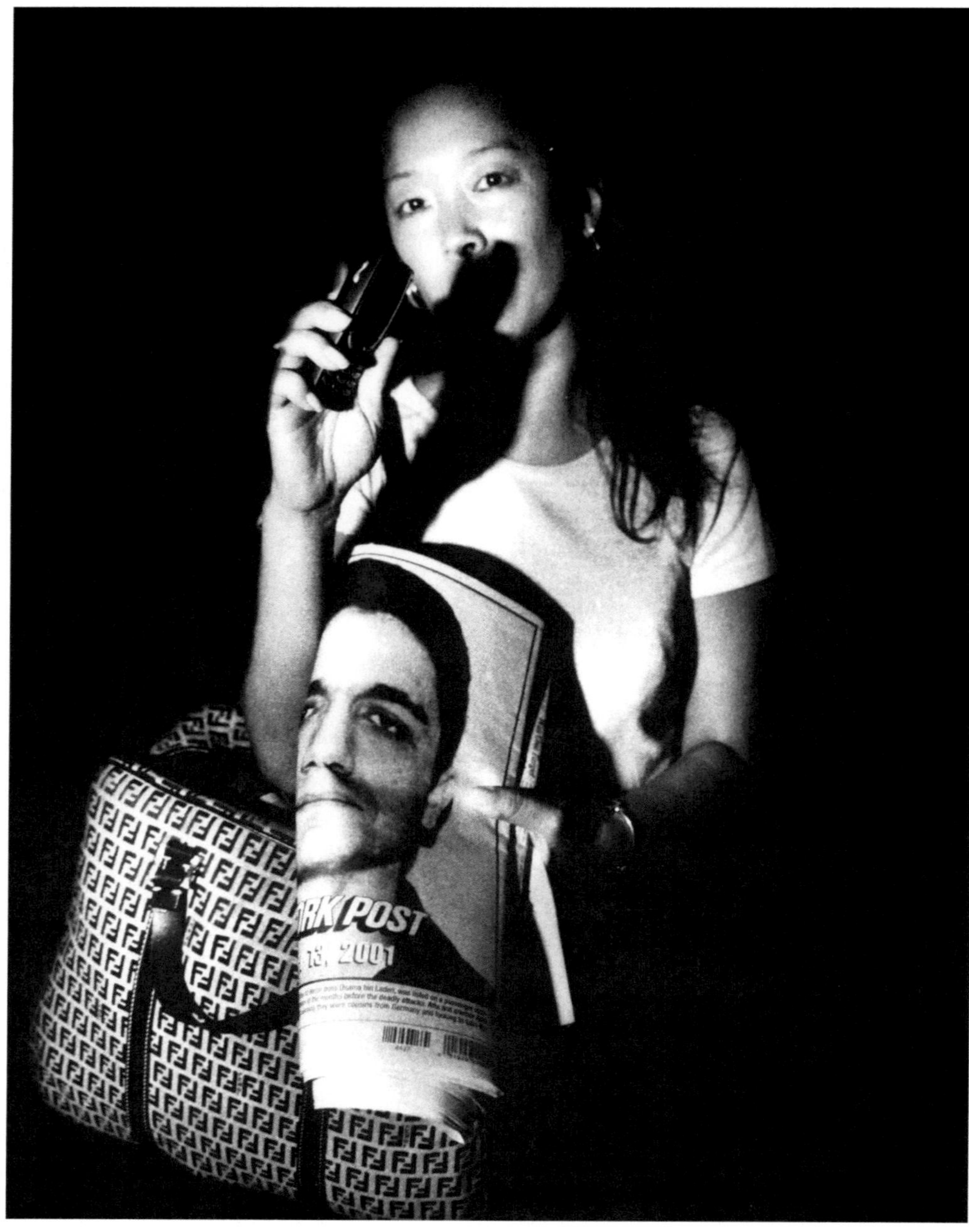

Fig. 13 and 14
**Touhami Ennadre, from the series "New York, September 11",** 2001, b-&-w photographs. Courtesy the artist.

## ART PROJECTS FROM AFRICA

The Paris-based Moroccan photographer Touhami Ennadre arrived in New York on September 10, 2001 with an airplane from Chicago and – by pure chance – became an eyewitness to the attacks. Although his friends warned him not to, he took his bulky 6 x 6 camera and strolled through downtown Manhattan taking pictures of affecting moments, in which time seems to be shock-frozen. The result was a series of 26 large-format black-and-white prints that were first presented at the Documenta 11 in Kassel in 2002 (Fietzek 2002:264ff). Ennadre's photographs belong to the aforementioned artworks that focus on the immediate post 9/11 trauma, panic, loss, and grief. His approach, however, is

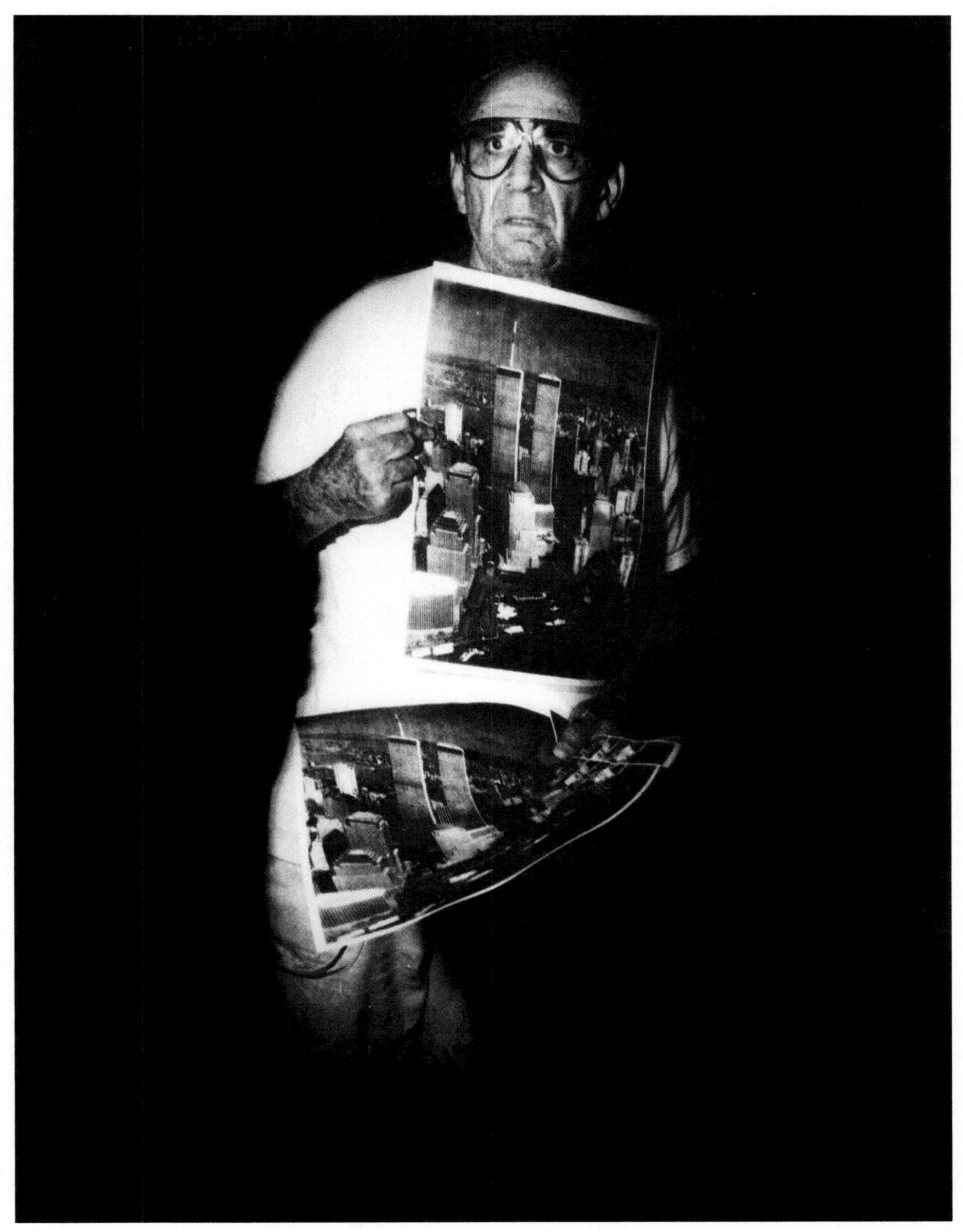

different from the more official and widely mediated imagery of concern and dismay.

Working with special torch lights in the smoky and dusty night of Manhattan, Ennadre has created quite unusual theatrical compositions that explore how light and shadows create forms and figures, simultaneously appearing out of and disappearing into their black apocalyptic surroundings (fig. 13, 14). His series portrays and memorializes the vigorous, enraged, and at times witty image testimonies of New Yorkers of all colors coping with the injuries inflicted upon their city.

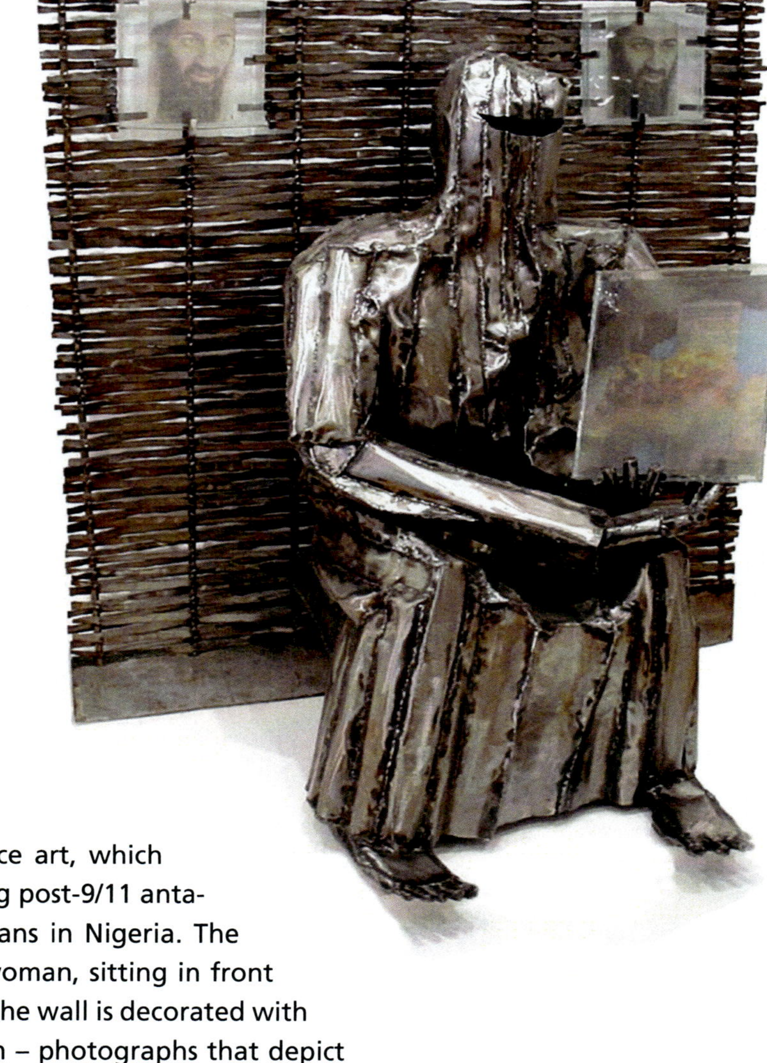

Sokari Douglas Camp was born in southeastern Nigeria. She studied at the California College of Art and Craft in Oakland and later gained a Master's degree from the Royal College of Art in London. She works mainly in welded steel, fusing the realities of London and Nigeria. Several of her sculptures make direct references to the masquerade traditions of the Kalabari and Yoruba.[5] Her 2002 steel sculpture evokes life-sized eastern Nigerian shrine figures, although the title "Osama Bin Laden Pietá" (fig. 15) places the work in the well-established "pieta" genre of Christian Renaissance art, which the artist adopted to address the rising post-9/11 antagonism between Muslims and Christians in Nigeria. The statue depicts a fully veiled Muslim woman, sitting in front of a small wall made of cane or reed. The wall is decorated with two photographs of Osama bin Laden – photographs that depict him as a popular Robin Hood hero – reminiscent of the imagery of Che Guevara, Nelson Mandela, or Patrice Lumumba. The female protagonist holds and contemplates a picture of the burning Twin Towers, enshrined in fiberglass. As a genre in the visual arts, the "pieta" depicts Mary as a "mater dolorosa", lamenting while holding the dead body of her son in her arms. In Sokari Douglas Camp's rendering, the seated Muslim woman seems to be in the position of such a "mater dolorosa"; but the dead body of Christ has been substituted by the burning towers of the World Trade Center, which appear as a meditation picture enshrined in acrylic glass. This substitution remains enigmatic. One is tempted to read it as a symbol of the death of the 3,000 victims who lost their lives in the attacks, but probably also of those other 100,000 civilians and soldiers who would lose their lives in the subsequent wars in Afghanistan and Iraq. Sokari Douglas Camp dedicated her piece to all Muslim mothers in the world. Yet, the substitution of the Christian Redeemer's body by the image-body of the burning Twin Towers also illustrates that the media turned the iconoclasm of 9/11 into an icon itself.

Fig. 15
**Sokari Douglas Camp, Bin Laden Pietà,** steel, acetate, and glass (140 x 88 x 125 cm). VG Bildkunst, Bonn 2002.

[5] See the artist's website: http://www.sokari.co.uk/ accessed January 06, 2015.

Fig. 16
**Sam Nzima, Hector Pieterson being carried by Mbuyisa Makhubo after being shot by South African police,** b-&-w photograph 1976.

Fig. 17
**Ousmane Dago,** Untitled C Print 2001. Courtesy the artist.

In this context, it is interesting to note that the genre of the "pieta" was also operative in the iconization process of a famous photograph during the Soweto uprisings in 1976 (Fig. 16). It depicts the dying student Hector Pieterson, who is carried in the arms of a young comrade, whose face reflects the weight and horror of his burden. Hector's sister, Antoinette, runs alongside holding her hands in a gesture of grief. Sam Nzima's famous photograph first appeared in a local newspaper, but later became one of the icons of the anti-apartheid struggle. Its striking resemblance to the Christian "pieta" recently inspired South African artist Kevin Brand to process the photograph further into a mosaic, which he first prepared at the Castle of Good Hope in Cape Town and later on Potsdamer Platz in Berlin.

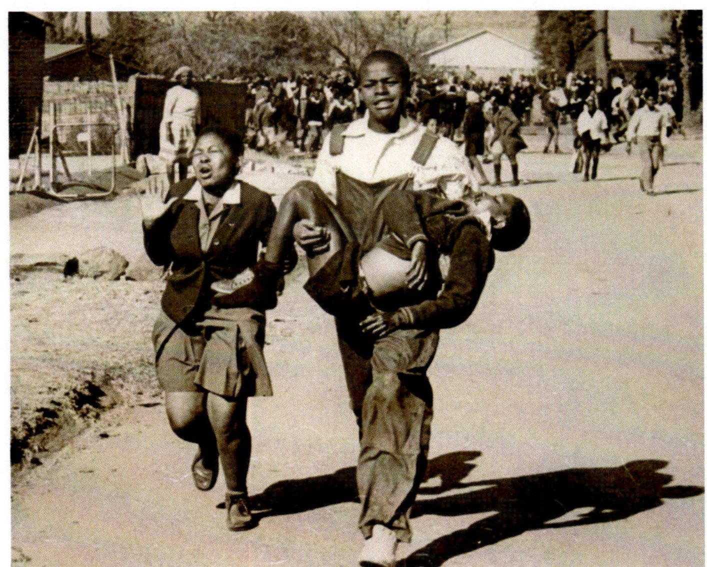

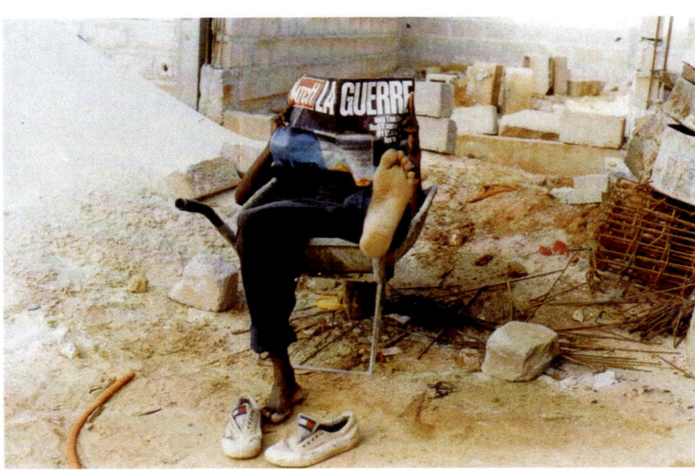


Sokari's "Bin Laden Pietà" also evokes reflectiveness, meditation, and contemplation – a topos that emerges in many other artworks as well. It seems that regarding the image of the burning Twin Towers is both an expression of the fundamental ambivalence toward the event itself and an attempt to critically reflect on the experience of its mass mediation live and in real time through its endless looping, which created a hitherto unknown conflation between the event and its image. A photograph from 2001 by the Senegalese artist Ousmane Dago depicts a construction worker relaxing in a pushcart while reading the Paris Match special 9/11 issue. At first glance, the photograph's subject is the mass-mediation experience mentioned above. Then one discovers the bare left foot of the protagonist directed to the viewer, evoking an involuntary insult but also an uncanny resonance between the collapsing iron skeleton on the cover page and the real iron at the construction site.

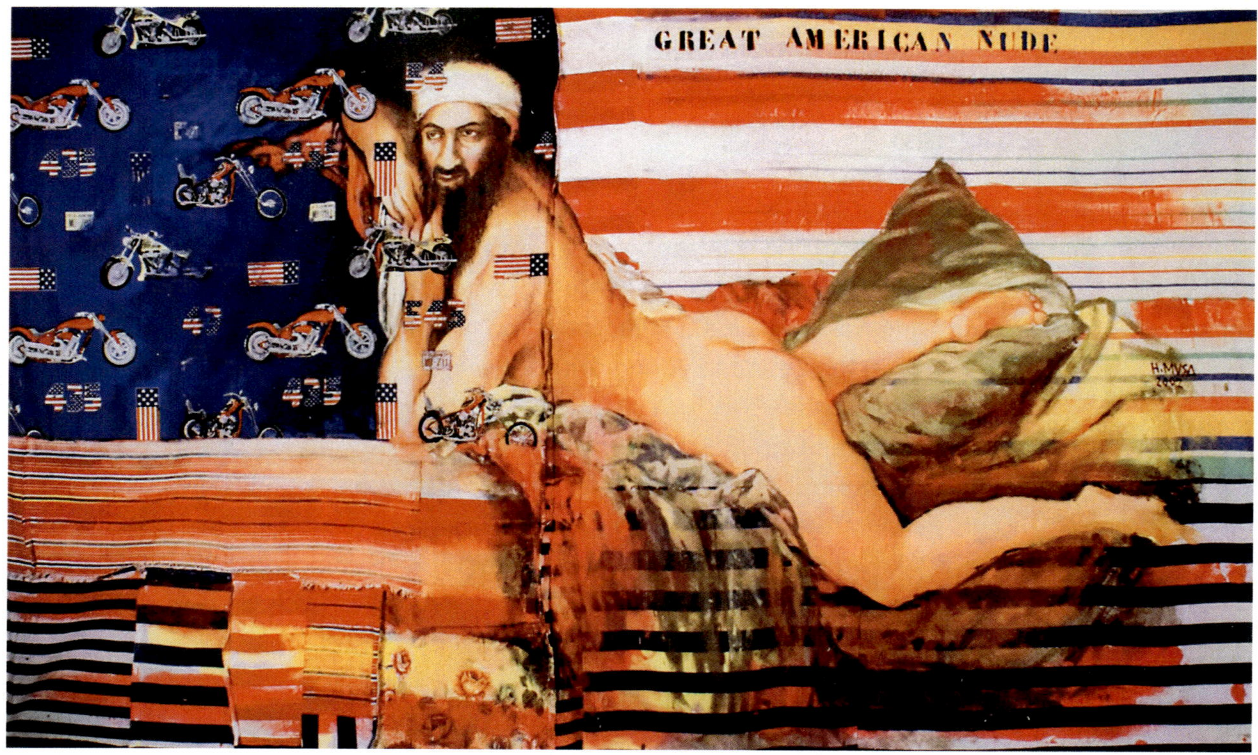


Fig. 18
**Hassan Musa, Great American Nude,**
ink on textile
(204 x 357 cm)
VG Bildkunst, Bonn
2004.

In his "Great American Nude", Hassan Musa ironically comments on the clash between Islamic fundamentalism and American capitalist hegemony in a pastiche of iconic images superimposing a key French Rococo painting, Francois Boucher's pedophile nude, onto a bedspread of patterned African fabrics, which, in turn, are blended into the stripes of the US flag (fig. 18). Boucher's model of the "Reclining Girl" (1751) on the right is matched with the face of Osama bin Laden on the left. The white stars of "Old Glory" in the upper left part have faded away to make way for a collage of motorbikes and a variety of small newly composed US flags, underscoring the necessity to find a new US identity. The painting borrows its title from Tom Wesselmann's series "Great American Nudes" of the 1960s and stresses the erotic qualities associated with the creation of Osama bin Laden as a global icon of resistance in a new world setting reminiscent of David's battle with Goliath.

As Matthias Krings has shown, the increasing popularity of Osama bin Laden in posters, videos, T-shirts, and stickers in countries like Nigeria resulted from a successful re-mapping of global conflicts – simplified and reduced to „Bin Laden versus Bush" – onto the local conflict between Muslims and Christians, which had deepened in Nigeria since 1999 due to the introduction of Sharia law in the North. For many Nigerian and Sudanese Muslims, Osama bin Laden emerged as a new hero and prophet and his face successfully filled the bill of uniting radical Muslims in their aspiration to overcome the corrupt political and economic elites of their own countries (Krings 2009:31ff).

In 2006, Richard Onyango, who started out as a sign and billboard painter in Malindi, produced a series of six large-format paintings based on cartoons and real media coverage that dramatically re-visualize the well-known 9/11 story in a didactic manner (see page 4). First, we see the hijacking of the airplane crew. Then the first plane is seen heading toward the World Trade Center and attacking it in a semi close-up. In painting No. 5, we see the first tower in flames and smoke, while the second airplane crashes into the second tower. And finally, we see – again in a long shot – the second tower collapsing. Onyango's last painting also includes the spectators who watch the inferno from a secure distance on the Brooklyn promenade. The artist says that his primary motivation for carrying out the 9/11 series was his wish to create a visual memory to hand down to those who were not yet born in 2001 or those who already have forgotten.

Chéri Samba from the Congolese capital of Kinshasa has a similar affiliation with and affinity to popular culture. For quite a while now, he has been the most famous and best-selling painter of Africa. And though he stayed for long periods abroad, in Paris and Brussels, he has always returned home to Kinshasa to his workshop, where he employs many assistants and apprentices who help

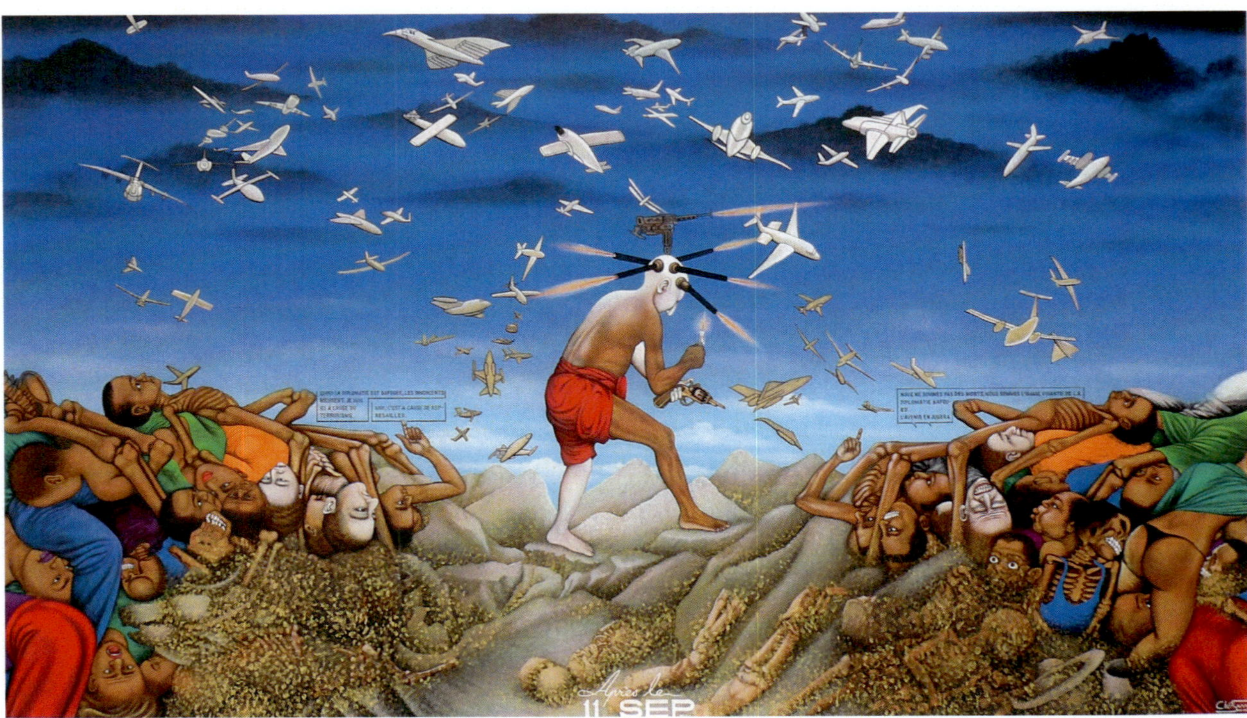

Fig. 19
**Chéri Samba, Après le 11 séptembre 2001,** oil on canvas (200 x 350 cm) 2002. Courtesy the artist and CAAC collection Jean Pigozzi Geneva.

him meet the growing demand for his works on the international art market. Trained as both a billboard painter and a comic strip artist, Chéri Samba has created his very personal and distinctive style, by borrowing from comic art the device of "speech balloons", which allow him to put verbal narrative and commentary into his figurative, often photorealistic compositions. Chéri Samba has remained a moralist and critical commentator not only of the politics and social issues in Congo/Zaire, but also in the contemporary art world. In many of his recent paintings, he is himself the main subject and reflects on the world around him and his position in it (Jewsiewicki 1995 and Magnin 2004). His painting "Apres le 11 séptembre" (fig. 19) from 2002 stages an apocalyptic vision of the future. The sky is overcrowded with airplanes and fighter jets, flying like swarms of birds or mosquitos without clear direction or destination. In the center, we see the terrorist protagonist, armed with revolver and hand grenade and a strange firing device on his hand, trying to make his way through a landscape of devastation. The victims piled up to the left and right are not the victims of the terrorist attacks in Manhattan, but the victims of disasters in Africa – victims who run the risk of being forgotten and ignored in the post-9/11 world. The text in the speech balloons speaks of the collapse and mockery of diplomacy. On the left side, we see two dead bodies in a dialogue: "Quand la diplomacie est bafouée, les innocents meurent. Je suis ici à cause du terrorisme." Whereupon the other responds: "Moi c'est à cause des repressailles." On the right side we are told: "Nous sommes pas des morts. Nous sommes l'image vivante de la diplomacie bafouée – L'avenir en jugera."

The South African video artist Thando Mama formulates a very similar concern. His video piece "We are afraid" is normally presented in a dark tunnel that absorbs the viewer in a black hole. The visual appears at first glance as an electrostatic flickering, before we gradually recognize the contours of a black man's face. It is an unstable self-portrait of Thando Mama himself, recorded in a dark room, in which the only light source was a TV monitor, presenting the BBC world news during the bombings of Iraq in 2003. Thando Mama's face appears only faintly as a reflection of events on the TV screens; it mirrors the pixel array of the news (fig. 20). The visual noise is supplemented by a looped audio track that eerily fills the viewing space with random samples of a BBC news broadcast. A stiff British voice repeats the mantra-like phrase: "The world has forgotten about Africa", at times shortened to "Forgotten about Africa". And in between the glossolalic Iraq news fragments and the "Forgotten about Africa" theme, we hear a girl's voice intoning, "We are afraid".[6] The whole piece runs for two and a half minutes. The authoritative male BBC speaker seems to frame the

[6] See: Lipp, Thorolf and Wendl, Tobias, I want this Feeling. Conversations with Thando Mama, Documentary Film, (2010, 20 min.): http://www.geschkult.fu-berlin.de/e/khi/abteilung_afrika/afrika_forschung/dokureihe/conversations_thando/index.html accessed January 06, 2015.

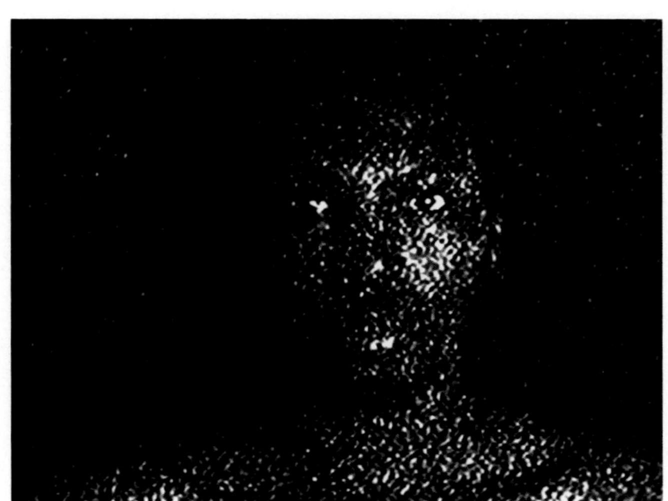

Fig. 20
**Thando Mama,**
**We are afraid,**
video still (2003).
Courtesy the artist.

future reality of "an Africa being forgotten" because the world's media attention is now exclusively focused on Iraq. And at the same time, the girl's voice seems to respond, "Africans feel threatened and are afraid." Thando's work provides a disturbing viewing and auditive experience. One feels afraid oneself, as in a haunted space, reminiscent of the house at the end of the Blair Witch Project, where one has only a single wish: to escape.

Another artist who has taken up the 9/11 issue in a completely different, subtle, and witty manner, is the Moroccan artist Mounir Fatmi, who lives and works mostly in Paris. He conceived of a project he titled "Save Manhattan" that refers to the Platonic idea of images as moving shadows. "Save Manhattan" includes a series of three installations made between 2003 and 2007 (Hunsinger 2008). The first was composed of a variety of books, all of which were written following the events of September 11th, except for the two copies of the Quran. The books were arranged on a table in such a way that a light projected from a distance creates a sharp outline of the original, pre 9/11 Manhattan skyline against the wall behind; whereby the two copies of the Quran create a spectral image of the twin towers on the back wall (fig. 21).

All the books displayed were written after 9/11 – on the left are hawkish books on the war against terror, and on the right books with 9/11-related conspiracy theories. In version No. 02, the books have been replaced by VCR cassettes, which are a recurrent material in Fatmi's work. Here the piled-up tapes can be understood as a reference and reflection of the frenetic media coverage and harsh imagery that TV audiences worldwide had consumed during and after the events. At the same time, the tapes also seem to form a kind of memorial or monument to the media, evoking a moment of silence surrounding all the chaos that was magnified by the media around the world. The last and final version, No. 03 (fig. 22), which was presented at the Venice Biennale in 2007, is based on sounds and sound equipment. The installation includes 90 loudspeakers of varying size and shape arranged on the floor. The speakers provide a concert of noises, real sounds recorded in New York. They recreate the congested city life: horns, screeching tires, approaching subways and crashing cars, but also

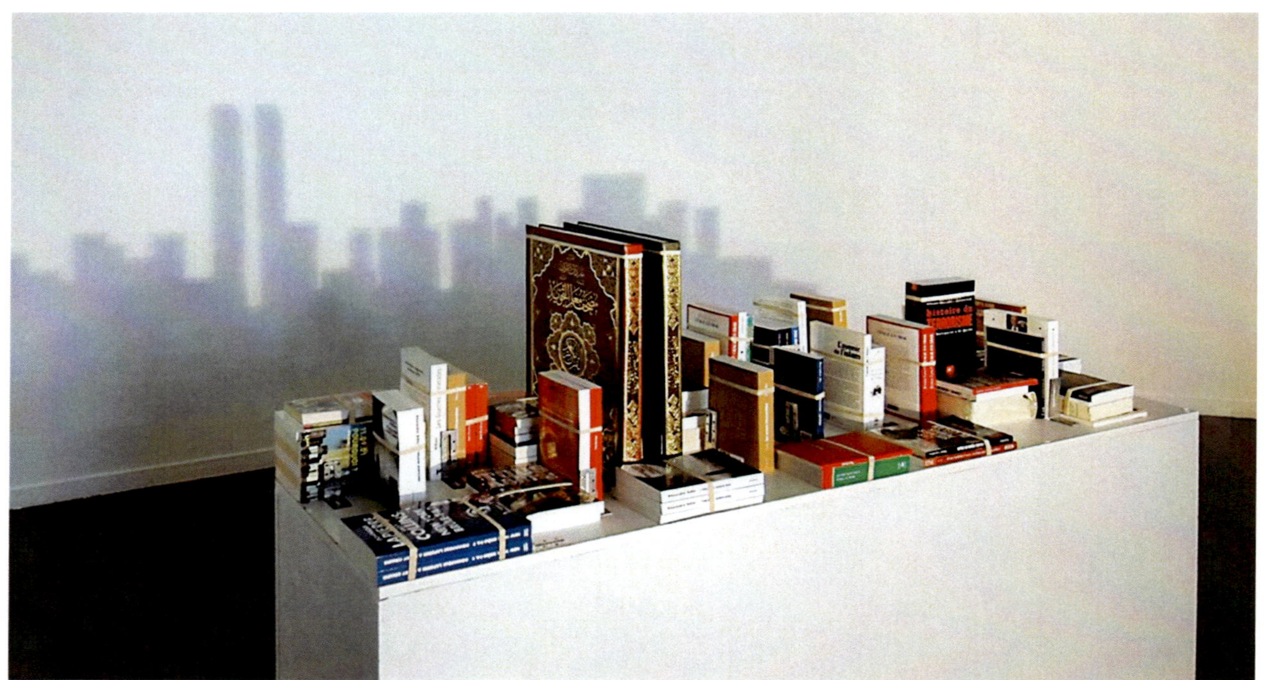

fictional sounds of explosions, which were extracted from Hollywood movies. The synchronized sounds are looped in three parts, which correspond to the architecture of the speakers. The installation evokes an image of New York City as a breathing body, as an energetic organism that suffers and struggles to overcome even the worst disaster.[7]

[7] See also Mounir Fatmi's website: http://www.mounirfatmi.com/2installation/savemanhattan03.html accessed January 06, 2015.

The Algerian artist Adel Abdessemed, who lived as an artist in residence in New York, felt increasingly unwanted after the attacks because of the growing mistrust and tendency to scapegoat Arabs, Middle Easterners, and Muslims as potential terror suspects. His 2003 installation *Habibi* (literally "Darling") (fig. 23) consists of a 17-meter-long floating skeleton made of fiberglass with its arms and legs stretched out. It is suspended from the ceiling and is clearly reminiscent of Gino de Domenici's "Calamita cosmica" (1990); both works draw on the allegory of vanity associated with the human skeleton and the ephemerality of life. In Abdessemed's installation, however, the skeleton is presented in combination with an aircraft turbine in the background, from which the skeleton seems to have been spit out – a subtle hint at the post-9/11 fear of terrorism, which reverberates with the chilling relationship between airplanes and destruction, tragedy and sacrifice.

Another work by Abdessemed he created in reaction to the xenophobic climate after the attacks in New York is his video titled "God Is Design". It is based on more than 3,000 animated sketches of ornamental motifs from the visual legacies of Islam, Judaism and Christianity, constantly mixed and remixed with abs-

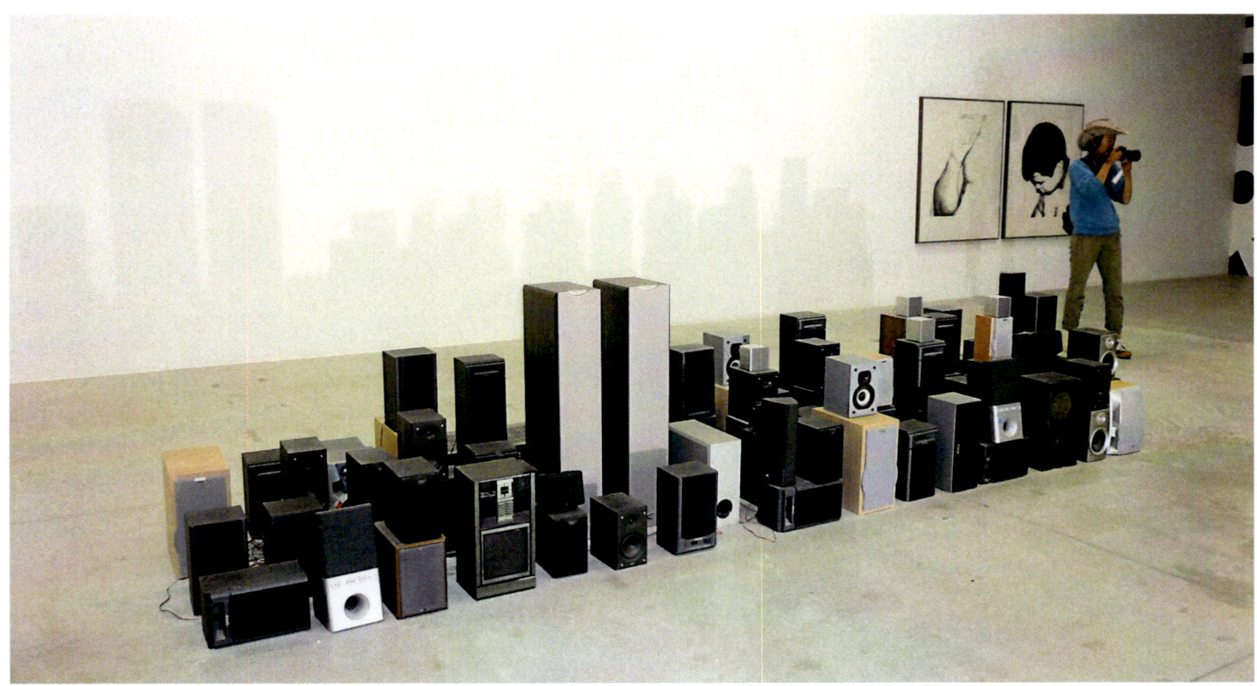

Fig. 21
**Mounir Fatmi, Save Manhattan 01,** installation, books, light, shadows. VG Bildkunst, Bonn 2003.

Fig. 22
**Mounir Fatmi, Save Manhattan 03,** sound architecture, speakers, sound system, soundtrack, light and shadow, 500 x 250 x 100 cm. VG Bildkunst, Bonn 2007.

tract patterns and human cell structures into a „visual Esperanto" whose flow questions the supremacy of any single esthetic canon as well as all attempts at branding corporate religious identities (Abdessemed et al. 2012).

As a result of the rising post-9/11 Arabophobia in the US and Europe, international curators and art critics became interested in the artistic production of the Arab and Muslim worlds, and several group exhibitions have focused on the predicaments and developments in the area (Chakar 2002, Odenthal 2003, Kunstwerke 2006). In his book *Reel Bad Arabs* (2001), Jack Shaheen extensively analyzed the (mis-) representation of Arab characters in 900 Hollywood productions in which Arabs have been targeted as religious fanatics, violent, and money-mad. Inspired by this book, Jackie Salloum produced a video titled *Planet of the Arabs* that compiles key scenes from some of the most spectacular examples into a cinematic collage.[8] Being Arab and being associated with terrorism in the post-9/11 media regime is also a topic for the Cairo-based painter and video artist Khaled Hafez. His video "Idler's Logic" (2003), funded by the Young Arab Theatre Fund and awarded the "prix de la francopohonie" at the Dakar Biennale in 2004, depicts three idlers with stereotyped North African/Arab/Middle Eastern features. Although they are "no-goods", excessively drinking and smoking, they seem to be creative and talented: the protagonist turns out to be a trained singer, another character is obsessed with Hollywood action movies and acts out James Bond-like scenes, and the third creates and plays musical instruments. The Hollywood-obsessed character handles guns and pistols throughout the film, without uttering a single word. With his Arab

[8] See: Jackie Salloum, Planet of the Arabs. Video (2005, 9 min.), http://www.youtube.com/watch?v=Mi1ZNEjEarw accessed January 06, 2015.

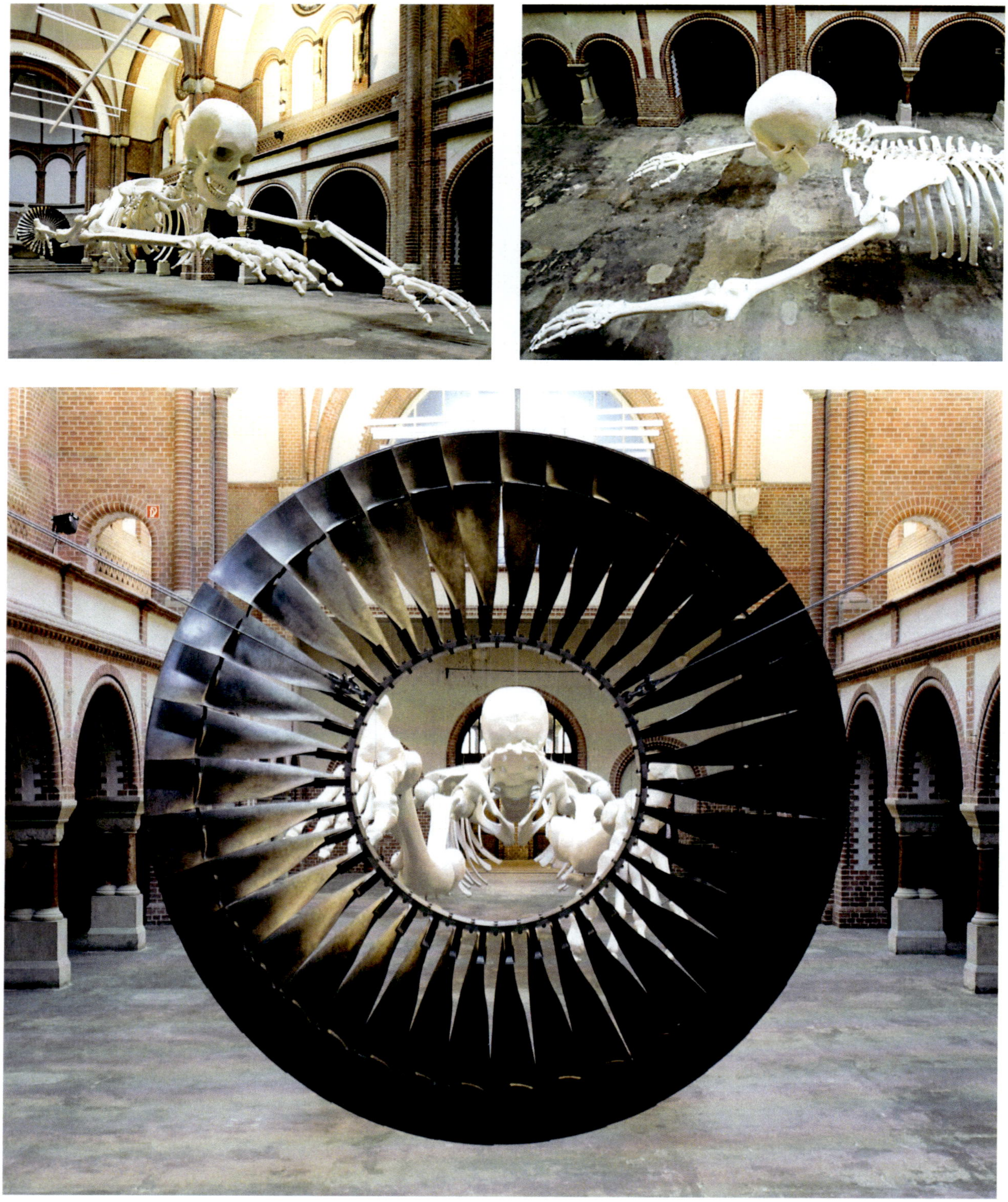

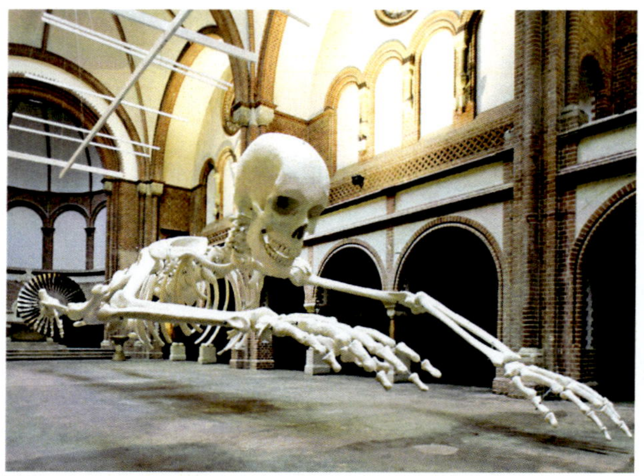

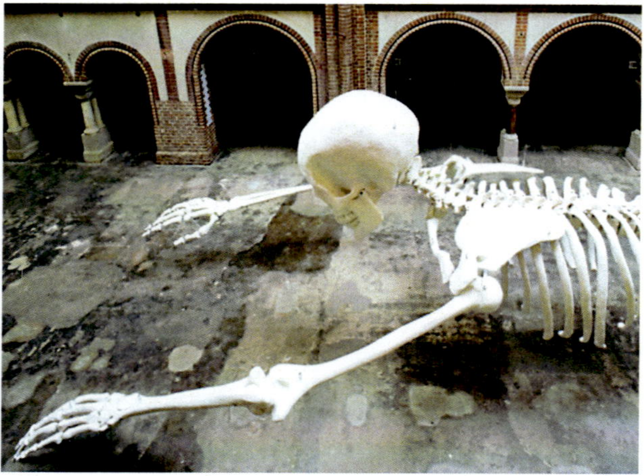

Fig. 23
**Adel Abdessemed, Habibi,**
installation, resin, fiberglass, polystyrene and airplane engine turbine (17 m).
VG Bildkunst, Bonn 2003.

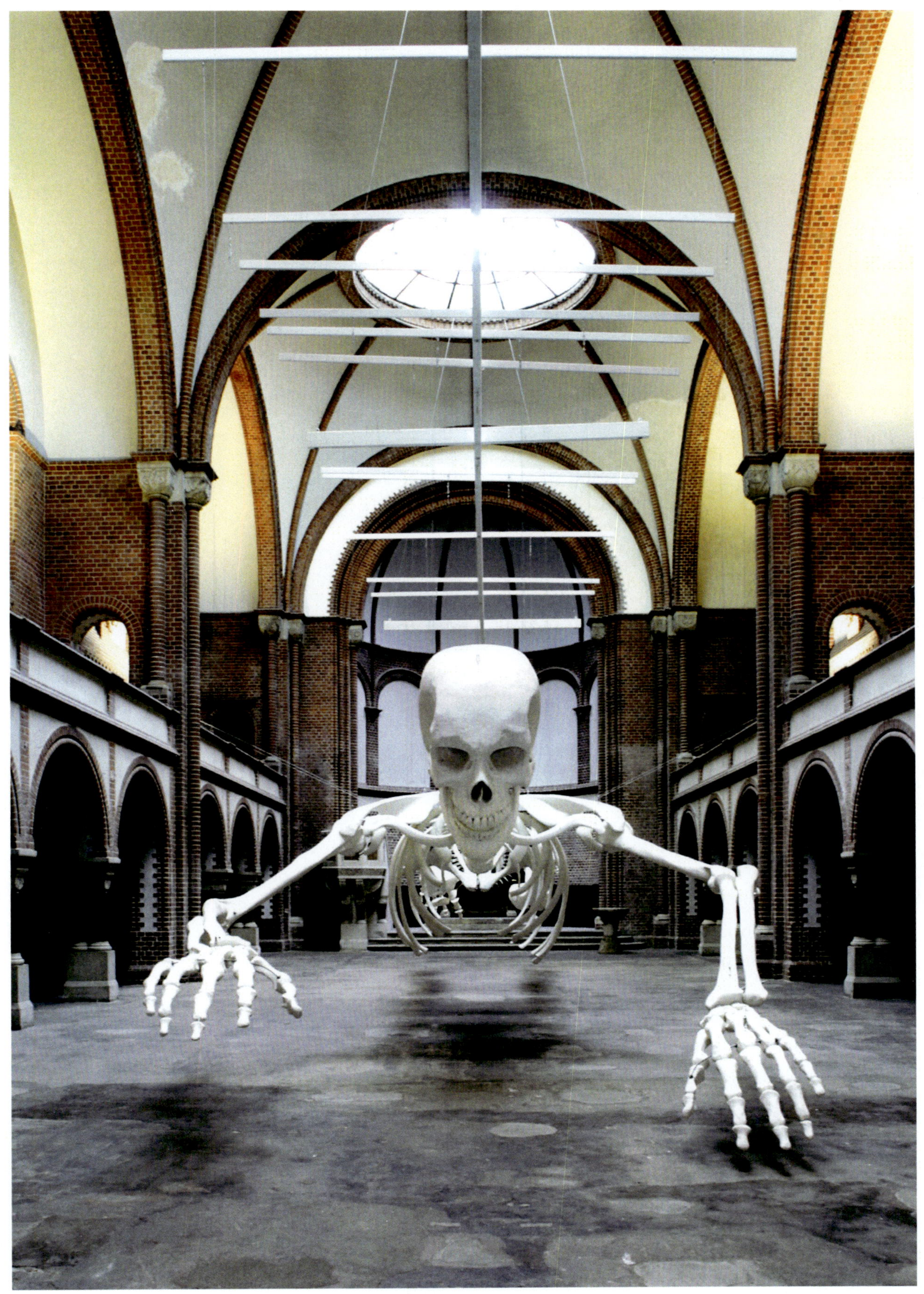

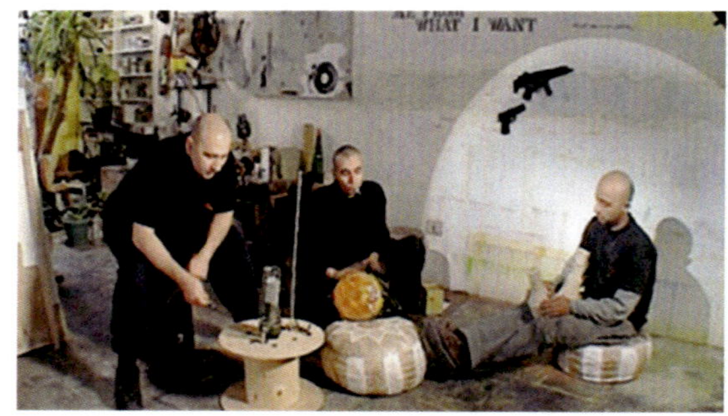

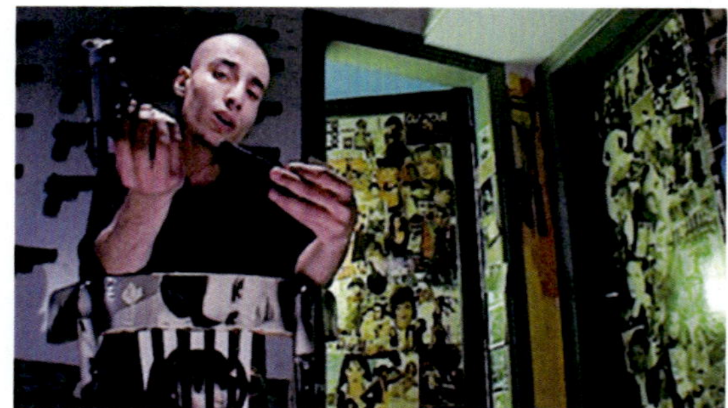
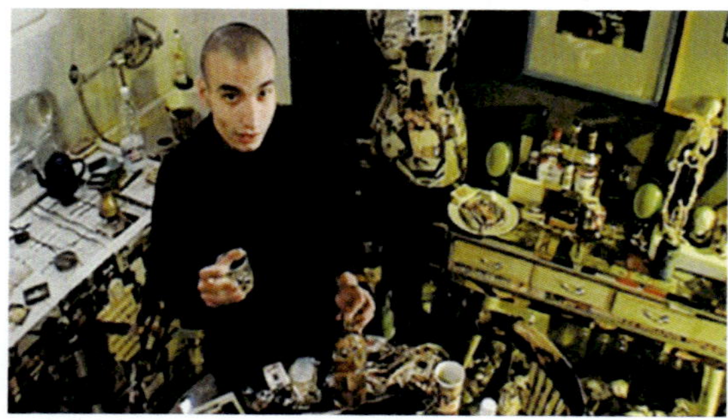
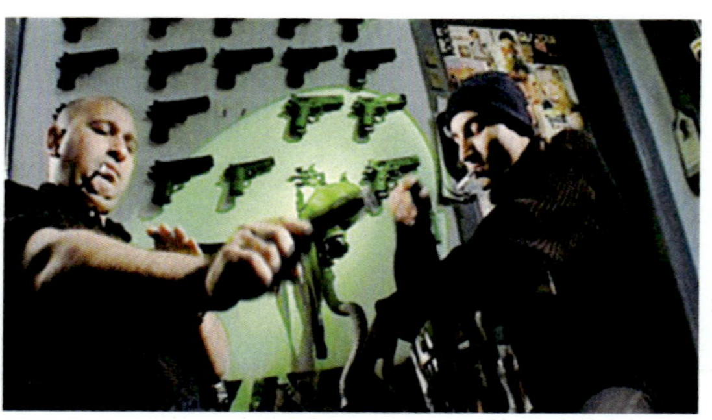

Fig. 24
**Khaled Hafez, Idler's Logic,**
video stills
(2003 – 24 min.)
Courtesy the artist.

features and his toying with guns, he delivers a virtual message that defies all labels – or as Hafez has put it himself: „I am Egyptian, I am North African, I am Middle Eastern, I am Arab. I like guns that I did not invent. I get all my ideas and inspiration from your movies, and I do not care if you terrorist-label me or not." [9] The video stages and deconstructs the stereotypes of the evil Arab male "Other", but also questions the notions of the authentic Egyptian or Middle Easterner. Hafez' idlers perform in a de-territorialized space that is permeable to the flows of global images and sounds as well as to the legacy of Egyptian popular culture, music, and cinema (fig. 24).

Artistic responses to 9/11 and the subsequent war on terror reached their peak in the years between 2002 and 2005. With the election of Barak Obama in 2008, the topic gradually lost its impact, although it did not completely disappear. In May 2011, when a CIA-led Navy Seal commando liquidated Osama Bin Laden in his hideout compound in Abbottabad in northeastern Pakistan, the world's most concentrated media attention had already shifted to the revolutionary events of the Arab Spring in Tunisia, Egypt, and Libya and to the escalating civil war in Syria. The killing of Osama Bin Laden constituted the final act in the 9/11 drama. President Obama commented on it with his famous "Justice has been done", and the US press subsequently hailed it with blunt headlines such as:

[9] See also Khaled Hafez' website: http://www.khaledhafez.net/videos/idlers.htm accessed January 06, 2015.

"We got the Bastard" (Philadelphia Daily News) and "Rot in Hell" (New York Daily News). The White House explained its decision to not release any pictures of the dead Osama Bin Laden with security considerations. Similar reasons were given for the rapid disposing of Bin Laden's body in the open sea. The US celebrated its victory by circulating the official photograph of the "situation room", which showed the US political elite watching the very liquidation that it withheld from the international audience (Kauppert and Leser 2014).

It took about a year before Osama Bin Laden's denied body returned. It returned during the 11th Havana Biennale in May 2012. The Cuban artists Alberto Lorente, Manolo Castro, and Julio Lorente presented a lifelike wax dummy of the dead Al Qaida leader at the Superior Institute of Arts on a rug (fig. 25). His eyes are closed; his head rests on a pillow with a completely peaceful facial expression. The title "He" is an obvious tribute to Mauricio Catelan's controversial sculpture "Him" of the praying Adolf Hitler in a tweed suit (2001). The human remains of both have been disposed of and denied in a similar way. Although several critics have referred to the waxwork as "eerie" and "macabre", it soon turned out to

Fig. 25
**Alberto Lorente, Manolo Castro and Julio Lorente, He,** wax sculpture 2012. Courtesy the artists.

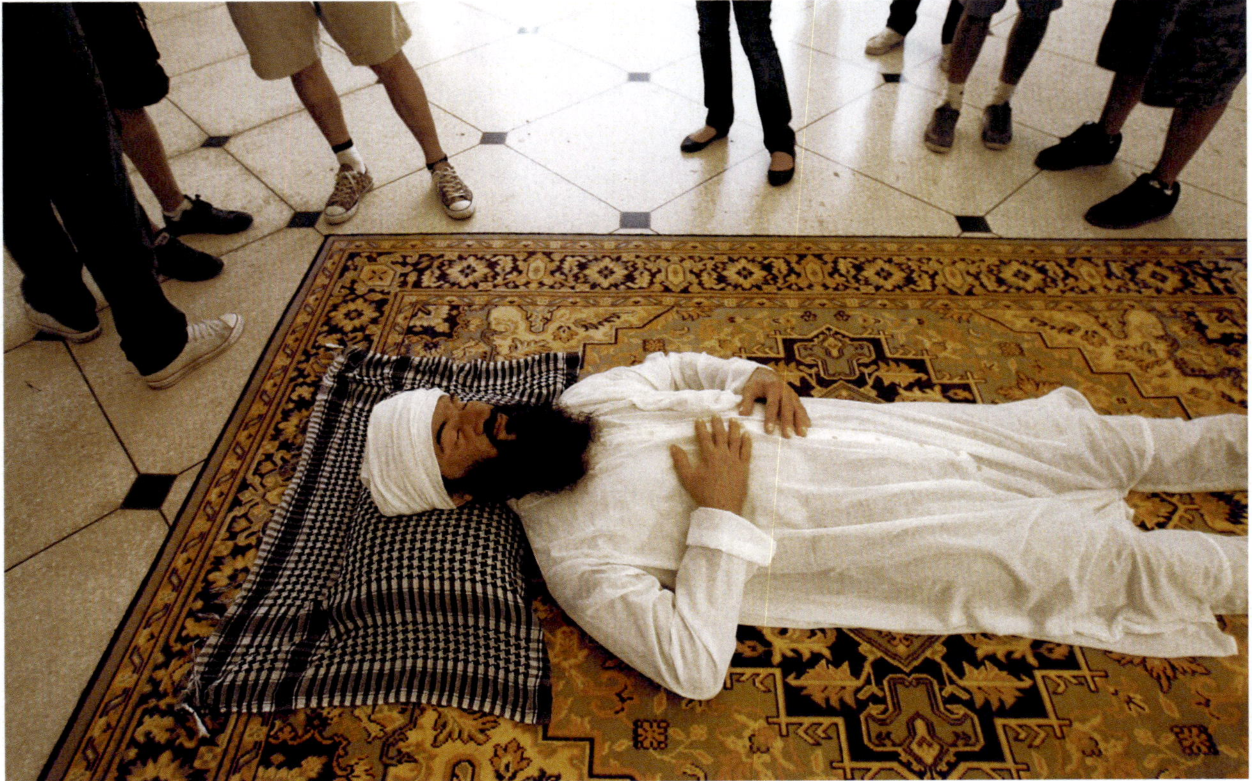

be the 11th Havana Biennale's secret lightning rod. Osama Bin Laden's bearded face and his index finger kept us company as a "digital ghost" for a whole decade – printed on newspaper front pages, appearing on TV and the web, on coffee mugs, t-shirts, and stickers. Yet, his real corpse was judged so dangerous that it was preferable to hide it and dump it into the depths of the ocean to prevent the creation of any pilgrimage site (Donghi 2014:1ff). "Osama Bin Laden is the most famous man on the Internet," says the artist Alberto Lorento, "and many people in Cuba don't believe that he is dead" (Slenske 2012).

## CONCLUSION

In October 2014, thirteen years after the attacks and intense debates about rebuilding the area, the newly constructed One World Trade Center with its mirrored glass façade was officially opened; other buildings, framing the future Ground Zero memorial site with the footprints of the former Twin Towers, still await their completion. The traumatic experience of vulnerability and the void in Lower Manhattan still lurk there. Numerous studies have addressed the aesthetic reactions and coping strategies to come to terms with the cultural break and rupture that 9/11 has created, especially in journalism, cinema, and literature (Irsigler and Jürgensen 2008; Lorenz 2004). The void not only provided fertile ground for the proliferation of conspiracy theories, it also prompted silence, diffuse concern, and dismay. The artistic responses in the US in the immediate aftermath were preoccupied with digesting the shock and easing the trauma and national tragedy and subsequently with criticizing the Bush administration's "war on terror" and its atrocities (Abu Ghraib). In Africa other aspects and perspectives came to the fore: 9/11 as a distant, yet global media experience, its re-mediation in popular culture with the emergence of Osama bin Laden and (to a lesser extent) Saddam Hussein as heroes and the subsequent outbreak of new antagonisms and fault lines on the geopolitical map. Another recurrent issue was the concern that the world would deprive Africa of attention. Although the examples that I have presented in my survey were selected more or less randomly, they indicate the spectrum of the artistic endeavors and questions raised by artists in Africa and the African diaspora.

## BIBLIOGRAPHY


Abdessemed, Adel; Michaud, Philippe-Alain; Centre Georges Pompidou (Eds.), *Adel Abdessemed. Je suis Innocent.* Göttingen: Steidl 2012.

Appadurai, Arjun, *Fear of Small Numbers. An Essay on the Geography of Anger.* Durham: Duke University Press 2006.

Barber, Karin (Ed.), *Readings in African Popular Culture.* London: International African Institute 1997.

Baudrillard, Jean, "The Spirit of Terrorism". In: *Le Monde* (Paris), November 2, 2001.

Becker, Anne, *9/11 als Bildereignis. Zur visuellen Bewältigung des Anschlags.* Bielefeld: Transcript 2013.

Chakar, Tony et al., *Tamáss: Contemporary Arab Representations: [Beirut Lebanon].* Barcelona: Fundació Antoni Tápies 2002.

Donghi, Lorenco, "Replacing Bodies with Pictures: Al Qaeda's Visual Strategies of Self-Configurations". In: *Diffractions* 3 (2014), pp. 1-15.

Fabian, Johannes, *Moments of Freedom. Anthropology and Popular Culture.* Charlottesville: University of Virginia Press 1998.

Fietzek, Gerti (Ed.), *Documenta 11 Plattform 5* (Exhib.-Cat.). Ostfildern-Ruit: Hatje Cantz 2002.

Groys, Boris, *Art Power.* Cambridge MA: MIT Press 2008.

Horkheimer, Max and Adorno, Theodor W., *Dialectic of Enlightenment.* New York: Herder & Herder 1972.

Hunsinger, Wolfgang, *Zeitgenössische Werke marokkanischer Künstler: Traditionsverankerung und emanzipatorische Bestrebungen.* Weimar: VDG 2008.

Irsigler, Ingo and Jürgensen, Christoph (Eds.), *Nine Eleven. Ästhetische Verarbeitungen des 11. September 2001.* Heidelberg: Winter: 2008.

Jewsiewicki, Bogumil, *Chéri Samba – The Hybridity of Art.* Québec: Amrad 1995.

Kauppert, Michael and Leser, Irene (Eds.), *Hillary's Hand: Zur politischen Ikonographie der Gegenwart.* Bielefeld: Transcript 2014.

Krings, Matthias, „Marke 'Osama'. Über Kommunikation und Kommerz mit Bin-Laden-Bildern in Nigeria". In: *Peripherie* 113/29 (2009), pp. 31-55.

Kröner, Magdalena (Ed.), „New York nach 9/11". In: *Kunstforum* 189, 2008.

Kunstwerke (Ed.), *The Iraqi Equation - Contemporary Arab Representations.* Berlin: Kunst-Werke 2006.

Lang, Karen, „Eric Fischl's ‚Tumbling Woman 9/11', and ‚Timeless Time'". In: *Future Anterior* 8/2 (2011), pp. 21-35.

Lorenz, Matthias N. (Ed.), *Narrative des Entsetzens: Künstlerische, mediale und intellektuelle Deutungen des 11. Septembers 2001.* Würzburg: Königshausen & Neumann 2004.

Magnin, André, *Arts of Africa. Jean Pigozzi's Contemporary Collection.* Milan: Skira 2005.

Magnin, André, *J'aime Chéri Samba.* Paris: Fondation Cartier 2004.

Mitchell, William J.T., *Das Klonen und der Terror. Der Krieg der Bilder seit 9/11.* Berlin: Suhrkamp 2011.

Mitchell, William J. T., *What Do Pictures Want? The Lives and Loves of Images.* Chicago: Chicago University Press 2005.

Odenthal, Johannes, *DisORIENTation: Contemporary Arab artists from the Middle East. Literature, Film, Performance, Music, Theatre, Visual Arts.* Berlin: Haus der Kulturen der Welt 2003.

Page, Max, *The City's End. Two Centuries of Fantasies, Fears, and Premonitions of New York's Destruction.* New Haven and London: Yale University Press 2008.

Schechner, Richard, "9/11 as Avant-Garde Art?". In: *PMLA* 124/5 (2009), pp. 1820-29.

Shaheen, Jack and Greider, William, *Reel Bad Arabs: How Hollywood Vilifies a People.* New York: Olive Branch Press 2001.

Seiler, Sascha (Ed.), *9/11 als kulturelle Zäsur: Repräsentationen des 11. September 2001 in kulturellen Diskursen, Literatur und visuellen Medien.* Bielefeld: Transcript 2009.

Storr, Robert (Ed.), *Think with the Senses – Feel with the Mind. Art in the Present Tense.* New York: Rizzoli International, 2007.

Taussig, Michael, "Old Glory". In: Latour, Bruno and Weibel, Peter (Eds.), *Iconoclash. Beyond the Image Wars in Science, Religion, and Art.* Karlsruhe: ZKM and Cambridge MA: MIT Press. pp. 82-84.

Wähner Matthias, „Drei Kriege in vier Jahren sind keine schlechte Bilanz". In: Jürgens-Kirchhoff, Annegret and Matthias, Agnes (Eds.), *Warshots. Krieg, Kunst und Medien.* Weimar: VDG, Verlag und Datenbank für Geisteswissenschaften 2006.

**ONLINE**

Danto, Arthur, *9/11 Art as a Gloss on Wittgenstein.* © 2005. www.apexart.org/exhibitions/danto.htm accessed June 25, 2010.

Mitchell, William J.T., "Echoes of a Christian Symbol. Photo reverberates with raw power of Christ on cross". In: *Chicago Tribune*, 2004. http://articles.chicagotribune.com/2004-06-27/news/0406270291_1_torture-humiliation-image accessed January 15, 2015.

Serra, Richard, *Man weiss nicht wer schlimmer ist – Bush oder Osama* (Interview). In: Die Zeit, September 2, 2004. http://www.zeit.de/2004/37/Statement accessed January 05, 2015.

Slenske, Michael, "Stars and Students at the Havana Biennale". In: *Art in America*, May 22, 2012. http://www.artinamericamagazine.com/news-features/news/havana-biennale/ accessed January 05, 2015.